"OUR TROOPS ARE IN GENERAL ALMOST NAKED"

The Delaware and New York Infantry
at the Valley Forge Encampment
1777-1778

Joseph Lee Boyle

CLEARFIELD

Printed for Clearfield Company by
Genealogical Publishing Company
Baltimore, Maryland
2017

ISBN 978-0-8063-5857-4

TABLE OF CONTENTS

PREFACE

While the six-month encampment of the Continental Army at Valley Forge in 1777-1778 has been part of America's folklore for generations, most of the men who served there have remained anonymous. The names of over 30,000 men of all ranks appear on the surviving monthly muster and payroll records. This compilation is the fourth volume of an effort to recognize some of these heroes of the Revolutionary War. Connecticut, New Hampshire, New Jersey, and Rhode Island have already been completed.

The information in the Name Index has been abstracted from Record Group 93, M 246, "Revolutionary War Rolls, 1775-1783," at the National Archives in Washington, D.C. Microfilm copies can be found at the branches of the National Archives and at some larger libraries. Microfilm rolls 30-31 cover the Delaware Regiment from 1777-1783; rolls 65-66 the First New York; rolls 67-70 the Second; rolls 70-71 for the Fourth, and roll 125 for Malcom's/Malcolm's Regiment. It should be remembered that Colonel William Malcom spelled his name without the second l, though numerous publications through the years show it as "Malcolm." This list does not include men in the cavalry and artillery regiments.

It must be noted that men were not required to enlist in a regiment from their home state. There was always competition for recruits, and as the Delaware regiment spent over a year in New York, New Jersey and Pennsylvania, it is likely that some men from these states joined the Delaware ranks.

The information which follows in the Name Index has been taken from the muster and payrolls. The muster rolls were usually compiled in the early part of each month for the preceding month. Men are shown by company, with name and rank. Any alterations which happened during the month are shown, usually with the date it occurred. These include men joining and leaving the company for various causes and being promoted. Though the reports are for the preceding month, it cannot be assumed that a man who appears as "on command" for example, was in that status for an entire month. Such annotation indicates a soldier's status on the day a given roll was compiled.

The rolls were not compiled within consistent periods after the end of the month. Most of the rolls for December 1777 are dated January 2 and 4, 1778. However, the rolls for June 1778 are largely dated the latter part of July. The latter can be accounted for by the fact that the Army had been on the move for several weeks after leaving Valley Forge and had fought in the Battle of Monmouth on June 28. As these were status reports, a man who appears as "sick absent" on a June roll may not have been sick at all in June, but become sick in July.

The payrolls were derived from the muster rolls. These were also kept on a monthly basis and ideally, though rarely, the men were paid on a monthly basis for the preceding month. In practice, the pay was usually several months behind and the non-financial notations on payrolls may be less accurate. Where discrepancies are noted on the date a man enters or leaves the service, the payroll is probably more accurate than the muster roll, as the regimental paymaster was audited on his disbursements.

Though the rolls were supposed to be done monthly, it did not always happen. The Second and Fourth New York's December rolls, dated January 2, 1778, actually covered the period from September 1, through December 31, 1777, probably due to the fact that these units were actively moving. Why the rolls for January were not completed until February 21, is a matter of conjecture. The rolls for June were not completed until July 22.

Not all the rolls for the period survive. On the nine companies in Malcom's, there are no rolls for June alone, nor for the Field Officers. Kirkwood's Delaware company has only payrolls for the period. Rhodes; has payrolls only as well, but nothing for January.

The companies are known by the name of the company captain. In some cases the captain had left the army, but his company continued to be listed for some months under his name, which sometimes causes confusion. Captain Barent Ten Eyck was discharged in January, but the company continued to bear his name through June. Captain James Moore was captured on January 16, 1778, and remained a prisoner until November, 1778. His company was commanded by John Willson In other cases a captaincy was left vacant and the company went by the lieutenant's name. For example Captain Thomas Holland died on October 13, 1777, but Lieutenant John Rhodes commanded the company until September 1778.

For the most part the original rolls are reasonably legible. However, in some cases they are extremely poor. Brackets indicate illegible or questionable words.

The reader should be very much aware that many of the names on the original lists have multiple spellings. For last and first names, the two most common spellings are shown. Some names appear with numerous variations such as those of Micijah/Micajah Sherwood/Shearwood/Sheirwood of the Fourth New York, John Lincamore/Linkenmoore/ Lindechamor/Lingamore of Malcom's Regiment, and Joel Tuttle/Tuthill/Toutell/Tuttel/Tuttell/Tutle/Touttell of the Second New York. Was Philip Kole/Koole of the Second New York really Philip Cole?

There are probably other spelling variations for the time periods before and after Valley Forge. In cases where no dominant spelling appears, the rolls have been checked forwards or backwards from the Valley Forge time period to find the most common variations. Additional variations can be found for some men on the rolls before and after the Valley Forge period. In these cases only the names shown on the rolls from December 1777 through June 1778 inclusive are used.

A common problem was that the record keeping was often months behind for men who had been sent to distant hospitals or were left behind on special duty. Some men were fortunate in being resurrected from the grave by the Army's paperwork. A number of men appear as deserting and then returning. This may account for some of the gaps in the records for other men. Some may have deserted for a month or two, then returned, and the individual preparing the roll never noted the soldier's absence. Those who are interested in a particular individual before or after the Valley Forge Encampment should check the rolls for the months before or after Valley Forge, or request a copy of the soldier's service record from the National Archives in Washington.

There are some men who appear on a single roll and then disappear without notation. They may have enlisted and then rapidly deserted or died. Some of these notations could be clerical errors or extreme errors in spelling, and some of these mysteries will never be clarified.

James Low of Delaware is shown as enlisting on March 10, but deserting on March 27. However he appears as joined on April 1. William Hewlin of the Delaware Regiment. The April payroll shows he deserted on April 18, but the April muster roll shows he deserted on May 18. Men such as William Smith who were on the rolls for the entire time, but was absent sick at various hospitals.

John Campbell of the Second New York is shown on furlough from December through May, but the June roll shows he deserted on January 1, 1778. Thomas Duncan of the Second appears as sick at Albany December-February, then on the rolls with no comment for March, then sick at Albany for April. Not likely he was sick at Albany, well at Valley Forge in March, and then back sick at Albany.

The Second New York shows that a Charles Powers deserted on December 17, and that a Charles Powers enlisted on May 1, 1778. The assumption is that it was two different men, but the same Powers may have been forgiven his crime if he reenlisted. A Cornelius Van Ness is shown as having deserted from the same regiment in October, and as enlisted on June 5. Perhaps another sinner forgiven. Others were not so fortunate. Edward McConnel/McConnell of the Delawares was "Brought back from desertion" on February first, but deserted again on March 19. He was brought back again on May 16, and shot on May 25. William Grimes was perhaps a slicker fellow. He enlisted on May 22, and apparently successfully deserted the next day.

INTRODUCTION

There are few regimental histories for units in the Revolutionary War. In several cases there are histories of the regulars, then called the Continental Line, of a given state. The *Delaware Continentals* is an exception, but it was published over seventy years ago and needs to be updated.

The best single source is Robert K. Wright's *The Continental Army*. This gives a short sketch of each regiment with an excellent bibliography for further reading.

In June 1775, the Continental Congress adopted the army of New Englanders besieging the British in Boston and appointed George Washington of Virginia as Commander in Chief of the Continental Army. Washington inherited what were essentially New England state forces with short terms of enlistment. Throughout the Fall of 1775 into the Spring of 1776, Congress authorized the formation of various regiments by the states in a piecemeal fashion while Washington and his officers strove to establish a coherent organization. These new units also had short term enlistments.

In December 1775, Congress assigned the State of Delaware the task of raising one Continental regiment which it promptly accomplished. In August the regiment marched to New York where it served with distinction at the Battle of Long Island and other engagements in Washington's efforts to hold New York. Badly depleted in numbers the regiment fought again at Princeton, where it's leader John Haslet was killed.

The regiment was reorganized and recruited in 1777, and assigned to serve with the First Maryland Brigade in Washington's army. One of the two major British initiative of the year, found General William Howe in late August with a British fleet at the head of the Chesapeake Bay. Howe landed in Cecil County, Maryland, and began to advance, defeated Washington at the Battle of Brandywine, and captured the American capital of Philadelphia.

Washington launched a surprise attack on the enemy positions on October 4, but he was defeated and forced to withdraw. After Germantown, the opposing armies licked their wounds. The British withdrew and fortified themselves in Philadelphia. They also began their "river assault" of nearly six weeks to clear the Delaware of obstructions and subdue the American strong points of Fort Mifflin south of Philadelphia and Fort Mercer on the New Jersey side of the river. This was critical for the British to be able to communicate with their fleet and bring up supplies and reinforcements. The American's stubborn resistance on the river was critical in delaying further land movements by the enemy for several months.[1]

On December 4, General Howe led his army out of Philadelphia to confront Washington. By this time the Americans were well fortified on the hills at White Marsh in present day Montgomery County. They had also been reinforced by three more brigades of men, fresh from victory over Burgoyne at Saratoga. Howe looked things over for three days and tried to maneuver for an engagement, but Washington was too wise to leave his stronghold and engage the British in the open field.

After the British retired to Philadelphia, Washington remained at White Marsh until December 11. The army crossed the Schuylkill River to a place called the Gulph and remained there from December 12 until December 19. Exactly when it was decided to encamp the army at Valley Forge for the winter is not certain, but it was on December 17 that Washington told the men in General Orders that the army would take post in the neighborhood. On December 19, the Continental Army left the Gulph and marched into Valley Forge.

But that day Washington ordered William Smallwood to take command of Sullivan's division, as he wrote to the Delaware's president George Read, "I have recd information, which I have great reason to believe is true, that the Enemy mean to establish a post at Wilmington for the purpose of countenancing the disaffected in the Delaware State, drawing supplies from that Country and the lower parts of Chester County, and securing a post upon Delaware River during the Winter. As the advantages resulting to the Enemy from such a position are most obvious I have determined, and shall accordingly, this day, send off Genl Smallwood with a respectable continental Force to take post at Wilmington before them."[2]

On December 21 the Delawares arrived back home, with eight other regiments in the division. The high point of their time was probably the capture of the grounded British brig *Symetry*, loaded with stores, clothing, and arms. With the exception of alarms when enemy ships appeared in the Delaware River, mundane military duties occupied the garrison for the next months, while they suffered from a shortage of provisions, and desertions, the latter likely exacerbated as the men were closer to home. The regiment showed a grand total of all ranks at the end of December of 279 men, just 90 privates were present fit for duty. By the end of May the total was 321 men, with 160 privates present fit for duty.

As the withdrawal of the enemy from Philadelphia became increasingly likely, Washington ordered the Wilmington garrison to Valley Forge. Smallwood was told "I am to request that you will immediately detach the first Brigade of the Troops under your command, with all their Baggage, Artillery &ca. to come to Valley Forge."[3] Smallwood responded the next day and Commissary John Chaloner wrote that Smallwood had arrived at camp on May 29. The Delawares with the main army fought the British at the Battle of Monmouth on June 28, and served under Washington in New York and New Jersey well into 1780.

On May 5, 1780, the Delawares, in the Maryland Division were ordered to the Southern Department, and were part of Gates crushing defeat at Camden, S. C., but fought extremely well. After Camden, "The heart of the Southern Army remained the infantry regiments from Maryland and Delaware.[4] The Delawares served in the South for the rest of the war, heroically battling at Guilford Court House, Hobkirk's Hill, and Ninety-Six and were finally sent home in December 1782.

At the end of 1776, most of the enlistments for Continental troops expired. Congress had anticipated the problem of a disappearing army and had passed a resolve for eighty-eight battalions, or regiments, on September 16, 1776. This was intended to be an army for the duration of the war. However, efforts to recruit the new organization were ineffectual, and in January 1777, Washington was left with only a small cadre of veterans.

On December 27, 1776 the Continental Congress had passed one of it's more useless resolves, authorizing Washington to recruit "sixteen additonal regiments" that were not tied to a specific state. As might be expected, there was not much trouble in finding field officers for the units, but none were ever close to full strenght.

One of the Additonal regiments was led by William Malcom, a New York City businessman, who had commanded militia units. The regiment was assigned on June 27, 1777 to the Highlands Department, where it participated in the defense of the Hudson River. On September 23, 1777, it was assigned to the Main Army, in the Third Pennsylvania, also known as Thomas Conway's Brigade, and spent the winter at Valley Forge. The regiment had 231 men of all ranks at the end of December, with 109 privates present fit for duty. By the end of May this had dropped to a total of 175 men of all ranks, with just 62 privates present fit for duty, and only 48 by the end of June, when a single infantry company was supposed to have 76 men.

Malcom himself asked for leave of absence, which request was denied by Washington. Malcom replied that "I am therefore unavoidably oblig'd to leave the Service—" Washington does not appear to have been impressed by Malcom's military zeal when he replied: "When you reflect how lately you Joined the Army—What indulgencies you have had, and how long you were at & in the Neighbourhood of your Home, after your Appointment, you cannot be surpized, that I disapproved your Application for a Furlough with some degree of displeasure."[5]

Lieutenant Colonel Aaron Burr, later Vice-President, among other things, commanded the unit for the rest of the Encampment. Despite the off-told tale of Burr cutting off a mutinous soldier's arm, there is absolutely no primary evidence that this occurred. An infamous act was committed by one of its lieutenants, Frederick Gotthold Enslin, who was drummed out of the army in February 1778, for allegedly attempting sodomy.

The regiment next saw action in the Battle of Monmouth, and then spent its remaining time in the Highlands Department, where Colonel Malcolm was at times commander at West Point. The regiment was broken up in early 1779, as follows: the Pennsylvania companies were assigned to the 11th Pennsylvania Regiment, and the New York companies assigned to Spencer's Additional Continental Regiment.

The First New York, along with the Delawares, was another regiment that arrived late at Valley Forge. The regiment that came to be known as the First New York was actually authorized as the Second New York Regiment of the Continental Line on May 25, 1775. It was assigned to the Northern Department in Albany, NY with 10 companies from Albany, Tryon, Charlotte, and Cumberland Counties. In April 1776, Colonel Goose Van Schaick was designated as commander. He reorganized the regiment to consist of eight companies. They were promptly assigned to the Canadian Department. After only a month, on June 9, 1776, they were again reassigned to the Northern Department. As the Second New York Regiment, they participated in the failed American invasion of Canada and the debatably successful Battle of Valcour Island (Lake Champlain).

On January 26, 1777, the Second and Fourth New York were consolidated under Goose Van Schaick's command into a unit to be known as the First New York. They were assigned to the Northern Department under the overall command of General Philip Schuyler at Albany.

As the British invasion of New York State changed from a threat into a reality (with the attacks and take take-over of New York City in mid-1776, and the subsequent Siege of Fort Stanwix and invasion of the Champlain Valley in the summer of 1777), Schuyler made the decision to split his forces and send a contingent to help the Third New York Regiment at Fort Stanwix. A portion of the First became part of this relief column, and arrived at the fort around August 23, 1777. They remained as part of the Fort Stanwix garrison until the winter, and were at Saratoga in February.

Washington had ordered the First New York to the Highlands of New York, but ten days later, on March 31, Washington ordered Van Schaick's regiment from New York to Valley Forge, "march without delay." On April 26, Thomas Ewing recorded that: "This evening Coll Van Swiks Regt arivd in Camp from Albany consisting of 400 men."[6] On May 7, Washington ordered the regiment "to relieve the picquit, at Cuckholdtown until further orders." The regiment's muster rolls for March 17 to May are dated May 5 and May 7, at "Traydiffrin Camp Valley Forge." "Cuckholdtown/Cuckold's Town" was likely the area once known as "Cockletown" on the Lancaster Road, in Tredyffrin Township, Chester County. The regiment totalled 484 men at the end of May, of whom 325 were rank and file, present and fit for duty.

Private Richard Mount of the First wrote he was "Three Miles from Head Quarters" and that "here we behold the Effects of Rapine, Plunder and Devastation and People who once lived in ease and affluence barely subsisting. Here the distressed Farmer has not spirit to cultivate his Fields not knowing who may reap the profit—"[7] This was likely a widespread problem in Southeast Pennsylvania.

On June 18, the First was moved into the Second Pennsylvania Brigade fought at Monmouth and the next month was moved into the new New York Brigade. In November the unit was ordered to relieve the garrison at Fort Stanwix. While at the frontier outpost, in April 1779, Van Schaick led the First on a raid against the Onondaga Indians. Not loosing a man on this raid which was considered a great success, he was voted the thanks of the Continental Congress.

On January 1, 1781, the First was consolidated with the Third New York Regiment (which was not at Valley Forge). The regiment, with the main army, marched south and successfully participated in the Siege of Yorktown. In the spring of 1782, the First went into final quarters at New Windsor, New York, as the war wound down. In June, many of the men were furloughed home; and in November 1783, with the coming of peace, the men of the old First New York Regiment were honorably discharged.

The Second and Fourth New York followed a different path to Valley Forge. Each had been authorized in May 1775, the Second, began its existence as the Third New York, but was designated as the Second in January 1777. The Fourth began as the Third, was then called the Second, and finally designated as the Fourth New York in January 1777. Elements of both participated in invasion of Canada, Battle of Valcour Island, and the failed American efforts to defend New York City in 1776..

The British plan in 1777 was to cut the United States in half with a British army advancing south from Canada under General John Burgoyne. Burgoyne was to advance to Albany while other British troops moved up along the Hudson River from New York and down the Mohawk River Valley to meet him.

The Second and Fourth were at Fort Ticonderoga with other units. They remained there until the advance of John Burgoyne's army from Canada force forced the evacuation of that and the nearby posts. Over two months later, the Continental

Army in the north had been reinforced enough to stand and fight. On September 19, at the Battle of Freeman's Farm, the left wing of the army, including the New York men, now brigaded with Enoch Poor's New Hampshire men, fought three desperate hours under Major General Benedict Arnold against the best in the British Army, while the enemy held the field; the nearly 600 casualties they suffered crippled their advance.

Burgoyne waited eighteen days and sent out a reconnaissance in force to determine if an assault on left of the American position would be successful. The Continentals replied with three columns, one of which was Enoch Poor's Brigade with the New York troops, which fought against the elite British grenadiers who were "swept away by the ferocious charge."[8] This led to the Burgoyne's surrender at Saratoga on October 17, the biggest American victory to date.

After his victory at Saratoga, Horatio Gates ordered four of his brigades, including Poor's Brigade, to march down the Hudson River Valley and join Israel Putnam. Washington in turn ordered the New Hampshire men, as well as other brigades, to reinforce him in Pennsylvania. But Major General demurred stating: "The New York Regiments being annex'd to General Poors Brigade they are exceeding unwilling to be seperated, and I knowing the disadvantages that would arrise from their being here have presumed in some measure to deviate from your excellencys Orders—Those Regiments are principally composed of men who former Residence was within the Enemys Lines and the little time they were down in this Quarter last summer, there was upwards of one hundred Deserters from them; mostly to the Enemy—that we should soon loose the greater part of them here."[9]

Poor's Brigade, which included two regiments of New York men, arrived at Washington's camp at White Marsh on November 22. Washington was happy to receive the reinforcements but was dismayed to discover that "many of them are very deficient in the Articles of Shoes, Stockings, Breeches and Blankets."[10]

On December 27, eight days after the army entered Valley Forge, Adjutant General Timothy Pickering reported on the status of the regiments. The Second had 18 Sergeants and 91 rank and file present fit for duty, while the Fourth had 22 Sergeants and 116 rank and file present fit for duty. The Second actually had more men sick present and absent, 98, than fit, and the Fourth, 84, nearly as bad off.[11] Two musicians in the Fourth New York are named only as "Cato" and "Dick." It is assumed these are Patriots of African Descent, and there were probably others in the ranks as well.

The tale of the Continental Army at Valley Forge has often been told. Recent books include: Thomas Fleming, *Washington's Secret War: The Hidden History of Valley Forge* (2005), Nancy K. Loane, *Following the Drum: Women at the Valle Forge Encampment,* (2009), John W. Jackson, *Valley Forge: Pinnacle of*

Courage (1992), Herman O. Benninghoff III, *Valley Forge: A Genesis for Command and Control* (2001), and Dr. Wayne K. Bodle, The Valley Forge *Winter: Civilians and Soldiers in War* (2002). However, a body of folklore and myth has so encompassed the six-month encampment that the historical facts are sometimes difficult to discern.

The first few days of the Valley Forge Encampment and mid-February 1778 were the hardest times for the troops. Worn out after a hard campaign, they had to build log huts for their winter lodging. At the same time a food shortage so severe occurred that Washington wrote to the President of Congress on December 22 that if something was not done immediately "this Army must dissolve."[12]

Washington was forced to send details out from the camp to take food from the citizenry to feed his men. The citizens were not considered pleasant neighbors, but suffered from both armies. Captain James Gray of the Third New Hampshire wrote to his wife Susan the day before Christmas that "In this State we find a people who are, (generally speaking), the most unfriendly of any we have passed through; insomuch that we are put to the disagreable necessity of taking our necessary support from them, by armed force—" Gray was doubtless pleased to be on furlough from January through June. Despite this food supplies were so critically low that Washington wrote: "The occasional deficiencies in the Article of Provisions, which we have often severely felt, seem now on the point of resolving themselves into this fatal Crisis, total want and a dissolution of the Army." [13]

Thousands of troops were too ill-clad to be out of doors or participate in any work details. On December 24, the Colonel of the Fourth New York wrote: Our Troops "are in General Almost Naked & very often in a Starveing Condition through the Mismanagement of our Commissaries who are Treading in the Paths of our Quarter Masters and Forrage Masters who have already Starved our Horses Burgoins Army was not worse [provided] with Forrage when in their Greatest Distress. The Enemy are rolling in the Fat of the Land having played the Soldier Sufficiently to secure them the Best of Quarters. All my men except 18 are unfit for duty for want of Shoes Stockings and Shirts." Nearly two months later, the Colonel to the Second New York lamented: "it is beyond description to Conceive what the men Suffer, for want of Shoes, Stockings, Shirts, Breeches and Hats. I have upwards of Seventy men unfit for Duty, only for want of the articles of Clothing; Twenty of which have no Breeches at all, so that they are obliged to take their Blankets to Cover their Nakedness, and as many without a Single Shirt, Stocking or Shoe; about Thirty fit for Duty; the Rest Sick or lame, and God knows it wont be long before they will all be laid up, as the poor Fellows are obliged to fitch wood and water on their Backs, half a mile with bare legs in Snow or mud.[14]

Many men left the Army in January 1778, as their terms of service were up. For the next few months few new enlistments appear. However, by April the number of recruits began to increase. Some historians have remarked that General Howe missed a golden opportunity to attack Washington at Valley Forge when the Continental Army was at a low ebb. This might be so, but if Washington could have kept a full complement of men at Valley Forge, there would have been no chance of feeding them and his army would have dissolved.

There was much discontent among the officers at Valley Forge. Ensign Peter Dolson of the Second New York wrote to General Washington on January 1, 1778, that "I am very sorry that the low Value set on Continental Money renders my present pay incapable of Supporting me in the Character of an Officer & Consequently that I am Oblig'd to make A request Otherwise the Most distant from my soul of being discharg'd the Continental Service." His request to resign was granted. Lieutenant Colonel Pierre Regnier de Roussi of the Fourth New York, wrote to Washington on March 24, complaining about the treatment he received from Colonel Henry B. Livingston, requesting a discharge or to be transferred to another regiment, as he was "doing my best, to abbate Tiranney, I am myself treated like a slave, & cant bear it no longer." He had been acquitted at a court martial the day before, but despite his problems he continued with the regiment.[15] In Steel's Company of Malcom's Regiment three of four officers resigned in March.

All the men of the army suffered gravely from the disastrous food and clothing shortages, until Spring weather improved the roads Nathanael Greene became Quartermaster General. There were few opportunities for glory or excitement at Valley Forge. After the huts were constructed, many of the soldiers were given the opportunity to go home on furlough. Those who remained stood guard duty, cut firewood, drilled, and were sometimes sent out of camp "on command." This catchall term might mean guarding stores at an outlying post, collecting forage for the army's horses, or guarding prisoners. Throughout the six months the British were in Philadelphia and the Continental Army at Valley Forge, detachments were rotated to the "lines"–the area close to the British fortifications to stop civilians going into the city and to harass enemy patrols. These assignments were probably a welcome break from the tedium of camp, but they were not without risk as men were killed, wounded, or captured in skirmishes.

In March 1778, the arrival of "Baron" Frederick Wilhelm von Steuben brought a new drill for the army. The Commander in Chief's guard was enlarged to serve as the model company. Several men of the New York regiments were transferred to were transferred to the guard at this time. Steuben introduced a simple but highly efficient drill which was critical to the success of American arms. Washington's last letter as Commander-in-Chief, four and a half years later was to the Baron: "I wish to make use of this last moment of my public life, to signifie in the strongest terms my entire approbation of your conduct, and to express my sense of the obligations the public is under to you, for your faithful and meritorious Services.[16]

The high point of the Encampment was reached on May 6, 1778. Word of the American alliance with France was announced a few days before, and the entire army celebrated with an orchestrated *feude de joie*. Major Richard Fish closed a letter to a friend saying: The Afternoon was celebrated by all the Officers of the Army in the most rational and jocund Amusemts at Head Quarters, and the Day concluded with universal Happiness & the strictest Propriety."[17]

Further good news arrived shortly after this when it became certain that the British were preparing to evacuate Philadelphia. No one in the American camp knew what the new British commander Henry Clinton was planning to do, but the simple fact that the American capital would be free was enough reason for joy.

Philadelphia was evacuated on June 18, and the Continental Army left Valley Forge in pursuit the next day. At the Battle of Monmouth, New Jersey, on June 28, Poor's Brigade, with the Second and Fourth New York was on the field, but was not engaged in the action.

The Second and Fourth became part of the newly organized New York Brigade on July 22, 1778, which was assigned to the Northern Department. Under General James Clinton they participated in the successful Sullivan Expedition against the Six Nations in 1779, and the Battle of Newtown.

They were stationed Morristown, the Highland, and Fort Schuyler, until January 1781, when the Second was consolidated with the Fourth and Fifth New York, and designated as the Second New York Regiment. The Second and the new First New York marched to Yorktown and participated in the actions which led to the surrender of Cornwallis. In 1782, the Second went into final quarters at New Windsor, New York. In June 1783, many of the men were furloughed home; and in November, with the coming of peace, the men were honorably discharged.

---

[1]. John F. Reed, *Campaign to Valley Forge*, (Pioneer Press, 1965), 269-87.

[2]. Washington to Read, 19 December 1777, Washington Papers, Library of Congress.

[3]. Washington to Smallwood, 25 May 1777, Washington Papers, Library of Congress.

[4]. Robert K. Wright, Jr., *The Continental Army* (Washington, D. C.: Government Printing Office, 1983), 163.

[5]. Malcom to Washington, 4 January 1778, George Washington Papers, Library of Congress; Washington to Malcom, 6 January 1778. GWP Papers.

[6]. Thomas Ewing, *George Ewing, Gentleman: A Soldier of Valley Forge* (Yonkers, N.Y., 1928), 41.

[7]. Richard Mount to William Engen, 7 June 1778, Jacob, Cornelius & Henry Glen Papers, Manuscript Department, The New-York Historical Society.

[8]. For a description of this campaign see: Richard M. Ketchum, *Saratoga: Turning Point of the Revolutionary War,* New York: Henry Holt, 1997.

[9]. Putnam to Washington, 14 November 1777, George Washington Papers, Library of Congress.

[10]. Alexander Hamilton to Washington, 12 November 1777, Hamilton Papers, Library of Congress. Washington to Henry Laurens, 23 November 1777, *The Writings of George Washington from the Original Manuscript Sources, 1745-1799,* ed. John C. Fitzpatrick (Washington: Government Printing Office, 1933), *WGW,* 10:101.

[11]. Timothy Pickering, State of the Non-Commissioned Officers & Privates...., 27 December 1777, New-York Historical Society.

[12]. Washington to Henry Laurens, 22 December 1777, *WGW,* 10:183.

[13]. James Gray to Susan Gray, 24 December 1777, HM 22016, The Huntington Library, San Marino, California. Washington to William Buchanan, 7 February 1778, *WGW,* 10:427-28.

[14]. Henry Beekman Livingston to Robert Livingston, 24 December 1777, Livingston/Bancroft Transcripts, New York Public Library; Philip Van Cortlandt to George Clinton, 13 February 1778, *Public Papers of George Clinton, First Governor of New York.* (New York: Wynkoop Hallenbeck Crawford Co., 1900), 2:843-44.

[15]. Record Group 93, M 859, Roll 23, Document 7450, National Archives; Washington Papers, Library of Congress.

[16]. Wright, *Continental Army,* 141-42; Washington to Steuben, *Writings of George Washington,* 27:283.

[17]. Fish to Richard Varick, 9 May 1778, "Extract of a letter from Major Nicholas Fish to Lieutenant-colonel Richard Varick," *Historical Magazine,* 5 (March 1869), 204.

DELAWARE

Name/ Rank	Enlistment or Commission Date/Term of Enlistment	Company	Remarks
Adams, Berthol/ Bartholomew Private	June 1, 1777, March 18, 1778, Duration of War	Jaquett	April-June 1778.
Adams/Addams, James Private	Nov 1777, Duration of War	Patten	Dec 1777-May 1778; June 13, 1778 died.
Ake, William/ Wm Private	March 15, 1778, Duration of War	Learmouth	June 22, 1778 left sick. Sept 1778 roll shows him sick at Morris Town, June 22, 1778.
Alcorn/Allcorn, William Private	Jan 10, 1777	Kirkwood	Dec 1777; Jan-Feb 1778 on command waiter; March-June 1778.
Alfred, John Private	Dec 1, 1777, Duration of War	Anderson	Dec 12, 1777 deserted.
Anderson, Enoch Captain	Dec 3, 1776	Anderson	Dec 1777-June 1778.
Anderson, Herdman Drummer/ Drum Major	March 10, 1777	Anderson	Dec 1777-May 1778; June 1778 promoted to Drum Major; June 1778.
Anderson, Thomas Quartermaster	Sept 15, 1777		June 1778.
Andrews, Charles Private	Jan 4, 1777, Duration of War	Anderson	Dec 1777; Jan 4, 1778 deserted.
Andrew/ Andrews, John Private	Aug 17, 1777	Moore	Dec 1777-May 1778. He was crossed off the June 1778 payroll without comment. Roll dated Sept 10, 1778, shows him sick absent June 15, 1778.
Archdale, Thomas Private	Nov 1777, Duration of War	Patten	Died about Dec 20, 1777.
Arnage/Arnott, Nathan Private	April 16, 1778	Patten	April-May 1778; June 1778 returned from hospital.
Arnett/Arnet, Jacob Private	March 10, 1778, Duration of War	Rhodes	April-May 1778; June 1778 sick hospital. Muster roll dated Sept 9, 1778 shows him sick at Valley Forge.
Arnett/Arnold, Nathan Private	March 16, 1778, Duration of War	Patten	April-May 1778; June 1778 "Retd. from Hospital."

Name	Enlistment	Officer	Service Record
Atkins, Every/Evory Private	April 3, 1778, Duration of War	Jaquett	April 22, 1778 sick in hospital; April-May 1778; June 1778 sick hospital, Nottingham May 22.
Barns/Barnes, Lantre/Lanty Private	June 23, 1777	Moore	Dec 1777 missing or deserted from a scouting Party Sept 16, 1777.
Benign/Bernign, James Private	Feb 14, 1778, Duration of War	Patten	April 1778 muster roll shows he was taken prisoner on March 15, 1778; July, 1778 returned.
Bennet, Joseph Private	March 2, 1778		Deserted, no record he ever served.
Bennett/Bennet, Benjamin Private	Jan 20, 1777, Duration of War	Kirkwood	Dec 1777-Jan 1778; Feb 1778 sick absent; March 1778.
Bennett, Caleb Ensign	April 5, 1777	Rhodes	Dec 1777; Feb-June 1778.
Bennett/Bennet, Jeames/James Private	Dec 1776	Anderson	Dec 1777-June 1778.
Bennett, John Private	April 6, 1778	Kirkwood	April 1778; May 1778 under inoculation; June 1778 sick at Nottingham. Muster roll dated Sept 9, 1778 shows him sick at Nottingham May 1.
Bennett, John Private	April 14, 1778, Duration of War	Learmouth	June 1778 roll shows he deserted on April 16, 1778.
Benson/Benston, John/Jehu Private	March 5, 1778	Patten	April-May 1778; June 1778 sick at Brunswick; July 1778 sick at Trenton.
Bentley, John Sergeant	Oct 1777, Duration of War	Wild	Dec 1777-April 1778; June 1778. Undated roll, probably Sept 1778 shows him "on Command Newark Delaware State" Feb 5, 1778.
Berry/Berrey, Mordecai/ Mordica Corporal	May 1777; June 2, 1777	Jaquett	Dec 1777-June 1778.
Berry/Barry, Thomas Ensign	April 5, 1777	Moore	Dec 1777-June 1778.
Beatson/ Beatsman, John Ensign	April 5, 1777	Kirkwood	Dec 1777-April 1778; May 1778 on command; June 1778.
Black, David Sergeant	March 16, 1777, Duration of War	Rhodes	Dec 1777; Feb-May8; June-Aug 1778 sick hospital; Sept 1778 on furlough from hospital.
Black, William Corporal	April 27, 1777, Duration of War	Rhodes	Dec 1777; Feb-June 1778.

Name	Date	Commander	Notes
Blackshire/ Blacksher, Ebenezer/Ebenz Private	March 29, 1778, Duration of War	Anderson	May-June 1778.
Blake, John Private	May 10, 1777, Duration of War	Rhodes	Dec 1777; Feb-June 1778.
Bostock/ Bostwick, George Private	Feb 8, 1778, Duration of War	Kirkwood	April 1, 1778 joined; April 1778; May 1778 under inoculation; June 1778 sick absent.
Bostridge, Thomas Private	March 22, 1777, Duration of War	Learmouth	Dec 5, 1777 died.
Bowen/Bowing, Stephen Private		Wild	Jan-April 1778; June 1778.
Bowen, William Private	April 28, 1778	Rhodes	April-May 1778; June 1778 sick in hospital.
Boyce, Daniel Sergeant	March 2, 1778, Duration of War	Learmouth	June 1778.
Boyd, James Private	May 3, 1778, Duration of War	Learmouth	May 26, 1778 deserted.
Bradeye/Bradey, Ezekiel/Ezekeal Private	March 17, 1778	Rhodes	April-June 1778.
Brannan/ Brannon, William Private	May 1, 1778, Duration of War	Kirkwood	May 1778 picquett; June 1778 on piquett.
Brattan/Bratten, James 2nd. Lt.	Jan 1, 1777; April 5, 1777	Moore	Dec 1777-June 1778.
Bride see McBride			
Briann/Brown, Jeremiah Private	April 25, 1778, Duration of War	Learmouth	May 1778 not joined the regiment. May 26, 1778 deserted. Appears on Sept 1778 muster roll.
Brooks, Seth Corporal	Jan 3, 1777	Learmouth	Dec 1777-June 1778.
Brown, Andrew Private	May 29, 1778, Duration of War	Kirkwood	May 1778 under inoculation; June 1778 under inoculation at Nottingham. Muster roll dated Sept 9, 1778 shows him sick at Nottingham June 5.
Brown, Caleb 2nd. Lt.	April 5, 1777	Rhodes	Dec 1777; Feb-June 1778.
Brown, John Private	Jan 3, 1777	Kirkwood	Dec 1777; Jan-Feb 1778 on command as waiter; March-June 1778.
Brown, Joseph Private	May 7, 1777	Rhodes	December 25, 1777 died.

Name/Rank	Enlistment	Company	Service
Brown, Joshua Private	March 28, 1778	Patten	April-May 1778; June 1778 sick at Brunswick; July 1778 sick at Trenton.
Brown, Stephen Private	March 31, 1778	Rhodes	April-May 1778; June 1778 joined from hospital.
Brown, William/ Wm Private	June 22, 1777, Duration of War	Anderson	Dec 1777-June 1778. Muster roll dated Sept 9, 1778 shows "Wounded 4th October 77. on Furlough from 19."
Bryan, Jeremiah Private	March 22, 1778		Date of enlistment is the only record found.
Bulling, John Private	March 17, 1778, Duration of War		Date of enlistment is the only record found.
Burcham, John Private	Nov 23, 1777, Duration of War	Moore	Dec 1777-May 1778. He was crossed off the June 1778 payroll without comment. July 17, 1778 died.
Burchard, John Private	April 8, 1778, Duration of War	Kirkwood	May 1778 under inoculation; June 1778 sick absent. See Richard, John.
Burchard, William Private		Kirkwood	June 1778 sick at Nottingham. Muster roll dated Sept 9, 1778 shows him sick at Nottingham May 1.
Burke/Burk, Patrick Private	Dec 31, 1776	Anderson	Dec 1777-June 1778.
Burns,Barns, John Private	March 6, 1778	Rhodes	April 8, 1778 deserted.
Burris/Burows, Joseph Private	Jan 1. 1777; Feb 7, 1777, Duration of War	Moore	Dec 1777 sick present; Jan-May 1778; June 3, 1778 discharged.
Burrous/Burrows, Patton Private	Dec 26, 1777, Duration of War	Moore	Dec 1777-May 1778. He was crossed off the June 1778 payroll without comment.
Butcher/ Burtchen, William/Wm Private	March 8, 1778	Anderson	May-June 1778.
Burton, Jacob Private	May 11, 1778, Duration of War	Jaquett	May-June 1778.
Caimon, Patrick Private		Kirkwood	March 1778 muster roll is the only record.
Camford/ Comford, Valentine/ Valentint Private	Aug 21, 1777, Duration of War	Kirkwood	Dec 1777-Jan 1778; Feb 1778 on command; March 1778; April-May 1778 weaving stockings; June 1778 on command at stocking factory.

Cammell/ Campbell, Colin/Collen Private	April 6, 1778, Duration of War	Wild	June 1778.
Campbell, George Private	May 18, 1778, Duration of War	Kirkwood	May 1778 sick in hospital; June 1778 sick at Valley Forge. Muster roll dated Sept 9, 1778 shows him sick at Valley Forge June 16.
Campbell/ Campell, James/Jeams Ensign	Jan 1, 1777; April 5, 1777, Duration of War	Anderson	Dec 1777-June 1778.
Campbell/Camble, James, Private	Nov 29, 1776; Jan 1, 1777	Kirkwood	Dec 1777-Jan 1778 sick absent; Feb-June 1778.
Carr, John Private	Jan 3, 1777, Duration of War	Kirkwood	Dec 1777-June 1778.
Carson, James Private	Jan 20, 1777, Duration of War	Learmouth	Dec 1777-June 1778.
Carty, William Private	March 8, 1778; April 8, 1778, Duration of War	Jaquett	April 29, 1778 deserted.
Carvel/Connel, Isick/Isaac Private	Jan 1, 1777, Duration of War	Kirkwood	Dec 1777 on command as waiter; Jan-March 1778; April 1778 picquett; May 1778 under inoculation; June 1778.
Casson/Carson, James Private	Jan 20, 1777, Duration of War	Patten	Dec 1777-Feb 1778; March 1778 on furlough; April 1778.
Casson/Cassin, Robert/Robt Private	Duration of War	Patten	May 1778.
Castle/Casels, John Private	June 24, 1777, Duration of War	Jaquett	Dec 1777-June 1778.
Cavender/ Cavander, Jeames/Jeemes Corporal/ Sergeant	March 1, 1777, Duration of War	Anderson	Dec 1777; Jan 1, 1778 appointed Sergeant; Jan-March 1778; April 17, 1778 died.
Cayton/Keaton, James Private	May 25, 1777, Duration of War	Moore	Dec 1777 on guard; Jan-June 1778.
Cazier/Casier, John Sergeant	April 12, 1778, Duration of War	Anderson	April 12, 1778 enlisted and appointed a Sergeant; April-June 1778.
Christian, John Private	June 21, 1777	Jaquett	Dec 1777.

Cimmey see
Kimmey

Clark/Clerk, Alexander/Alexdr Private	April 7, 1778	Anderson	April-June 1778.
Clark, Harman/Herman Private	March 17, 1777 Duration of War	Patten	Dec 1777-June 1778.
Clark, James Private	April 26, 1778, Duration of War	Patten	April-June 1778.
Clark, John Private	June 4, 1777; June 17, 1777, Duration of War	Kirkwood	Dec 1777-Feb 1778 sick absent; March-June 1778.
Clark, Thomas/ Thos Drummer	June 4, 1777	Kirkwood	Dec 1777-April 1778.
Clifton, Bosman/ Boseman Private	May 23, 1778, Duration of War	Kirkwood	June 1778. Muster roll dated Sept 9, 1778 shows him sick at Nottingham June 13.
Clifton, George Private	Feb 17, 1778; March 13, 1778, Duration of War	Patten	April-May 1778; June 1778 returned from hospital.
Clifton, John Private	Jan 1, 1777, Duration of War	Wild	Dec 1777-April 1778; June 1778 returned from hospital.
Clifton, Whittington/ Williston Private	Feb 16, 1778; March 16, 1778, Duration of War	Kirkwood	March 22, 1778 joined; April-June 1778.
Cochern/ Cochran, Daniel Sergeant/ Sergeant Major	Jan 1, 1777, Duration of War	Kirkwood	Dec 1777. In January he was apparently promoted to Sergeant Major for the regiment and appears at that rank in June 1778.
Cochran/ Cochren, James Private		Patten	Dec 1777-June 1778.
Cochran, John Private		Patten	Only notation March 23, 1778 deserted
Cody/Coadey, William/Wm Private	March 1, 1778	Anderson	March-May 1778; June 1778 Prior Inlistment taken 21 June.
Coffhile, Richard Private	Oct 1777, Duration of War	Anderson	Dec 1777-June 1778.
Conoffill/ Conoffeld, Hugh Private	Jan 16, 1777	Kirkwood	Dec 1777-Jan 1778; Feb-March 1778 on bullock guard; April 1778 standing guard; May 1778 guard; June 1778.
Cole, Zebulon/ Zebeloun Private	March 28, 1778, Duration of War	Jaquett	April-June 1778.

Name/Rank	Enlistment	Captain	Record
Coleman/ Colman, Patrick/Patt Private	June 1777; Aug 1, 1777, Duration of War	Kirkwood	Dec 1777-June 1778.
Collins/Collings, George Private	May 10, 1778, Duration of War	Patten	May-June 1778.
Collins/Collens, John Private	Jan 28, 1778, Duration of War	Patten	Jan 1778; Feb 1778 "Joyned from Desertion 1st Febry"; March 1778 payroll shows he deserted on March 26. The May payroll shows he deserted on May 23.
Collins/Collings, Thomas/Tho. Private	Oct 1777, Duration of War	Wild	Dec 1777-April 1778; June 1778.
Comine, Nathan Private	March 14, 1778, Duration of War	Learmouth	Date of enlistment is the only record found.
Conner/Connor, John Private	Dec 4, 1776; Jan 4, 1777, Duration of War	Kirkwood	Dec 1777-Jan 1778 sick absent; Feb 1778; March 1778 on furlough March 1; April-June 1778.
Connor/Conner, Edward Private	Oct 1777, Duration of War	Anderson	Dec 1777-June 1778.
Connelly/ Connolly, Charles Private	Feb 25, 1778, Duration of War	Learmouth	June 1778.
Coock/Cooch, Jonathan/ Jonothon Private	Oct 1777, Duration of War	Anderson	Dec 1777-June 1778. Sept 1778 muster roll shows "Shoemaking in Newark Factory 20 Jan 1778."
Cook/Cooke, James Drummer/ Private	Feb 18, 1777, Duration of War	Learmouth	Dec 1777-April 1778; April 20, 1778 "joined ranks" which means reduced to private; May-June 1778.
Cook, John Private	Feb 28, 1778, Duration of War	Kirkwood	April 1778 at ye factory; May 1778 Newark factory; June 1778 clothing factory.
Cook, Timothy Fifer	Jan 10, 1777, Duration of War	Learmouth	Dec 1777-June 1778.
Cork/Cook, Jacob Private	April 6, 1778 Duration of War	Rhodes	June 1778.
Correy/Curry, John Private	May 27, 1777	Kirkwood	Dec 1777; Jan 1778 on furlough; Feb-April 1778; May 1778 on party; June 1778.
Corse, John 1st. Lt.	Dec 3, 1776	Anderson	Dec 1777-June 1778.

Coulter, Charles Sergeant	Feb 27, 1777, Duration of War	Learmouth	Dec 1777-March 1778; March 15, 1778 taken prisoner; June 21, 1778 returned from prison.
Coverdil/ Coverdale, Benjamin Private	Duration of War	Wild	Dec 1777-April 1778; June 1778.
Cox, Daniel/Dannal Powell 2nd. Lt.	Jan 4, 1777; April 5, 1777	Wild	Dec 1777-April 1778; June 1778.
Cox, John/Jno Sergeant	Jan 3, 1777	Learmouth	Dec 1777-June 1778.
Cox, Matthew Private	April 24, 1778, Duration of War	Learmouth	June 1778.
Cox, Nathan/ Nathanl. Private	April 21, 1778; April 23, 1778, Duration of War	Kirkwood/ Moore	April 1778; May 1778 under inoculation; June 3, 1778 transferred to Moore's Company.
Crawford, Alexander Corporal	April 28, 1778	Anderson	Enlisted and appointed a Corporal on April 28, 1778; April-June 1778.
Crawford, Alexander Private	April 12, 1778, Duration of War	Rhodes	June 1778 joined from hospital.
Croft/Cronofft, Peter/Pett Private	Dec 31, 1776	Kirkwood	Dec 1777-Feb 1778; March 1778 absent for want of shoes April 1778 pioneer; May-June 1778.
Crosby/Crosbey, John Private	Oct 1777, Duration of War	Anderson	Dec 1777; Jan 12, 1778 died.
Cross, Samuel/ Saml Corporal	May 20, 1777, Duration of War	Moore	Dec 1777 sick absent; Jan-June 1778.
Cullen, John Private	March 17, 1778, Duration of War	Rhodes	April-May 1778; June 21, 1778 supposed deserted.
Culver/Culvert, Levin Private	Feb 11, 1778; March 11, 1778, Duration of War	Kirkwood	March 22, 1778 joined; April-May 1778 under inoculation; June 1778 sick at Nottingham. Muster roll dated Sept 9, 1778 shows him sick at Nottingham May 1.
Curry/Currey, John Private	April 10, 1777; May 27, 1777, Duration of War	Kirkwood	Dec 1777; Jan 1778 on furlough; Feb 1778 on command; March 1778 on command; March 1778 on furlough; April 1778; May 1778 on party; June 1778.
Curry, Nathan Private	April 24, 1778, Duration of War	Kirkwood	April 1778; May 1778 under inoculation; June 1778 deserted from hospital at Nottingham.

Currypool, Richard Private	Feb 8, 1778; March 8, 1778, Duration of War	Kirkwood	April 1, 1778 joined; April 1778; May 1778 under inoculation; June 1778 on bullock guard.
Daily/Dailey, Andrew/Ander Drummer/Private	May 30, 1777, Duration of War	Jaquett	Dec 1777-June 1778. March 1, 1778 reduced to private
Dailey/Dayly, Daniel/Dan. Private	March 2, 1777 Duration of War	Patten	Dec 1777-June 1778.
Daily/Dailey, Thomas/Tho. Private	March 16, 1777, Duration of War	Rhodes	Dec 1777; Feb-March 1778.
Dangherty, Michael Private		Patten	May 1778.
Darnill/Darnell, Isick/Isaac Private	March 1, 1778, Duration of War	Learmouth	June 1778.
Daugerty/ Dougharty, Michael Private	May 21, 1777, Duration of War	Jaquett	Dec 1777-March 1778; April 1778 muster roll shows he deserted on May 17. April 1778 payroll shows he deserted on April 17. Oct 1778 rejoined.
Davis, Patrick Private	Jan 16, 1777	Learmouth	Dec 1777; Jan 1, 1778 deserted.
Davis/Daviss, Samuel Sergeant	Jan 8, 1777, Duration of War	Rhodes	Dec 1777; Feb 1778-June 1778.
Dawars/Dawors, William Private	Feb 22, 1777, Duration of War	Anderson	Dec 1777-May 1778; June 4, 1778 deserted.
Deman/Demarr, James Private	April 21, 1778, Duration of War	Kirkwood	April 1778; May 1778 under inoculation; June 1778 sick at Nottingham. Muster roll dated Sept 9, 1778 shows him sick at Nottingham May 1.
Dempsy/ Dempsey, Dennis Private/Corporal	Oct 1777, Duration of War	Anderson	Dec 1777-Jan 1778; Jan 24, 1778 promoted to Corporal; Feb-June 1778.
Denny, James Private	April 20, 1778, Duration of War	Learmouth	May 1778 enlisted not yet joined; June 4, 1778 deserted.
Deusey/Dewsey, Patrick Private	May 24, 1777, Duration of War	Anderson	Dec 1777-June 1778.
Dixon, Andrew Private	April 18, 1777	Learmouth	Dec 1777-June 1778.
Dixon/Dixen, William/Wm Private	June 11, 1777, Duration of War	Anderson	Dec 1777-June 1778.

Donaldson/ Donnaldson, William Private	April 24, 1778	Kirkwood	April 16, 1778 joined; April 1778; May-June 1778 clothing factory.
Donnally/ Donnelly, Hugh Private	Jan 4, 1777; Oct 1777, Duration of War	Anderson	Dec 1777-June 1778.
Donneho/ Donohow, Thomas/Thos Private	April 19, 1777	Learmouth	Dec 1777-March 1778; April 1, 1778 deserted.
Dorman, Mathew Private	April 7, 1777 Duration of War	Patten	May 1778 smallpox at Dover; June 22, 1778 died at Dover.
Dormant/Dorment, Michael/Micheal Private	Feb 7, 1777; Oct 1777, Duration of War	Anderson	Dec 1777-June 1778. September 1778 payroll shows "Tayloring Factory at Newark 28 March." Muster Roll dated Sept 9, 1778 shows him "Taylor in Newark" Jan 20, 1778.
Dougherty/ Daugharty, James Sergeant	Jan 1, 1777, Duration of War	Kirkwood	Dec 1777; Jan 1778 sick absent; Feb 1778; March 1778 sick in quarters; April 1778 sick in quarters; May 1778 sick absent; June 3, 1778 discharged.
Dougherty/ Daugherty, Nathaniel Corporal/Private	Jan 20, 1777	Learmouth	Dec 1777-Jan 1778; Jan 18, 1778 reduced to private; Feb-April 1778; May 12, 1778 deserted.
Douglass/ Douglas, Peter Fifer	Feb 10, 1778, Duration of War	Jaquett	Feb-March 1778; April 1778 roll shows he went on furlough March 12; May 1778; June 1778 on furlough March 12, 1778.
Dowds/Downs, Charles/Chars. Private	Jan 6, 1777; May 1778, Duration of War	Patten	April 22, 1778, received for McLaughlin the same day; May 1778; June 1778 orderly at Trenton.
Dowds, William Corporal	Jan 1, 1777; Jan 7, 1777, Duration of War	Kirkwood	Dec 1777; Jan 1778 on furlough; Feb 1778 sick absent; March-April 1778 recruiting; May 1778 on command; June 1778.
Downs, Robert Private	April 2, 1778, Duration of War	Patten	April-June 1778.
Drew, William Private	May 24, 1778, Duration of War	Kirkwood	May 1778 under inoculation; June 1778 joined.
Duff, Henry 2nd. Lt.	Jan 1, 1777; April 5, 1777	Anderson	Dec 1777-June 1778.
Duffy, Laughlin Private		Patten	May 1778.

Duncle/Duncley, William Private	May 20, 1777, Duration of War	Moore	Dec 1777 missing or deserted from scouting party near Philadelphia Nov. 5; Feb 1778 taken prisoner Nov 5, 1777 and returned Feb 7; Feb-May 1778.
Dunn/Dounn, Patrick/Patt Private/Corporal	July 16, 1777	Kirkwood	Dec 1777; Jan 1778 promoted to Corporal; Jan 1778-June 1778.
Dunn, Thomas Private	Duration of War	Anderson	Jan 14, 1778 came back from desertion; Jan-May 1778; June 1778 returned from hospital.
Durnett, Charles Private	Feb 23, 1778, Duration of War	Kirkwood	April-May 1778 at ye Cross Roads; June 1778; July 11, 1778 Duration of War.
Dyer/Dyar, James Private	March 6 1778; March 12, 1778, Duration of War	Rhodes	April 14, 1778 deserted.
Edgess/Edgliss, John Private	March 6, 1778, Duration of War	Rhodes	April 14, 1778 deserted.
Edwards, Edward Private	June 20, 1777, Duration of War	Jaquett	Dec 1777-Jan 1778; Feb 1778 waggoner for G. Sullivan; March 1778.
Elliot, Moses Private	March 10, 1778, Duration of War	Patten	One reference is April 1778 payroll which shows he deserted on March 27, 1778.
Ellis/Elliss, David Private	Nov 1777, Duration of War	Patten	Dec 1777-May 1778; June 1778 returned from hospital.
Emerton/ Emorton, Joseph Private/Corporal	June 18, 1777, Duration of War	Rhodes	Dec 1777; Feb-May 1778; June 1, 1778 promoted to Corporal; June 1778.
Emmory/Emery, William Private	April 1, 1778, Duration of War	Rhodes	April-May 1778; June 1778 sick in hospital. Muster roll dated Sept 9, 1778 shows him sick at Valley Forge.
English, Berthol/ Bartholomew Private	May 28, 1777; May 29, 1777, Duration of War	Jaquett	Feb 1778 command joined Feb 1; March-April 1778; April 30, 1778 sick in hospital; May-June 1778.
English, Thomas Private	March 10, 1778, Duration of War	Kirkwood	April 1, 1778 joined; March 27, 1778 deserted.
English, William Private	Feb 27, 1778	Jaquett	Only record is the Feb 1778 muster roll which shows his enlistment date.
Engram/Ingram, Eli Private	April 16, 1778; May 16, 1778, Duration of War	Jaquett	April 1778.
Ermine, William Private	March 8, 1778	Jaquett	Only record is the enlistment date.

Eshon/Easom, John Sergeant	Oct 1777. Duration of War	Wild	Dec 1777-April 1778; June 1778.
Evans, Jenkin Private	June 7, 1777, Duration of War	Jaquett	Dec 1777-March 1778; April 1778 on guard; May-June 1778.
Evans/Eavens, William Private	March 4, 1778; March 6, 1778, Duration of War	Jaquett	April 1778; April 22, 1778 sick in hospital; June 1778 sick hospital Valley Forge. June 19. Muster roll dated Sept 8, 1778 shows him "in Hospital 19 June."
Everite/Everigtt, John/Jno Private/Corporal	April 27, 1778, Duration of War	Jaquett	April-June 1778. June 1778 promoted to Corporal.
Fagan/Fagen, Garrett/Garet Private	Jan 1, 1777, Nov 1777, Duration of War	Patten	Oct-Nov 1777 Bethlehem Hospital; Dec 1777-Jan 1778 at hospital; Feb 1778 sick in hospital; March 1778; April 1778 unfit for duty; May 1778 Phila Hospital; June 16, 1778 discharged.
Farguson/ Fargusson, Robert Private	Jan 14, 1777, Duration of War	Kirkwood	Dec 1777-May 1778; June 1778 sick at Valley Forge. Muster roll dated Sept 9, 1778 shows him sick at Valley Forge June 16.
Fegin/Fagen, Cato Private	Oct 1777, Duration of War	Learmouth	Dec 1777-May 1778; June 14, 1778 deserted.
Ferguson/ Farguson, Joseph/Jos Private	May 1, 1778	Kirkwood	May-June 1778.
Figgs, Charles Private	March 5, 1778, Duration of War	Patten	April-May 1778; June 1778 returned from hospital.
Fink, George Private	June 17, 1777; July 17, 1777, Duration of War	Kirkwood	Dec 1777-Feb 1778 sick absent; March 1778; April-May 1778 sick absent; June 1778 sick at Nottingham. Muster roll dated Sept 9, 1778 shows him sick at Nottingham May 1.
Fish/Fich, William Private	Nov 27, 1777; Dec 1, 1777, Duration of War	Kirkwood	Dec 1777-Feb 1778 on command as waiter; March 1778 on command Feb 15; April-May 1778 on command; June 1778 at Nottingham hospital.
Fleetwood, Jonson/Johnson Private	Oct 1777, Duration of War	Wild	Jan-April 1778; May 16, 1778 deserted. Feb 1779 roll shows him returned from desertion.
Fleming/ Flemming, Hugh Private	Oct 1777, Duration of War	Wild	Dec 1777-April 1778; June 1778.

Name	Enlistment	Company	Service
Flemming/ Flemin, William Private	Aug 4, 1777, Duration of War	Patten	Dec 1777 at hospital; Jan 1778 "Hosp'l"; Feb-March 1778 1778 sick in hospital.
Flinn, Patrick Private	Duration of War	Anderson	Dec 1777-June 1778.
Flower/Flowers, Alexander Private	May 30, 1778	Kirkwood	May 1778 under inoculation; June 1778. Muster roll dated Sept 9, 1778 shows him sick at Nottingham May 10.
Flowers, Elias/Ellis Private	Duration of War	Wild	Dec 1777-April 1778; June 1778 returned from hospital.
Foplis, John/ Jno C. Private		Jaquett	Jan 1778-March 1778; April 22 sick hospital; May-June 1778.
Ford, Andrew Private	May 3, 1778, Duration of War	Learmouth	June 1778 shows he deserted on May 26, 1778.
Foster, William/Wm Private	Jan 21, 1777, Duration of War	Patten	Dec 1777-June 1778.
Freeland, Emanuel Private	May 20, 1778	Kirkwood	May 23, 1778 deserted.
Furbush, John Private	Duration of War	Wild	Dec 1777-April 1778; June 1778 returned from hospital.
Furbush, William Private	March 15, 1778, Duration of War	Jaquett	April-May 1778; June 22 1778 sick hospital Coords Ferry.
Gamble, James Corporal		Patten	May 1778 absent.
Gardiner/ Gardner, Christopher/ Christ./ Private	Feb 24, 1777; Oct 1777, Duration of War	Anderson	Dec 1777-May 1778; Payroll shows he deserted on June 16, 1778; Muster roll shows he deserted on June 1.
Garrett, Nathan Private		Patten	May 1778.
Garrett/Garret, Richard/Richd Private	Nov 1777, Duration of War	Anderson	Dec 1777-May 1778; June 1778 sick in country.
Gilder, Reuben Surgeon	April 5, 1777		June 1778.
Giles/Joyles, Thomas Private	May 23, 1777, Duration of War	Rhodes	Dec 1777; Feb-May 1778; June 1778 sick hospital. Muster roll dated Sept 9, 1778 shows him sick at Valley Forge. Dec 1778 died at Yellow Springs.
Gorden/Garden, Jeemes/James Private	March 16, 1778	Anderson	March 27, 1778 deserted.

Gordon, Thomas/Tho. Private	April 27, 1778, Duration of War	Learmouth	June 10, 1778 left sick; Sept 9, 1778 "Sick at Valley forge June 10 1778"
Gorman/Garman, John Private	May 19, 1777, Duration of War	Jaquett	Dec 1777-Jan 1778; Feb 1778 on command Feb 5; March 1778; April 1778 on command Feb 5; May-June 1778. Muster roll dated Sept 8, 1778 shows him "on Command February 5."
Goter/Gouther, Charles Private	March 1, 1778, Duration of War	Rhodes	In Sept 1778 he first appears on the rolls and drew seven months pay.
Grace, William/Wm Private	Feb 7, 1778, Duration of War	Kirkwood	March 22, 1778 joined; April 1778; May 1778 under guard; June 1778.
Green, Michael/Michl Fifer	April 5, 1777; Nov 1777, Duration of War	Patten	Dec 1777-Jan 1778; Feb 1778 sick in hospital; March-June 1778.
Greenwood, John Private	Feb 26, 1778	Jaquett	Only record is of his enlistment. A Johnson Fleetwood appears in 1779 as having returned from desertion.
Griffin/Griffing, Edward Private		Wild	Dec 1777-April 1778; June 1778.
Griffith/Griffin, Curtis/Curt Private	Feb 16, 1778; March 16, 1778, Duration of War	Kirkwood	March 22, 1778 joined; April-May 1778; June 1778 at Peekskiln.
Griffith/Griffen, Isick/Isaac Private	Feb 16, 1778; March 16, 1778, Duration of War	Kirkwood	March 22, 1778 joined; April-May 1778; June 1778 at Peeks Kill.
Griffith/Griffiths, William Private	April 29, 1778, Duration of War	Learmouth	April-June 1778.
Grimes/Grahams, Cornelius Private	Jan 12, 1777, Duration of War	Kirkwood	Dec 1777-March 1778; April 1778 sick present; May 1778 sick absent; June 1778 sick at Valley Forge. Muster roll dated Sept 9, 1778 shows him sick at Valley Forge June 16.
Grimes, William Private	April 22, 1778, Duration of War	Kirkwood	April 23, 1778 deserted.
Gutrey/Gutery, William Private	Jan 2, 1777; Oct 1777, Duration of War	Anderson	June 1778.
Hackney, John Private	March 10, 1778, Duration of War	Rhodes	April-May 1778; June 1778 sick hospital. Muster roll dated Sept 9, 1778 shows him sick at Valley Forge.

Hagney/Heagnea, Cornelius/ Corneleus Private	1776; Oct 1777, Duration of War	Anderson	Dec 1777; Jan 1778 on furlough; Feb-May 1778; June 1778 returned from hospital.
Haigans/Haigns, William Private	Jan 1, 1777	Kirkwood	Dec 1777-June 1778.
Hall, David Colonel	Jan 4 1777; April 5, 1777		June 1778.
Hamelton/ Hamilton, John Private	Feb 5, March 5, 1778, Duration of War	Kirkwood	March 22, 1778 joined; April-May 1778; June 1778 Missing June 28.
Hamilton/ Hambleton, Charles Corporal	Jan 13, 1777, Duration of War	Kirkwood	Dec 1777; Jan 1778 sick absent; Feb-April 1778; May 1778 sick in quarters; June 1778 sick at Valley Forge.
Handley/Hanley, Daniel/Danl Private	Feb 9, 1777, Duration of War	Moore	Dec 1777-June 1778. Roll dated Sept 10, 1778, shows him "at the Factory" Feby. 1, 1778.
Harbert/Harbet, John Private	Feb 20, 1777	Moore	Dec 1777 on furlough; Jan-June 1778.
Harney/Harnney, Ginnathaw/ Genthan 1st. Lt.		Patten	Dec 1777-April 1778 absent; May 1778 prisoner Long Island.
Harper/Hearper, Thomas Private	Jan 12, 1778, Duration of War	Kirkwood	Jan-March 1778; April 1778 blacksmith; May 1778; June 1778 blacksmith.
Harris/Harrison, Richard/Richd Private	Oct 1777, Duration of War	Learmouth	Dec 1777-March 1778; April 1, 1778 deserted; April-June 1778.
Harris, Thomas Private	April 7, 1778, Duration of War	Learmouth	April-June 1778.
Harry, Daniel Private	June 1, 1778, Duration of War	Jaquett	June 1778.
Hask, Frederick Private		Anderson	June 1778.
Haslet, Kenler/Kenlar Private	Nov 1777, Duration of War	Patten	Dec 1777-June 1778.
Hasty/Heasty, Robert Private		Wild	Dec 1777-April 1778; June 1778.
Hatfield, John Private	April 23, 1778, Duration of War	Learmouth	June 1778.
Hawkes/Hawks, Richard Private	Feb 23, 1778, Duration of War	Patten	April 1778 payroll shows he was taken prisoner March 15, 1778.

Name / Rank	Enlistment	Company	Notes
Hays/Hayes, Charles, Private	Oct 1777, Duration of War	Anderson	Dec 23, 1777 died.
Hazzard, Cord, Captain	April 5, 1777	Wild	Dec 1777; Jan 27, 1778 resigned.
Hearny/Harney, Ginnathan/ Gennathan, 1st. Lt.	Jan 15, 1776; Nov 30, 1776	Patten	Nov, 1777; "Returned from Imprisonment 25th Novr.—absent with leave"; Dec 1777-April 1778 absent; May-June 1778. Though he appears on the payrolls, no amount is listed for pay.
Helford, Matthew/Mattw, Private	Feb 15, 1777, Duration of War	Moore	Dec 1777 on guard; Jan-June 1778.
Hewlin/Hewling, William, Private	April 16, 1778; April 27, 1778, Duration of War	Jaquett	April 1778 muster roll shows he deserted on May 18. April payroll shows he deserted April 18, 1778.
Hibbard/Hebbard, Joseph/Jos, Private	April 1, 1778	Jaquett	April 19, 1778 on command; April-May 1778; June 1778 on command Delaware State April 9.
Higman/ Heighman, Joshua/Joseph, Private	March 6, 1778, Duration of War	Jaquett	April-May 1778; June 1778 muster roll shows him sick hospital, Kings Ferry, July 19. June 1778 payroll shows him in hospital June 19, returned June 27.
Higman, Meniah/Nemiah, Private	March 16, 1778, Duration of War	Jaquett	April-June 1778.
Hignet/Hignitt, John/Jno, Private	June 20, June 21, 1777	Jaquett	Jan-March 1778 prisoner at Philadelphia.
Hill, Absolom, Private	March 4, 1778, Duration of War	Patten	April-June 1778
Hill, John, Private	March 6, 1778, Duration of War	Rhodes	April-June 1778.
Hilton, John, Artificer		Anderson	April 1778 payroll shows him paid from April 1, 1777 to April 1, 1778.
Hinds, James, Private	April 3, 1778, Duration of War		Date of enlistment is the only record found.
Hines, Thomas, Private		Patten	May 1778.
Hine/Hines, William, Corporal	May 23, 1777	Jaquett	Dec 1777-Jan 1778; Feb 1778 on command March 8; March 20, 1778 deserted.
Hinnis, John, Private		Patten	May 1778 muster roll shows he deserted in March 1778.

Holdeton/ Holdston, Thomas/Tho. Private	April 4, 1778, Duration of War	Learmouth	June 1778.
Hollingsworth/ Holingsworth, Charles Private	Feb 14, 1778, Duration of War	Rhodes	April-May 1778; June 1778 sick hospital. Muster roll dated Sept 9, 1778 shows him sick at Valley Forge.
Holt/Hoult, William Private	March 12, 1778, Duration of War	Jaquett	April-May 1778; June 1778 sick hospital, June 19.
Hook, William Private	April 27, 1778, Duration of War	Learmouth	June 1778.
Hosea/Hozea, John Private/Corporal	Feb 11, 1778; March 11, 1778, Duration of War	Kirkwood	March 22, 1778 joined; April-May 1778; May 1778 promoted to Corporal; June 1778 returned from hospital.
Hoskins/ Hoskens, Robert Private	Feb 20, 1777, Duration of War	Rhodes	Dec 1777; February-June 1778.
Hosman, Joseph Ensign	April 5, 1777; April 15, 1777	Learmouth	Dec 1777-June 1778.
Houston, Elijah Private	March 30, 1778	Kirkwood	April 13, 1778 deserted.
Hugg, Benjamin Private	Feb 4, 1777; Oct 1777, Duration of War	Anderson	Dec 1777-May 1778. September 1778 roll lists him as "in the Army 26 March".
Hughes/Huse, Robert Sergeant	Dec 30, 1776; Jan 1, 1777 Duration of War	Kirkwood	Jan 1778 "Escaped from the Enemy was taken Germantown Battle Oct 4, 1777"; Feb-June 1778.
Husbands/ Husbands, James Corporal	July 16, 1777, Duration of War	Patten	Dec 1777-June 1778.
Hutchison/ Heutchison, John/Jno Private	May 1, 1777	Jaquett	April 17, 1778 deserted.
Hyatt, John Vance 2nd. Lt.	March 1, 1777; April 5, 1777	Jaquett	Dec 1777-Jan 1778; Feb 1778 sick quarters; March 1778; April 1778 prisoner at Philadelphia April 26. Muster roll dated Sept 8, 1778 shows him "Prisoner" on April 1. 1778.
Ingley/Inglery, William Private	Aug 5, 1777, Duration of War	Jaquett	Dec 1777-Jan 1778; Feb 23, 1778 died.

Ingram, Eli Private		Jaquett	April 22, sick in hospital.
Jackson, Ebenezer/Eleazer Private	April 23, 1778, Duration of War	Learmouth	Sept 9, 1778 "Sick Nottingham Hospital May 3d 1778" only record
Jackson, John Private	March 27, 1778, Duration of War	Rhodes	April-June 1778.
Jakes/Jackes, George/Geo Private	June 5, 1777; Oct 1777, Duration of War	Wild	Dec 1777-Feb 1778; March 18, 1778 "Prisond."
Jaquett/Jacquett, Peter Captain	Jan 4, 1777; April 5, 1777	Jaquett	Dec 1777March 1778; April 1778 on party; May 1778 ; June 1778 wound.
Jermin/Jermin, William	April 18, 1778, Duration of War	Jaquett	April 29, 1778 deserted.
Joab, Moses Private	Jan 3, 1777; Jan 9, 1777, Duration of War	Kirkwood	Dec 1777-Feb 1778 sick absent; March-April 1778; May 1778 sick absent; June 1778 sick at Nottingham. Muster roll dated Sept 9, 1778 shows him sick at Nottingham May 10.
John, James Private	Feb 17, 1778	Patten	Only reference is name on the April 1778 payroll.
Johnson/Jonson, John Private	Oct 1777, Duration of War	Wild	Dec 1777-March 1778; April 20, 1778 deserted.
Johnston/ Jonston, Adam/Addam Sergeant	Nov 22, 1776, Duration of War	Moore	Dec 1777-June 1778.
Jones, Francis Private	March 26, 1778, Duration of War	Jaquett	April-June 1778.
Jones, Stanford/ Private	April 21, 1778, Duration of War	Kirkwood	April 1778-May 1778; June 1778 sick absent.
Jordan, Jonathan/Jno Corporal/ Sergeant	Oct 1777, Duration of War	Learmouth	Dec 1777-March 1778; March 9, 1778 promoted to Sergeant; April-June 1778.
Joyles see Giles			
Kayton see Cayton			
Kearney/Kerney, Dennis Private	Jan 18, 1777, Duration of War	Kirkwood	Dec 1777; Jan 1778 sick absent; Feb 28, 1778 died.
Keaton see Cayton			
Kelty/Kilty, William/Wm Private	Dec 26, 1776, Duration of War	Kirkwood	Dec 1777 sick absent; Jan-March 1778; April 1778 on detachment; May-June 1778.

Kershaw/ Kirshaw, Mitchel/Mitch Sergeant	June 10, 1777, Duration of War	Jaquett	Dec 1777-Jan 1778; Feb 1778 on command; March 1778; April 1778 on command; May 1778; June 1778 on detachment July 26.
Keys, William/Wm Private	May 27, 1777, Duration of War	Moore	Dec 1777-June 1778.
Kidd, Charles Ensign	April 5, 1777	Jaquett	Dec 1777-March 1778; April 1778 recruting; May 1778; June 11, 1778 wounded. Muster roll dated Sept 8, 1778 shows him "Wounded 1 of June absent."
Kilcanny/ Kilkany, Timothy/Timy Private	May 14, 1777, Duration of War	Jaquett	Dec 1777-June 1778.
Kimmey/ Cimmey, James Private	March 6, 1778, Duration of War	Jaquett	April-June 1778.
Kinde/Kindle, John	July 25, 1777, Duration of War	Moore	Dec 1777-Jan 1778 not joined detained at home for trial at court.
Kindsley/ Kindsly, Mark Private	March 6, 1778	Rhodes	April 14, 1778 deserted.
King, John Private		Anderson	Dec 1777-June 1778.
King, John/Jno Private	April 23, 1778, Duration of War	Patten	April-June 1778.
King, John Private	Jan 24, 1777; April 21, 1777, Duration of War	Rhodes	Dec 1777; Feb-March 1778.
Kinner-See Skinner			
Kinney/Kenney, William Private	May 12, 1777, Duration of War	Moore	Dec 1777 sick absent; Jan-March 1778.
Kirby/Kerby, Griffith Private	April 14, 1778, Duration of War	Learmouth	June 22, 1778 left sick; Aug 12, 1778 died.
Kirkwood, Robert Captain	Dec 1, 1776	Kirkwood	Dec 1777-June 1778.
Knocks/Knoxs, George Private	Feb 4. 1778; March 4, 1778, Duration of War	Kirkwood	March 22, 1778 joined; April-June 1778.
Knotts/Knots, Harmond/ Herman Private	March 20, 1777, Duration of War	Moore	Dec 1777 sick present; Jan 1778; Feb 15, 1778 deserted.

Knotts, Henry/Henery Private	Feb 20, 1777	Moore	Dec 1777 missing in Staten Island, August 22, 1777.
Lacat/Laccat, Mitchel/Metekel Private	March 12, 1778, Duration of War	Patten	April-May 1778; June 1778 returned from hospital.
Lahea/Lehea, John Private	May 10, 1777, Duration of War	Rhodes	Feb-June 1778.
Langherty, Denis Private		Patten	May 1778 muster roll shows he deserted in April 1778.
Latimore, Samuel/Saml Private	April 1, 1778, Duration of War	Learmouth	May-June 1778.
Lawler/Lawly, Daniel Private		Patten	Dec 1777 with the train; Jan 1778-April 1778; May 1778 sick Yellow Springs; June 1778.
Layfield/Lafield, Timothy/ Timmithy Private	Oct 1777, Duration of War	Wild	Dec 1777-April 1778; June 1778.
Lea, George Private	April 21, 1778, Duration of War	Kirkwood	April-June 1778.
Learmouth, John Captain	Jan 4. 1777; April 5, 1777	Learmouth	Dec 1777-June 1778.
Leary/Lairey, Dennis Corporal	Oct 1777, Duration of War	Wild	Dec 1777-April 1778; June 1778.
Leaugue/ League, William/Wm Private	Jan 7, 1777; Oct 1777, Duration of War	Anderson	Dec 1777-June 1778. Roll dated Sept 9, 1778 shows him "Shoemaking in Newark" Jan 20, 1778.
Ledger, Nathaniel/Nathl Private	April 1, 1778; April 6, 1778, Duration of War	Learmouth	June 1778 rolls shows he deserted on April 6, 1778.
Levingston/ Levistan, Neil/Neal Private	Oct 1777, Duration of War	Wild	Dec 1777-April 1778; June 1778.
Lewis/Lewes, William/Wm Private	Jan 3, 1777	Kirkwood	Dec 1777-June 1778.
Lindsey, Samuel/Saml Private	Dec 24, 1776, Duration of War	Kirkwood	Dec 1777-Feb 1778; March 1778 on furlough March 16; April-June 1778.
Lirty, Nicholas Private	Feb 13, 1778, Duration of War	Patten	Only reference is the April 1778 muster roll which shows he was taken prisoner on March 15, 1778.

Long, Samuel Private	Feb 9, 1777; Nov 1777, Duration of War	Moore	Dec 1777 on guard; Jan-June 1778.
Lover/Love James Drummer	March 1, 1778	Learmouth	June 1778.
Low, James/Jas Private	March 10, 1778, Duration of War	Kirkwood	April 1, 1778 joined; March 27, 1778 deserted.
Luallen/ Lieuallen, John Private	May 15, 1777, Duration of War	Rhodes	Dec 1777; Feb-June 1778.
Lucas, James Adjutant	Nov 27, 1776		June 1778.
Macklin/Marklin, Eli Private	March 6, 1778, Duration of War	Rhodes	April 14, 1778 deserted.
Mapletuff, Samuel/Saml Private	March 5, 1778, Duration of War	Kirkwood	March 26, 1778 deserted.
Marshall, John Fifer	April 6, 1778, Duration of War	Wild	May-June 1778.
Marine/Mavine, Thomas Private	March 16, 1778, Duration of War	Jaquett	April 1778 roll shows him sick in quarters May 18; May-June 1778.
Mathews/ Matthews, Thomas Sergeant	May 23, 1777, Duration of War	Jaquett	Dec 1777-Feb 1778; March 20, 1778 deserted.
Matthews/ Mathes, John Private	Jan 5, 1777; Nov 1777. This date may be for the man below.	Patten	Dec 1777-Feb 1778; March 1778 on command; April-June 1778.
Matthews, John Private	Jan 12, 1778, Duration of War	Kirkwood	Jan 1778 roll shows him "Missing from 3rd Feb. (Supposed Deserted."
Mattingly/ Mattenby, Thomas Private	Oct 1777, Duration of War	Wild	Dec 1777-April 1778; June 1778. Undated roll, probably Sept 1778 shows him "on Command Delaware State" May 10, 1778.
Maxwell, William/Wm Corporal/ Sergeant	March 1, 1777, Duration of War	Anderson	Dec 1, 1777 promoted to Sergeant; Dec 1777-June 1778.
McAfee, Joseph Private	Jan 7, 1777; Oct 1777, Duration of War	Anderson	Dec 1777-March 1778. See below.
McAfee, Joseph Private	June 1, 1778	Patten	First appears on Oct 1778 rolls. May be the man above who re-enlisted.

Name	Enlistment	Recruiter	Record
McBride/Brede, Archibald/Archd Corporal/ Sergeant	Jan 1, 1777; Jan 3, 1777, Duration of War	;	Dec 1777; Jan 1778 sick absent; Feb-April 1778; May 1, 1778 promoted to Sergeant; May-June 1778
McCabe, John Private	Jan 17, 1777; Oct 1777, Duration of War	Anderson	Dec 1777-June 1778.
McCallaster/ McCalloster, Patrick/Patt Private	Dec 24, 1776, Duration of War	Kirkwood	Dec 1777-Jan 1778 sick absent; Feb-March 1778; April 1778 store guard; May-June 1778.
McCally/ McCalley, Patrick Private	April 20, 1778	Learmouth	May 1778 enlisted not yet joined; June 12, 1778 deserted.
McCann/ McKann, Neal/Neil Private	April 24, 1778, Duration of War	Wild	April 1778; June 1778.
McCann/McCan, Thomas Private	Oct 1777, Duration of War	Anderson	Dec 1777-June 1778.
McCew, John Private	Dec 8, 1777	Kirkwood	Dec 29, 1777 Duration of War.
McClean/ McLane, Benjamin Ensign	Dec 4, 1776	Patten	Dec 1777-April 1778; May 20 1778 resigned.
McClemmons McClemons, James/Jas Private	April 2, 1777, Duration of War	Patten	Dec 1777-March 1778 sick absent; April-May 1778; June 1778 sick absent.
McCode, William Private	March 6, 1778 Duration of War	Anderson	Enlistment date is the only record.
McConnel/ McConnell, Edward Private	Feb 25, 1777	Learmouth	Feb 1778 "Brought back from desertion Feby. 1st"; March 19, 1778 deserted; May 1778 payroll states "Brought back from Desertion May 16 & shot for sd. Crime May 25th."
McConoughy/ McConnoughey, John/Jno Private	Jan 1, 1777, Duration of War	Kirkwood	Dec 1777-Jan 1778 sick absent; Feb-June 1778.
McCord/ McKorde, Patrick Private		Anderson	Only record is the March muster roll which shows he deserted on March 27, 1778.
McCue/McCaue, Patrick Private	May 27, 1777, Duration of War	Jaquett	Dec 1777-June 1778.

McCurdy/ McMurdy, James Private	April 12, 1778, Duration of War	Learmouth	May 1778 not joined the regiment. Roll dated Sept 9, 1778 shows him sick at Wilmington, May 26, 1778.
McDaniel, James Private	March 10, 1778, Duration of War	Patten	On reference is the April 1778 payroll which shows he deserted on April 1, 1778.
McDonald/ McDonnald, Daniel/Danl Private/Corporal	May 16, 1777, Duration of War	Jaquett	Dec 1777-Feb 1778; March 1, 1778 promoted to Corporal; March-June 1778.
McDonald, Alexander/ Allexander Private	April 17, 1778, Duration of War	Patten	May 1778; June-July 1778 sick Valley Forge.
McDowell McDowel, John/Jno Private	June 1, 1777, Duration of War	Kirkwood	Dec 1777; Jan-Feb 1778 sick absent; March 1778; April 12, 1778 dead.
McDowill/ McDowell, Joseph Private	Nov 1777, Duration of War	Patten	Dec 1777-June 1778.
McGill, John Private	May 17, 1778, Duration of War	Anderson	May-June 1778.
McGinnis/ McGinnes, John/Jno Private	Oct 1777, Duration of War	Anderson	Dec 1777-June 1778.
McGinnis/ Mginnis, Michael Sergeant	Jan 16, 1777; Sept 1, 1777, Duration of War	Patten	Dec 1777-Jan 1778; Feb-March 1778 recruiting; April-June 1778
McGuffin McGuffing, James Sergeant	Oct 1777, Duration of War	Wild	Dec 1777-March 1778; April 20, 1778 deserted.
McGuire, Thomas Corporal/ Sergeant	May 21, 1777, Duration of War	Anderson	Dec 1777-April 1778; May 21, 1778 promoted to Sergeant; May-June 1778.
McKennan, William 1st. Lt.	Jan 4, 1777; April 5, 1777	Learmouth	Dec 1777-June 1778.
McKinley/ McKinly, Jacob Private	Feb 5, 1778; March 5, 1778; April 17, 1778, Duration of War	Jaquett	April 1778; April 22, 1778 sick in hospital; May 28, 1778 deserted
McKorde/ McCorde, Patrick Private	March 6, 1778, Duration of War	Anderson	March 27, 1778 deserted.

McKurdy/ McCurdy, Patrick/Partrick Private	May 21, 1777, Duration of War	Rhodes	Dec 1777-June 1778.
McLaughlin/ Mlaughlin, Charles/Charls Private	Jan 6, 1777; Nov 1777, Duration of War	Patten	Dec 1777-March 1778; April 22, 1778 transferred to the Artillery. See Dowds, Charles.
McLaughlin/ McLauchlin, Cornelius/Corns Private	Jan 20, 1777, Duration of War	Learmouth	Dec 1777-Feb 1778; March 15, 1778 discharged.
McMullen, Alexander Private	Feb 1, 1778	Kirkwood	Jan 1778 not yet joined.
McMurry/ McMuray, Samuel/Saml Private	Jan 7, 1777; Oct 1777, Duration of War	Anderson	Dec 1777-June 1778.
McNight/ M. Night, John/Jno Private	Dec 30, 1776; Dec 31, 1776, Duration of War	Kirkwood	Dec 1777-June 1778.
McVicars/ McVicors, Archd. Private	May 24, 1777, Duration of War	Anderson	Dec 1777-Feb 1778; March 24, 1778 discharged.
Mears/Meers, Abraham/ Abrham Private	June 1, 1777; Nov 1777, Duration of War	Kirkwood	Dec 1777; Jan-Feb 1778 on command as a waggoner; March-May 1778 waggoner; June 1778 on command waggoner.
Meeker, Elias/Elius Private	Aug 3, 1777, Duration of War	Patten	Dec 1777-March 1778 on command; April 1778-June 1778. First name appears as Chas. on the May 1778 payroll.
Mercer/Messer, Benjamin Private	March 1, 1778; March 4, 1778, Duration of War	Learmouth	June 1778 muster roll shows he deserted on March 6, 1778.
Meredith/ Meredeth, Huriah/Urian Private	March 6, 1778, Duration of War	Rhodes	April-June 1778.
Meredith, John Private	March 6, 1778, Duration of War	Rhodes	April 8, 1778 deserted.
Meredith, Levin Private	March 6, 1778, Duration of War	Rhodes	April 8, 1778 deserted.
Michal/Michall, Isick/Isaac Private	Duration of War	Wild	Dec 1777-April 1778; June 1778.

Middleton/ Midleton, John/Jno Private/Corporal	Jan 10, 1777, Duration of War	Learmouth	Dec 1777-April 1778: May 1, 1778 promoted to Corporal; May-June 1778.
Millaway/ Milloway, Joseph Private	Jan 5, 1777	Moore	Dec 1777-April 1778; May 11, 1778 died.
Miller/Millar, David Drummer	Nov 25, 1776; Nov 29, 1776, Duration of War	Moore/ Kirkwood	Dec 1777-March 1778; April 18, 1778 transferred to Kirkwood's Company; April-June 1778.
Miller, Robert/Robart Private		Patten	March-June 1778.
Miller/Millar, Samuel/Saml Private	Jan 13, 1777, Duration of War	Kirkwood	Dec 1777-Jan 1778; Feb 1778 on command; March 1778; April-May 1778 waggoner; June 1778.
Miller/Millar, Samuel/Saml. Private	June 4, 1777; June 24, 1777, Duration of War	Patten	Dec 1777-Jan 1778; Feb 1778 on command; March-May 1778.
Miller, Thomas Private	Jan 4, 1777; June 24, 1777, Duration of War	Kirkwood	Dec 1777; Jan 1778 on command at Fogs manor; Feb-March 1778; April-June 1778 shoe factory.
Miller, Wm Private		Patten	May 1778 payroll shows he deserted on April 3, 1778.
Mills, Ricketts Private	March 4, 1778, Duration of War	Learmouth	July 1778 deserted.
Moody, Benjamin/Benn Private	Feb 28, 1777, Duration of War	Moore	Dec 1777-June 1778.
Moones/Moons, James/Jas Private	Jan 1, 1777, Duration of War	Kirkwood	Dec 1777-Jan 1778; Feb 1778 on command; March 1778 on command; April-June 1778.
Moore, Charles Private	March 16, 1778, Duration of War	Kirkwood	March 22, 1778 joined; April 1, 1778 deserted from Dover.
Moore, Epharim/Ephraim Private	March 13, 1778, Duration of War	Patten	Only reference is the April 1778 payroll which shows he deserted on April 4, 1778.
Moore, Isick/Isaac Private	March 13, 1778, Duration of War	Patten	Only reference is the April 1778 payroll which shows he deserted on April 4, 1778.
Moore, James Captain	Dec 2, 1776	Moore	Dec 1777 on furlough; Jan 21, 1778 taken prisoner at Newtown Square.
Moore/Moor, Richard Private	Feb 4, 1777, Duration of War	Patten	Feb 11, 1778 joined from desertion; Feb-June 1778.

Name	Enlistment	Company	Notes
Mornes, Steven Private	March 12, 1778, Duration of War	Kirkwood	March 22, 1778 joined; April 1, 1778 deserted from Dover.
Morriss/Morris, Zadock/Zedock Private	June 1, 1777, Duration of War	Rhodes	Dec 1777; Feb-June 1778.
Muncy, Patrick Private	April 11, 1778, Duration of War	Anderson	April 1778; June 1778 lists him and pays him for two months with the note "Left out in May.
Munday, Richard Private	May 8, 1777, Duration of War	Rhodes	Dec 1777.
Murphy/ Murphey, Elijah Private	March 6, 1778, Duration of War	Anderson	April 8, 1778 deserted.
Murphy/ Murphey, Elisha Private	June 8, 1778, Duration of War	Jaquett	June 12, 1778 deserted.
Murphy, James/Jeames Sergeant	Jan 1, 1777	Anderson	Dec 1777-Feb 1778; May 1778.
Murry/Murray, Daniel, Private	June 1, 1778	Jaquett	June 1778.
Murrey, Patrick Private	April 11, 1778	Anderson	April 1778; June 1778 left out of May payroll; June 1778.
Nash, Thomas Private/Corporal	Jan 1, 1778, Duration of War	Wild	Feb-March 1778; April 1, 1778 promoted to Corporal; April 1778; June 1778 returned from hospital.
Neal/O'Neal, Hamilton Private	Feb 14, 1778	Jaquett	April-June 1778. See O'Neal.
Neil/Neal, James Private	April 21, 1778, Duration of War	Kirkwood	April 1778-May 1778; June 1778 sick absent. Muster roll dated Sept 9, 1778 shows him sick at Valley Forge June 16.
Nelson, John Private	Nov 1777, Duration of War	Patten	Dec 1777-April 1778; May 1778 Philadelphia hospital; June 1778.
Nesbitt, Henry Private	Oct 1777, Duration of War	Learmouth	Dec 1777-June 1778.
Newell/Newill, William/Wm Private	Oct 1777, Duration of War	Wild	Dec 1777-April 1778; June 1778.
Newlin, William Private		Jaquett	April 1778 only record, April 18, 1778 deserted
Nichols/Nicols, Moses Private	Nov 1777, Duration of War	Patten	Dec 1777-June 1778.

Nicholas/ Nicholes, Samuel/Saml Private	Feb 30, [*sic*] 1777, Duration of War	Moore	Dec 1777-June 1778.
Nickolas/Nichols, Nehemiah Corporal	March 14, 1778, Duration of War	Rhodes	April-June 1778.
Noble, John Private	March 24, 1778; April 22, 1778, Duration of War	Jaquett	April 22, 1778 sick in hospital; April-May 1778; June 20, 1778 hospital.
Norris/Nories, John Private	Feb 15, 1778; Feb 19, 1778, Duration of War	Kirkwood	Feb 15, 1778 joined; Feb-April 1778; May 1778 on command; June 1778.
Norton, Nathan/Nath'l Private	Feb 16, 1777; Nov 1777, Duration of War	Patten	Dec 1777-Jan 1778; Feb-March 1778 on command; May 1778 Phila Hospital; June 1778.
Norwood, Henry Private	March 24, 1778, Duration of War	Jaquett	April-May 1778; June 2, 1778 deserted.
Nucheson, John Private		Jaquett	Feb 1778 roll shows he was a prisoner on Sept 11, returned March 17.
Nutter, Robert/Robt Private	March 6, 1778, Duration of War	Jaquett	April-June 1778.
O'Connell/ O. Camel, Francis Private	April 24, 1778, Duration of War	Learmouth	May 27, 1778 deserted.
O'Neal, Hamilton Private	April 1, 1778, Duration of War	Jaquett	April 8, 1778 joined. See Neal.
Oram/Orum, Robert/Robt Sergeant/ Quartermaster Sergeant	Jan 16, 1777; March 19, 1777, Duration of War	Patten	May 1778 on duty at Philadelphia; June 1778. In June he became the regimental Quartermaster Sergeant.
Orton, William Private	Oct 1777, Duration of War	Learmouth	Dec 1777-June 1778.
Owens/Owins, Robert Private	March 6, 1778, Duration of War	Jaquett	April-June 1778.
Owens/Oens, William/Wm Private	July 26, 1777, Duration of War	Patten	Dec 1777-Feb 1778. March 1778 payroll shows he deserted on March 20. The April 1778 payroll shows he deserted on April 10.
Pain/Paine, Benjamin/Benn Private	July 13, 1777	Moore	Dec 1777 sick absent; Jan-March 1778.
Paris, Eliakin/ Elicum Private	April 14, 1778; April 22, 1778, Duration of War	Jaquett	April 22, 1778 sick in hospital; April-June 1778.

Parker, John Private	Nov 22, 1777	Moore	Dec 1777 sick absent; Jan-May 1778. He was crossed off the June 1778 payroll without comment.
Parker, John Private	Nov 1777, Duration of War	Learmouth	Dec 1777-June 1778.
Parker, John Duration of War	April 22, 1777, Duration of War	Rhodes	Dec 1777.
Parsons, Dannaly/Danl/, Private	Oct 1777, Duration of War	Wild	Dec 1777; Jan 1, 1778 discharged.
Patten, John Captain	Nov 30, 1776	Patten	Dec 1777-Feb 1778; March 1778 on command; April-June 1778.
Patterson, Hugh Corporal/ Sergeant	May 30, 1777, Duration of War	Jaquett	Dec 1777-Feb 1778; March 1, 1778 promoted to Sergeant; March-June 1778.
Patterson, William/Wm Private	April 1, 1778, Duration of War	Learmouth	May 1778 not joined the regiment; Roll dated Sept 9, 1778 shows him sick at Wilmington, May 26, 1778.
Peate/Peete, William/Wm Private	Jan 1, 1777, Duration of War	Moore	Dec 1777-May 1778; June 1778 returned from hospital.
Pemberton/ Pembrton, John/Jno Private	Dec 26, 1776; Jan 6, 1777, Duration of War	Kirkwood	Dec 1777-Jan 1778; Feb 1778 store guard; March 1778 on the store guard; April 1778 store guard; May-June 1778.
Pennington, William Private	April 17, 1777; Oct 1777, Duration of War	Learmouth	Dec 1777-March 1778; April 1, 1778 Duration of War.
Perry/Perrey, Joshua/Jeashea Private/Sergeant	Jan 19, 1777, Duration of War	Anderson	Dec 1777; Jan 24, 1778 promoted to Sergeant; Jan-June 1778. Roll dated Sept 9, 1778 shows him "Shoemaking in Newark"
Perry/Perrey, William Private	Nov 1777, Duration of War	Patten	Dec 1777-June 1778
Peterson, John Private	April 5, 1777, Duration of War	Patten	Dec 1777-June 1778.
Peterson, Joseph Private	Feb 22, 1777; Nov 1777, Duration of War	Patten	May 14, 1778 transferred to Artificers.
Pheris/ Pharress, Moses/Mosis Sergeant	June 2, 1777, Duration of War	Moore	Dec 1777-June 1778.

Phillips/Philips, John Private	Jan 3, 1777, Duration of War	Patten	Dec 1777-Jan 1778 at hospital; Feb sick in hospital; March 1778 sick Yellow Springs; April 10, 1778 deserted.
Picheron, Littleton Private	June 5, 1778	Patten	First appears on Sept 1778 rolls. Same man as below?
Picker/Pickron, Littleton/Littelton Private	June 5, 1778, Duration of War	Jaquett	June 12, 1778 deserted. Same man as above?
Pierce, Andrew Private	April 16. 1778; April 24, 1778, Duration of War	Kirkwood	April 16, 1778 joined; April 1778; May 1778 sick absent; June 1778 sick at Wilmington. Muster roll dated Sept 9, 1778 shows him sick at Wilmington May 10.
Pierce/Price, Solomon Private	April 21, 1778	Kirkwood	April-May 1778; June 1778 sick absent. Muster roll dated Sept 9, 1778 shows him sick at Valley Forge June 16.
Pimm/Pim, William Private	April 16, 1777, Duration of War	Rhodes	Dec 1777; Feb-June 1778.
Platt, John Surgeon's Mate	April 1, 1777; April 5, 1777		June 1778.
Plowman/ Ploughman, William/Wm Private	Dec 23, 1776, Duration of War	Moore	Dec 1777-June 1778.
Pollard/Polord, Andrew/Adrew Private	Dec 21, 1776; Dec 26, 1776, Duration of War	Kirkwood	Dec 1777; Jan-Feb 1778 on command at Dover; March-June 1778.
Pope, Charles Lieutenant Colonel	Jan 4, 1777; April 5, 1777		June 1778.
Powell, John Private	Oct 1777, Duration of War	Learmouth	April 20, 1778 brought back from desertion; May 1778; June 10, 1778 left sick; roll dated Sept 9, 1778 shows him sick at Valley Forge June 10, 1778.
Preston, John Private	Dec 22, 1776, Duration of War	Moore	Dec 1777-June 1778.
Preston, Joseph Private	Dec 23, 1776	Kirkwood	Dec 1777-June 1778.
Proctor, John Private	April 23, 1778, Duration of War	Learmouth	June 1778 left sick June 22.
Purnall/Purnal, John/Joahn Private	Oct 1777, Duration of War	Anderson	Dec 1777; Feb-June 1778. Roll dated Sept 9, 1778 shows him "Shoemaking in Newark" Jan 20, 1778.

Purvis, George 2nd. Lt.	Dec 3, 1776; Dec 6, 1776; Oct 15, 1777	Patten	Dec 1777 sick present; Jan 1778; Feb-March 1778 recruiting; April-June 1778.
Pussell/Pursly, John Corporal	Nov 26, 1777	Learmouth	Dec 1777-Feb 1778; March 12, 1778 killed.
Quenault/ Queenanault, Paul 2nd. Lt./1st. Lt.	Dec 3, 1776; April 5, 1777	Kirkwood	Dec 1777 on furlough; Jan April 1778; May 1778 on command; June 1778. In Sept 1778 he was promoted to First Lieutenant retroactive to Jan 26, 1778.
Rambough/ Rambaugh, William/Wm Private	April 16 April 24, 1778, Duration of War	Kirkwood	April 16, 1778 joined; April 1778; May 1778 sick absent; June 1778 sick at Wilmington. Muster roll dated Sept 9, 1778 shows him sick at Wilmington May 10.
Random/ Randum, John Private	May 12, 1777, Duration of War	Rhodes	Dec 1777; June 1, 1778 joined.
Read, Fredric/ Frederic Private	Oct 1777, Duration of War	Anderson	Dec 1777-June 1778.
Read/Reed, Samuel/Saml Private	March 2, 1778	Anderson	April-June 1778.
Records, Samuel Private	Feb 25, 1778	Learmouth	June 1778.
Redden, William/ Wm Private/Corporal	Nov 1777, Duration of War	Patten	Dec 1777-Jan 1778 at hospital; Jan 1, 1778 promoted to Corporal; Feb-June 1778.
Redman/Redmon, James Private	June 24, 1777, Duration of War	Jaquett	Dec 1777-April 1778; May 1778 sick in hospital April 22; June 1778 muster roll shows him sick hospital, Kings Ferry, July 19. June 1778 payroll shows him in hospital June 19, Returned June 27.
Reily, Mark Private	May 28, 1778	Kirkwood	June 1778 muster roll shows "taken by prior enlistment."
Rhodes, John 1st. Lt.	Dec 4, 1776; Jan 4, 1777	Rhodes	Dec 1777; Feb-June 1778. Muster roll dated Sept 9, 1778 shows him wounded on May 13, 1778.
Rhodes, William Private	May 27, 1778	Jaquett	Only record is the enlistment date.
Richard, John Private	April 8, 1778	Kirkwood	April 1778. As this man disappears from the rolls, it is possible he is shown as Burchard, John.

Richardson/ Richeson, Benjamin/ Benjamon Private		Wild	Jan 1778-April 1778; June 1778. See Vickerson.
Ricketts, Peter Private	Feb 26, 1778	Learmouth	June 1778.
Ridgway, Zedk. Private	April 21, 1778, Duration of War	Kirkwood	April-June 1778.
Riggan/Riggin, Joseph Private	March 4, 1778, Duration of War	Learmouth	Only record is enlistment, July 1778 deserted.
Rhoades/Roades, Thomas/Thos Private	May 30, 1778, Duration of War	Kirkwood	May 1778 under inoculation; June 1778 joined.
Roberts, Henry Private		Patten	May 1778.
Roberts, John Private	June 24, 1777, Duration of War	Moore	Dec 1777 on guard; Jan-June 1778.
Robertson, Charles Private		Anderson	March 1778.
Robinson/ Robarson, Edward/Edwd Private/Drummer	March 2, 1778, Duration of War	Wild	March-April 1778; April 1778 promoted to Drummer; June 1778.
Robinson, James Private	Nov 1777, Duration of War	Patten	May 1778 left at Dover.
Robinson/ Roberson, John Private	Feb 24, 1778, Duration of War	Anderson	Feb-June 1778.
Roche, Edward Paymaster	June 21, 1777		June 1778.
Roe/Row, William Private	April 14, 1777, Duration of War	Rhodes	Dec 1777; Feb-June 1778.
Rowan, Henry Corporal	Nov 1777, Duration of War	Patten	Dec 1777-Feb 1778; March 1778 on furlough; April-June 1778.
Rowan, John Sergeant	Nov 1777, Duration of War	Patten	Dec 1777; Jan 1778 sick absent; Feb 1778; March 1778 on furlough; April 1778; May 1778 recruiting; June 1778.
Russell, Henry Private	June 15, 1778, Duration of War	Rhodes	June 21, 1778 supposed deserted.
Russell, Robert/Robt Private	April 23, 1778, Duration of War	Learmouth	June 1778.
Sappington/ Sapington, Thomas Private	Jan 3, 1778, Duration of War	Patten	Jan 1778 under guard.

Sapp, Joseph Private	April 3, 1778	Rhodes	April-June 1778.
Scantling, William Private	March 29, 1778, Duration of War	Patten	April-May 1778; June 1778 returned from hospital.
Scott, Joseph Private		Patten	May 1778
Scotten, Thomas, Sr. Private	April 24, 1778	Learmouth	Joined after the army left Valley Forge.
Scotten, Thomas, Jr. Private	April 24, 1778	Learmouth	Joined after the army left Valley Forge.
Sepple/Sipple, Martinus/ Marteenus Private	Feb 19, 1777; March 19, 1777, Duration of War	Moore	Dec 1777-June 1778.
Service/Servis, John/Jno Private	Sept 21. 1777; Nov 27, 1777, Duration of War	Kirkwood	Dec 1777-Jan 1778 on command as a waiter; Feb-March 1778; April 1778 picquett; May-June 1778.
Seymour/Seamer, William/Wm Corporal	April 1, 1777; May 3, 1777, Duration of War	Kirkwood	Dec 1777-May 1778; June 1778 sick absent. Roll dated Sept 9, 1778 shows him "sick at Valley Forge from 9th June."
Shadock/ Shaddock, John Private	Nov 25, 1776, Duration of War	Moore	Dec 1777 on fatigue; Jan 1778; Feb 26, 1778 deserted.
Shannon/Shehan, Joshua Private	April 21, 1778, Duration of War	Kirkwood	April-June 1778.
Shearmen, John Private		Anderson	May 20, 1778 discharged only record.
Sheron, John Private		Patten	May 1778
Showell, Eli Private	March 4, 1778, Duration of War	Jaquett	Only record is enlistment date.
Skillington, Elijah/Elijaah Ensign	April 5, 1777, Duration of War	Wild	Dec 1777-April 1778; June 1778.
Skinner/Kinner, William Fifer	April 24, 1777	Rhodes	Dec 1777; Feb-June 1778.
Slay, William Private	April 23, 1778, Duration of War	Kirkwood	April-May 1778; June 1778 sick at Peeks Kill.
Smith, James/Jeames Fifer/Drummer	March 2, 1778, Duration of War	Anderson	March-June 1778. He appears as a Fifer from March-May 1778, in June and July 1778 he is listed as a Drummer.

Name/Rank	Enlistment	Commander	Notes
Smith, John Private		Learmouth	Nov 1777 payroll shows him deserted which must have been an error, as the April 1778 payroll shows "Mustered for 6 mos" and pays him back to Nov 1, 1777. May 1778; Sept 1778 roll shows him sick at Nottingham Hospital May 24, 1778.
Smith, Robert Sergeant	May 14, 1777, Duration of War	Jaquett	Dec 1, 1777 deserted.
Smith, William Private	Aug 1, 1777, Duration of War	Jaquett	Dec 1777-Jan 1778; Feb 1778 sick in hospital; March 1778.
Smith, William Private	April 27, 1778, Duration of War	Learmouth	Enlistment is only record
Smith, William Private	Jan 5, 1777, Duration of War	Moore	Dec 1777 on command; Jan-June 1778.
Spear, Henry F. Private	Oct 1, 1777, Duration of War	Anderson	Dec 1777-June 1778. Muster roll for Sept 1778 shows him "with the Commissary 15 June 1778".
Spencer, John Corporal/ Sergeant	Feb 19, 1777, Duration of War	Moore	Dec 1777-May 1778; June 4, 1778 promoted to Sergeant; June 1778.
Stanford/ Stawford, Robert Private	March 20, 1778, Duration of War	Jaquett	April-June 1778.
Stears/Steers, Richard/Richd Corporal/Fifer/ Fife Major.	Oct 1777, Duration of War	Wild	Dec 1777; Feb-April 1778; Jan 1778. In Dec 1777 he appears as a Corporal, but earlier rolls and Jan 1778 show him as a Fifer. In February he was apparently promoted to Fife Major for the regiment and appears as that in June 1778.
Stevens/Stevins, John/Jno Private	Feb 16, 1778; March 16, 1778, Duration of War	Kirkwood	March 22, 1778 joined; April-June 1778.
Stevenson/ Stiveson, James Private	Jan 1, 1777; April 1, 1777, Duration of War	Kirkwood	Dec 1777-June 1778.,
Steward/Stewart, George Private	July 25, 1777; July 27, 1777, Duration of War	Moore	Dec 1777-Jan 1778 not joined detained at home for trial at court.
Stewart, Alexander 1st. Lt.	Nov 29, 1776	Kirkwood	August 27, 1776 taken prisoner at Battle of Long Island; Dec 1777-Jan 1778 prisoner; June 1778 "Exchanged Absent with Leave."

Stinchcomb, Christopher/ Christoper Sergeant		Wild/ Anderson	Dec 1777; Jan 1778 returned to his company; March 1778 taken [ ]; April 1778 returned from hospital on the 21 April; May 1778; June 1778 "Retd from Hospl on (the 1st taken sick the 27th April.)"
Streeps, Robert Private	Feb 18, 1778, Duration of War	Patten	April 1778 payroll shows he was taken prisoner on March 15, 1778
Sullivane, Edward Private	April 1, 1778, Duration of War		Date of enlistment is the only record found.
Tallan, Benjamin/Benjn Private	Feb 20, 1778; March 28, 1778	Anderson	May-June 1778.
Tallan, Hugh Private	March 28, 1778; April 20, 1778	Anderson	May 1778; June 1778 returned from hospital.
Taylor/Tayler, Richard/Richd Private	Jan 8, 1777, Duration of War	Kirkwood	Dec 1777; Jan 1778 sick present; Feb-April 1778 sick absent; May-June 1778.
Tevis, Daniel/Danl Private	April 26, 1778	Anderson	April-May 1778.
Thomas, William Private	March 17, 1778, Duration of War		Date of enlistment is the only record found.
Thompson, Benjamin Private	May 1, 1778, Duration of War	Kirkwood	May-June 1778.
Thompson/ Thomson, Robert Duration of War		Patten	Dec 1777-April 1778
Thompson, Thomas/Thos Sergeant	Nov 1777, Duration of War	Wild	Feb-May 1778; June 1778.
Thornton, Nathaniel/Nathan Private	March 6, 1778, Duration of War	Rhodes	April 8, 1778 deserted.
Timmins/ Timmons, Robert Private	Feb 10, 1778; March 10, 1778, Duration of War	Kirkwood	March 22, 1778 joined; April-June 1778.
Timmons, Jesse Private	March 10, 1778, Duration of War	Patten	Only reference is the April 1778 payroll which shows he deserted on March 27, 1778.
Timmons, Zadoc Private	March 26, 1778, Duration of War	Learmouth	Enlistment date is the only record.
Tirman, Thos Private		Patten	May 1778 payroll shows he deserted on May 4, 1778.
Tobin/Terbine, James Private	Feb 17, 1778, Duration of War	Patten	April-June 1778.

Todd, John Private	May 26, 1778, Duration of War	Anderson	May-June 1778.
Toland/Towland, Adam Private	April 1, 1778, Duration of War	Kirkwood	April-June 1778.
Toland/Towland, James Private	April 2, 1778, Duration of War	Kirkwood	April-May 1778; sick at Nottingham.
Toland/Towland, John Private	April 1, 1778, Duration of War	Kirkwood	April-June 1778.
Tool, Moses Private	June 1, 1778	Kirkwood	June 1778 sick absent.
Tool/Toole, Thomas Private	Dec 23, 1776, Duration of War	Kirkwood	Dec 1777-March 1778; April 1778 picquett; May-June 1778.
Townsend, Charles Private	Feb 18, 1778	Learmouth	June 1778 roll shows he deserted on April 1, 1778.
Townsend/ Towsend, Thomas/Thos. Private	Nov 1777, Duration of War	Patten	April-June 1778.
Townsend, William Private	April 27, 1778, Duration of War	Learmouth	Enlistment date is the only record.
Trayson/Trayton, Manuel/Emanuel Corporal	March 1, 1777, Duration of War	Anderson	Dec 1777-Feb 1778; March 20, 1778 taken prisoner.
Treasure/Tresure, Richard Private	Feb 16, 1777; April 16, 1777 Duration of War	Moore	Dec 1777 sick absent; Jan-June 1778.
Truit/Trewett, Philip/Phillip Private		Wild	Dec 1777-April 1778; June 1778. Undated roll, probably Sept 1778 shows him "on Command Delaware State" Feb 5, 1778.
Truitt/Truit, Purnal Private	April 19, 1778, Duration of War	Patten	April-June 1778.
Tucker, Zadock, Zedick Private	March 23, 1778	Jaquett	April 22, 1778 sick in hospital; April-May 1778; June 1778 sick hospital, Valley Forge June 19. Muster roll dated Sept 8, 1778 shows him "in Hospital 19 June."
Tully, John Private	Duration of War	Patten	Dec 1777; Jan 31, 1778 deserted.
Turner, James Private	Jan 13, 1777, Duration of War	Learmouth	Dec 1777-June 1778.

Turner, John Private	April 4, 177 368; April 7, 1778, Duration of War	Jaquett	April-June 1778.
Tully/Tulley, John Private	Nov 1777, Duration of War	Patten	Jan 31, 1778 deserted.
Vance, John Private	April 23, 1778, Duration of War	Anderson	April-May 1778; June 6, 1778 deserted.
Vanderlip/ Vandelip, Frederick/Fredr Private	Oct 1777, Duration of War	Anderson	Dec 1777-June 1778.
Vaughan, John Private	Nov 1777, Duration of War	Patten	Dec 1777-March 1778; April 23, 1778 deserted.
Vaughan, Joseph Major	Jan 4, 1777; April 5, 1777		June 1778.
Vaughan, Levin Private	March 5, 1778, Duration of War	Patten	April 1, 1778 deserted.
Veach/Veauch, Thomas/Thos Private	March 27, 1778, Duration of War	Kirkwood	March 27, 1778 joined; April 9, 1778 deserted.
Vickerson, Benjm Private		Wild	Dec 1777. This soldier is probably the man shown as Benjamin Richardson above.
Vinson, Ebenezer/Ebenr Private	Feb 27, 1778, Duration of War	Patten	Only reference is April 1778 payroll which shows he deserted on March 27, 1778.
Vinyard/Vingan, John Fifer/Corporal	Jan 5, 1777, Duration of War	Moore	Dec 1777-May 1778; June 4, 1778 promoted to Corporal; June 1778.
Walker, Thomas Private	Jan 1, 1777, Duration of War	Kirkwood	Dec 1777-Feb 1778; March 1778 on command March 12; April 1778 on detachment; May 1778 on party; June 1778.
Walker, William Private	April 2, 1778	Anderson	April-June 1778.
Wallace, William/Wm Private	Feb 28, 1778	Kirkwood	April 3, 1778 joined; April 1778- May 1778; June 1778 sick at Valley Forge. Muster roll dated Sept 9, 1778 shows him sick at Valley Forge June 16.
Watkins/ Wotkins, John Private	Dec 30, 1776	Kirkwood	Jan 1778 returned from desertion; Feb-May 1778; June 1778 on command.
Watkinson, Benjamin Private	May 11, 1778, Duration of War	Jaquett	April 1778 muster roll shows he enlisted on May 11; May-June 1778.

Webster/Webstor, John Private	May 23, 1777, Duration of War	Rhodes	Dec 1777; Feb-June 1778.
Weighnright/ Winright, James/Thomas Private	Jan 2, 1777, Duration of War	Kirkwood	Dec 1777-Feb 1778; March 1778 on command at Dover March 10; April-June 1778. In February and March, the first name appears as Thomas.
Welden/Weldon, Eli Private	April 16, 1778; April 24, 1778, Duration of War	Kirkwood	April 16, 1778 joined; April 1778; May 1778 sick absent; June 1778 sick at Wilmington. Muster roll dated Sept 9, 1778 shows him sick at Wilmington May 10.
Westor/Woster, George Private	May 13, 1777	Moore	Dec 1777 sick absent; Jan-Feb 1778.
Wharton/ Wharten, Charles Private		Anderson	Dec 1777-June 1778.
White/Wite, Henry Private	May 20, 1777; Dec 1777, Duration of War	Jaquett	Dec 1777-Jan 1778; Feb 1778 on command Jan 28; March 1778; April 1778 on command Jan 28; May 1778.
White, Joseph Private		Anderson	March 1778 roll shows he deserted on March 20, 1778.
Whiteworth/ Witeworth, William Private	May 9, 1777, Duration of War	Rhodes	Dec 1777; Feb-June 1778.
Whittington/ Whittenton, John Private	Nov 1777, Duration of War	Patten	Nov 1777-March 1778 on furlough; April 1778; May 6, 1778 discharged.
Wild/Wilds, Joseph 2nd. Lt.	April 5, 1777	Wild	Dec 1777-April 1778; June 1778.
Wild/Wilds, Richard 1st. Lt.	March 1, 1777; April 5, 1777	Jaquett	Dec 1777-Jan 1778; Feb 1778 wounded Oct 4 at Germantown; March 1778; April 1778 wounded October 4; May 1778; June 1778. wounded Oct 4 and disabled from doing any more duty.
Wilds, Solomon Private	April 14, 1778, Duration of War	Jaquett	Only record is date of enlistment.
Wiley/Wyley, John Private	Oct 1777, Duration of War	Wild	Dec 1777-April 1778; June 1778.

Wilkinson, James Private	Feb 8, 1777; March 8, 1777, Duration of War	Kirkwood	April 1, 1778 joined; April-June 1778.
Willett/Willet, Christopher/ Christ. Private	Jan 2, 1777, Duration of War	Kirkwood	Dec 1777-Jan 1778; Feb 1778 absent want of shoes; March-April 1778; May 1778 on party; June 1778.
Williams, Charles Private	March 19, 1778, Duration of War	Jaquett	June 1778 "under Qr. guard." Paid for three months and nineteen days in June.
Williams, Isick/Isaac Private	April 14, 1778; April 22, 1778, Duration of War	Jaquett	April 1778 sick in hospital; May 8; June 1778 on guard.
Williams, John Private		Patten	May 1778 payroll shows he deserted April 9. 1778.
Williams, Joseph Private	Oct 1777, Duration of War	Anderson	Dec 1777-May 1778; Roll dated Sept 9, 1778 shows him "Sick at Notingham" May 25, 1778.
Willis/Willes, Henry/Hennery Private	Dec 24, 1777, Duration of War	Kirkwood	Dec 1777; Jan-Feb 1778 on command at Dover; March 1778 on command at Dover March 10; April-May 1778; June 1778 sick at Valley Forge.
Willson/Wilson, John 1st Lt.	March 1, 1777	Moore	Dec 1777 on furlough; Jan-June 1778.
Wilson, Hosea Sergeant	Nov 1777, Duration of War	Patten	Dec 1777; Jan 1778 sick at Newport; Feb 1778; March 1778 on furlough; April-June 1778.
Wilson, Hugh Private	April 24, 1778, Duration of War	Kirkwood	April 4, 1778 joined. Only record.
Windsor, John Private	Feb 7, 1778, Duration of War	Kirkwood	March 22, 1778 joined; April-June 1778.
Wooden/ Woodin, Samuel/Saml Private	March 7, 1778, Duration of War	Patten	April-June 1778.
Wright, William Private	March 4, 1778; March 6, 1778, Duration of War	Jaquett	April 22, 1778 sick in hospital; June 1778.
Young, David Private/ Corporal	April 25, 1778	Anderson	Dec 1777; January 24, 1778 promoted to Corporal; Jan 1778 on furlough; Feb-June 1778.

NEW YORK

Name/ Rank	Enlistment or Commission Date/Term of Enlistment	Regiment/ Company	Remarks
Abel/Able, John Private	March 19, 1778, Duration of War	First, McCracken	April-June 1778.
Abel/Able, Mathias Private		Malcom's, Niven	Dec 1777 sick Lancaster; Jan-Feb 1778 sick hospital.
Ackerson, Jacob Private	Duration of War	First, Van Ness	April-May 1778; June 1778 left on the road sick Spotswoods.
Ackley, Joel Private	Dec 17, 1776, Duration of War	First, Copp	April-June 1778
Acklin, Francis Private	Dec 23, 1776, Duration of War	First, Wendell	April-June 1778.
Adams, Emanuel Private	Feb 10, 1778, Duration of War	First, McCracken	April-May 1778; June 1778 sick at Cuckolds Town.
Adams, James Private	March 9, 1777, Duration of War	First, Graham	April 1778; May 1778 on duty; June 1778.
Adams/ Adames, Jesse Private	Nov 28, 1776, Duration of War	Fourth, Pearsee	Dec 1777; Jan 1778 on party; Feb 1778 on duty; March 1778; April 1778 main guard; May 1778 sick in camp; June 1778 sick Valley Forge.
Adams, Nathan Sergeant	May 5, 1778	Fourth, Strong	June 1778.
Adams, Peleg/Pelig Private	June 1, 1777, Duration of War	Second, Lounsbery	Dec 1777 on command Col. Byard; Jan 1778 on command; Feb 1778 sick in camp; April-June 1778.
Adams, Samuel Private	May 5, 1778, Nine Months	Fourth, Strong	May 1778.
Addams/Adams, Daniel Sergeant	May 5, 1778, Nine Months	Fourth, Strong	June 1778.
Aikin see Eaken			
Aimes, Hugh Private	May 5, 1778, Nine Months	Second, Ten Eyck	June 1778 sick at Valley Forge.
Albright, Jacob Private	Jan 1, 1777 Feb 1, 1777	Second, Graham	Dec 1777 payroll only; Jan-March 1778 sick at Fishkill; April 1778; May 1778 tending sick; June 1778 sick Valley Forge.
Allan, John Corporal		Malcom's, Steel	Dec 1777; Jan 1778 absent with leave; Feb 1778; March-May 1778 sick quarters; June 1778 sick Yellow Springs.

Allen, James 1st. Lt.	Jan 22, 1777	Malcom's, Irvine	Dec 1777-Jan 1778; Jan 1, 1778 appointed Quartermaster to the Brigade. Oath on May 27 and May 28, 1778.
Allen, John Private	Oct 30, 1776, Duration of War	First, Copp	July 18, 1777 missing on a scout; March 9, 1778 joined; April 1778; May 1778 sick in Regimental hospital, June 1778 sick in Hospital Cuckolds Town.
Allen, John Private	Jan 12, 1777, Three Years	First, Van Ness	April-June 1778.
Alexander, John/Jno Private	Duration of War	Malcom's, Steel	Dec 1777; Jan-Feb 1778 sick hospital; March-June 1778.
Allis see Ellis			
Alport, John Armourer/ Armorers Mate	Oct 1, 1777, Duration of War	Fourth, Sacket	Dec 1777-April 1778 on command at Fishkill; May-June 1778.
Althiser, George Corporal	Nov 4, 1776, Duration of War	First, McCracken	April-May 1778 sick at Supus; June 1778.
Amberman, Cornelius Private	May 5, 1778, Nine Months	Second, Wright	First appears on rolls for Aug 1778.
Amberman, Derrick Private	May 7, 1778	Second, Pell	First appears on the rolls for August 1778.
Amerman, Obadiah/Obediah Private	Nov 22, 1776, Duration of War	First, Hicks	April-June 1778.
Anderson, James Private	Dec 25, 1777, Three Years	Fourth, Smith	Dec 1777; Jan-Feb 1778 sick in hospital; March-April 1778; May 1778 sick in camp; June 1778.
Anderson, Samuel Private	Duration of War	First, Ten Broeck	April-June 1778.
Andress, Joseph Private	May 5, 1778, Nine Months	Fourth, Davis	June 1778.
Anthony, Simon Private	May 5, 1778, Nine Months	Fourth, Pearsee	June 1778 sick in Jersey.
Antone, John Private	May 5, 1778	Fourth, Pearsee	May-June 1778.
Armstrong, Archibald/Archd Private	May 6, 1777, Three Years	Second, Graham	Dec 1777 payroll only; Jan 1778-Feb 1778; March 1778 on command at the lines; April 1778; May 1778 main guard; June 1778 wounded, at Princeton.
Armstrong, Edward 1st. Lt.	April 5, 1777	Malcom's, Kearsley	Dec 1777 on furlough; Jan-April 1778. Oath at Valley Forge on May 11, 1778.

Armstrong, Jonathan Private	Nov 21, 1776, Duration of War	Fourth, Titus	Dec 1777-May 1778; June 1778 sick in the Jersies.
Ashley/Ashly, Michael Sergeant	Duration of War	Malcom's, Kearsley	Dec 1777-Feb 1778; March 1778 on Lord Stirling's guard; April 1778.
Ashly, Aron Private	Dec 4, 1776, Duration of War	Second, Graham	Dec 1777 payroll only; Jan-Feb 1778 sick at Albany; March 1778 sick absent; April 1778 sick at Albany; May-June 1778 sick at Half Moon.
Astin, John Private	Dec 17, 1776, Three Years	Second, Hallett	Dec 1777-Feb 1778; March 1778; April 1778 on command one week; May 1778 on command.
Aston, Benoni Private	Dec 18, 1776, Duration of War	Fourth, Strong	Dec 1777-May 1778; June 1778 sick in Pennsylvania.
Atkinson, James Corporal	Dec 19, 1776, Duration of War	First, Wendell	April-May 1778; June 1778 on duty.
Atkinson/ Etkerson, Philip Private	Duration of War	Malcom's, Kearsley	Dec 1777-Jan 1778 sick absent; Feb 1778 sick hospital; March 1778 hospital; April-May 1778; June 1778 sick Princeton.
Avout see Evalt			
Babbott, Reubin Private	April 3, 1777, Duration of War	First, Ten Broeck	April 1778 sick at Fishkill; May 1, 1778 died.
Bachus, George Private	Aug 20, 1777 Three Years	First, Wendell	April-June 1778.
Bachus/Backus, John Private	May 11, 1777, Three Years	First, Wendell	April-June 1778.
Bacon, Penial Private	May 5, 1778, Nine Months	Second, Pelton	June 1778 sick in Pennsylvania.
Bacon, Thompson Corporal	July 23, 1777, Duration of War	First, Copp	April-June 1778.
Bailey/Bayly, Dannel/Daniel Private	Nov 29, 1776, Three Years	Fourth, Pearsee	Dec 1777-May 1778; June 1778 on command.
Bailey/Baily, Ebenezer Private	Aug 13, 1777, Duration of War	Second, Pelton	Dec 1777; Jan 1778 on command; Feb 1778 sick smallpox; March 1778; April payroll only; May 1778; June 1778 sick in Pennsylvania.
Baire, John Private	May 5, 1778, Nine Months	Second, Riker	First listed on muster roll dated September 10, 1778, at White Plains, New York.
Baker, Benjamin Private	May 5, 1778, Nine Months	Second, Pelton	June 1778.

Baker, Elnathan Private	Feb 13, 1778, Duration of War	First, Wendell	April 1778 sick in quarters; May 1778; June 1778 sick at Cuckolds Town in State of Pennsylvania.
Baker, Hendrick Private	March 21, 1778, Duration of War	First, Ten Broeck	April-June 1778.
Baker, Henry Sergeant	Nov 21, 1776, Duration of War	Fourth, Strong	Dec 1777-May 1778; June 1778 sick Pennsylvania.
Baker, John Private	Nov 3, 1776, Duration of War	First, Copp	April-June 1778
Baker, Pierce Private	Nov 21, 1776, Duration of War	Fourth, Titus	Dec 1777-March 1778; April-May 1778 sick in quarters; June 1778 sick in Pennsylvania.
Balding, Jehial Private	May 5, 1778	Fourth, Marvin	May 1778 in inoculation; June 1778; July 1778 sick in Valley Forge.
Balding, Nathaniel/Nathl Private	May 5, 1778, Nine Months	Fourth, Pearsee	May 1778; June 1778 sick in Jersey.
Ballantine, William Private	Jan 1, 1777, Three Years	First, Ten Broeck	April 1778; May 1778 sick present; June 1778 sick Valley Forge.
Bangell/Bangel, John Private	Jan 27, 1777, Duration of War	First, Finck	April 1778; May 1778 sick regimental hospital; June 1778 sick Cuckolds Town.
Banks, Benjamin Private	May 5, 1778, Nine Months	Second, Ten Eyck	June 1778 payroll only.
Baptist, John Private	Oct 28, 1776, Duration of War	First, Van Ness	April-May 1778; June 1778 on guard.
Barber, Jonathan Private		Fourth, Titus	Dec 1777-Jan 1778 sick absent; Feb-March 1778; April-May 1778 sick in quarters; June 1778 sick in Pennsylvania.
Barber/Barker, Stephen Private	April 9, 1777, Duration of War	Second, Pelton	Dec 1777-Feb 1778 sick absent; March 1778; April 1778 payroll only; May 1778 tending sick; June 1778 sick in Pennsylvania.
Barber, William Private	May 5, 1778, Nine Months	Second, Pelton	May 1778 smallpox; June 1778.
Barker, John Private	Duration of War	Malcom's, Kearsley	Dec 1777; Jan 1778 on command; Feb 1778; March 1778 tending sick over Schuylkill; April 1778.
Barker, Jonathan Private	Nov 21, 1776, Duration of War	Fourth, Titus	Dec 1777-Jan 1778 sick absent; Feb-March 1778; April-May 1778 sick in quarters; June 1778 sick in Pennsylvania.
Barnhart, David Private	May 5, 1778, Nine Months	Fourth, Strong	June 1778.

Barnhart, John Private	Nov 20, 1776, Duration of War	First, Hicks	April-May 1778; June 1778 left sick on road from Pennsylvania.
Barns/Barnes, Benoni Private	May 5, 1778	Second, Ten Eyck	June 1778 payroll only.
Barns, James Private	May 5, 1778, Nine Months	Second, Riker	June 1778 sick at Valley Forge.
Barns, Richard, Private	Feb 1, 1777, Duration of War	Second, Ten Eyck	Dec 1777-June 1778 sick at Albany.
Barnum, Samuel Private	Jan 1, 1777, Duration of War	Second, Pelton	Dec 1777; Jan-Feb 1778 on command; March 1778 sick absent; April payroll only; May-June 1778.
Barr, John Sergeant	Jan 1, 1777, Duration of War	Fourth, Titus	Dec 1777; Jan-March 1778 on command; April 1778 on command clerk to the Brigade Commissary; May 1778; June 1778 sick in camp.
Barratt/Barrett, John Private	Nov 20, 1777, Duration of War	First, Van Ness	April-June 1778.
Barrett/Barrit, Walter Private	March 11, 1777, Duration of War	First, McCracken	April-May 1778; June 1778 sick at Cuckolds Town.
Barrit/Barrett, James Ensign/2nd. Lt.	Nov 21, 1776	Fourth, Strong/ Sacket	Dec 1777; Jan 9, 1778 promoted to Second Lieutenant and transferred to Sacket's Company; Jan 1778 on command; Feb 1778 sick present; April-May 1778 acting Quartermaster from March 19; June 1778 on furlough.
Barry/Berry, Charles Private	Dec 1, 1776, Duration of War	Fourth, Sacket	Dec 1777; Jan 1778 sick in hospital; February 22, 1778 dead.
Bartholomew, John Private	May 5, 1778, Nine Months	Second, Pelton	June 1778.
Bartley, Andrew Private	March 1, 1777, Duration of War	Fourth, Strong	Dec 1777; Jan 1778 on command; Feb-March 1778; April 1778 on main guard; May 1778; June 1778 sick Pennsylvania.
Bartoe, Morrice/ Morris Private	Nov 21, 1776, Duration of War	Fourth, Titus	Dec 1777; Jan 1778 on command; Feb-March 1778; April 1778 on command at Radnor; May-June 1778.
Barton, Thomas Private	Duration of War	Malcom's. Niven	Dec 2, 1777 deserted.

Basemore, Jacobus Private	May 1, 1778, Nine Months	Second, Lounsbery	June 1778 sick Pennsylvania.
Basemer, Michael Private	May 1, 1778, Nine Months	Second, Lounsbery	May-June 1778.
Basil, Michael Private	Nov 17, 1776, Duration of War	First, Hicks	April-June 1778.
Bassett/Basset, William Private	Nov 21, 1776, Duration of War	Fourth, Davis	Dec 1777-April 1778; May 1778 sick in the hospital; June 1778 sick in Pennsylvania.
Bates, Joseph Private		Malcom's, Niven	Dec 29, 1777 deserted.
Battersby, Robert/Robt Private	Jan 1, 1777, Duration of War	Second, Ten Eyck	Dec 1777-May 1778; June-July 1778 sick at Valley Forge.
Baugh see Rough			
Baylis, Richard Private	May 5, 1778, Nine Months	Fourth, Walker	May 1778; June 1778 sick Crab Orchard.
Beadle, Moses Private	Nov 21, 1776, Duration of War	First, Hicks	April-June 1778.
Beagle, Silas Private	May 5, 1778, Nine Months	Second, Pell	June 1778 tending sick at Valley Forge; July 4, 1778 deserted. Aug-Sept 1778 muster roll shows him tending sick at Valley Forge.
Beats, Joseph Private	Duration of War	Malcom's, Niven	Dec 29, 1777 deserted.
Beaty, James/Jms Corporal	Duration of War	Malcom's, Kearsley	Dec 1777-March 1778; April 1778 on command at Carlisle.
Beckwith, Silas Private	May 5, 1778, Nine Months	Fourth, Strong	June 1778 sick at Peekskill.
Beddenger/ Biddenger, Philip Corporal	August 13, 1777, Three Years	First, Finck	April-June 1778.
Bednor/Bedner, John Chr Private	Duration of War	First, Wendell	April-June 1778.
Beebe/Beebee, Benergis/ Boanerges Private	Dec 18, 1776, Duration of War	Fourth, Sacket	Dec 1777-Jan 1778; Feb 1778 sick present; March 1778 sick in Hutts; April 1778; May 1778 sick present; June 1778 sick in Pennsylvania.
Beebe, Ezra Private	June 13, 1777, Duration of War	First, Copp	April-June 1778.
Beekman/ Beckman, Tjerck Ensign	Nov 21, 1776	Second, Pelton	Dec 1777-March 1778; April 1778 payroll only; May-June 1778.
Beesomer, John Private	May 7, 1778, Nine Months	Second, Pell	May 1778 in smallpox; June 1778 sick at Valley Forge.

Name / Rank	Enlistment	Company	Service
Begun/Bugun, Albert Private	Oct 28, 1777, Three Years	Malcom's, Tom	Dec 1777-March 1778; April 1778 sick present; May-June 1778.
Bell, John Corporal	Jan 1, 1777, Duration of War	First, Hicks	April-June 1778.
Bell, Robert Sergeant	Jan 8, 1777, Duration of War	First, McCracken	April-May 1778; June 1778 sick at Rareeton Landing; July 1778 sick at Brunswick.
Bellamy, Silas Private	March 1, 1777, Three Years	Fourth, Titus	Dec 1777-Jan 1778 sick absent; Feb-April 1778; May 27, 1778 died.
Benjamin, Daniel/Danl Private	May 2, 1777, Three Years	Malcom's, Tom	Dec 1777-Feb 1778; March 1778 command; April-June 1778.
Benjamin, Ebenezer Private	May 5, 1778	Second, Ten Eyck	June 1778 payroll only.
Benjamin/ Benjaman, Jonathan/Jonth Private	Feb 20, 1777, Duration of War	Second, Graham	Dec 1777 payroll only; Jan-June 1778.
Benjamin, McIntauch/Mach Private	June 4, 1777, Three Years	Malcom's, Tom	Dec 1777; Feb-March 1778; May 1778 sick Regimental Hospital; June 28, 1778 killed.
Benjamin/ Benjamon, Stephen Private	Nov 25, 1776, Duration of War	Fourth, Strong	Dec 1777-May 1778; June 1778 on command Pennsylvania tending sick.
Bennett/Bennet, Jacob Private	Nov 21, 1776, Duration of War	Fourth, Titus	Dec 1777-Feb 1778; March 1778 on command; April 1778; May 1778 sick in quarters; June 1778 sick in Pennsylvania.
Bennett/Bennit, Jeremiah/Jeremh Private	Dec 5, 1777 Three Years	Second, Hallett	Dec 1777-Jan 1778; Feb 1778 payroll only; March-April 1778; May 1778 payroll only; June 1778 sick in Pennsylvania.
Bennett/Bannett, John Private	Dec 5, 1776, Three Years	Second, Hallett	Dec 1777-Jan 1778 sick at Albany; Feb 1778 payroll only; March-April 1778 sick at Albany; May-June 1778 payroll only.
Bennett/Bennet, Joshua Private	Feb 4, 1777, Three Years	Second, Graham	Dec 1777 payroll only; Jan-May 1778; June 1778 sick at Princeton.
Bennett/Bennet, Timothy Private	Nov 21, 1776, Duration of War	Fourth, Titus	Dec 1777-March 1778 on furlough; April-June 1778.
Bennett/Bennit, William Private	July 13, 1777, Three Years	First, McCracken	April-June 1778.

Benscoten see Van
Beniscoten

Name	Enlistment	Company	Service Record
Benson, William Private	April 6, 1777, Duration of War	Second, Lounsbery	Dec 1777; Jan-Feb 1778 on command; March 1778 sick absent; April-June 1778.
Bently, George Private	May 5, 1778, Nine Months	Second, Pelton	May 1778; June 9, 1778 discharged.
Berry/Berrey, Thomas/Thos Private	May 8, 1778, Duration of War	Malcom's, Lucas	Dec 1777 confined in the Provo; Jan 1778; Feb 5, 1778 deserted.
Berryhill, John Private	Oct 26, 1776, Duration of War	First, Van Ness	April 1778 sick Albany State of New York; May 1778 sick in Albany New York State; June 1778 sick in Albany.
Bice/Bouse, Henry Private	May 18, 1778	First, McCracken	May 1778; June 1778 sick at Englishtown.
Bice/Bouse, Peter Private	Nov 28, 1776, Three Years	First, McCracken	April-June 1778.
Birch/Burch, William Private	May 6, 1777, Duration of War	Malcom's, Lucas	Dec 1777-Jan 1778; Feb 4, 1778 deserted.
Bishop, Ebenezer Private	May 5, 1778, Nine Months	Fourth, Pearsee	May 1778 sick in camp; June 17, 1778 died.
Bishop, John Private	Oct 24, 1777, Duration of War	First, Finck	April-May 1778; June 1778 wounded June 28, 1778.
Black, David Private	May 5, 1778, Private	Fourth, Davis	May 1778; June 1778 sick Pennsylvania.
Black, Jack Private	May 1, 1778, Nine Months	Second, Lounsbery	May-June 1778.
Black, James Captain	March 17, 1777	Malcom's, Black	Dec 1777-Feb 1778; March 1778 on furough; April-May 1778. Oath at Valley Forge on May 11, 1778.
Blakeney, John Private	May 5, 1778, Nine Months	Second, Riker	June 1778.
Blaar, Jacob Private	Oct 28, 1777, Duration of War	First, Finck	April-May 1778; June 1778 wounded June 28, 1778.
Blanchard, Ephraim Private	Dec 21, 1776, Duration of War	First, Wendell	April-June 1778.
Blank, Jasper Private	Feb 27, 1777, Three Years	Fourth, Walker	Dec 1777-Jan 1778; Feb 1778 sick in quarters; March-June 1778.
Blase/Blaze, Christopher Private	April 26, 1777, Duration of War	Fourth, Pearsee	Dec 1777; Jan 1778 on party; Feb-April 1778; May 1778 sick present; June 1778 sick Valley Forge.

Blie, John Christian Private	Oct 28, 1777, Duration of War	First, Finck	April-June 1778.
Blindberry, Elijah Private	April 25, 1777, Three Years	Fourth, Smith	Nov 12, 1777 deserted; July 1778 muster roll shows he died on July 1, 1778.
Block/Bullock, Archibald Private	Nov 28, 1776, Duration of War	First, Van Ness	April-June 1778.
Blum, Albert Private	Nov 25, 1776, Duration of War	First, Finck	April 1778 sick in quarters; May-June 1778.
Bogardus/ Bogardres, Peter Private	May 5, 1778, Nine Months	Second, Pelton	May 1778; June 1778 absent with leave.
Bogart, Gilbert Sergeant	Oct 25, 1776, Duration of War	First, Van Ness	April-May 1778; June 1778 sick at Cuckolds Town.
Bogart, John Fifer	Three Years	Malcom's, Steel	Dec 1777-March 1778; April 1778 sick at Cuckoldstown; May 1778.
Bogg, John Private	April 23, 1778, Three Years	Fourth, Pearsee	April 1778 weeks command; May 1778; June 1778 on guard.
Boils/Boyles, James Private	May 5, 1778, Nine Months	Fourth, Davis	May-June 1778.
Bolton, Jonathan/Jonn Sergeant	Dec 6, 1776, Duration of War	Second, Riker	Dec 1777-April 1778; May 18, 1778 died.
Bolton, Mathew Private	Feb 2, 1777, Three Years	First, Ten Broeck	April-June 1778.
Boom, John Private	Jan 8, 1777, Three Years	First, Ten Broeck	April 1778 command at hospital Schnectady; May 1778 sick at his own [ ] in Albany County; June 1778.
Bough/Bough, William/Wm. Private	Oct 29, 1777, Duration of War	First, Finck	April-May 1778 June 28, 1778 wounded.
Bovee, John Private	May 5, 1778, Nine Months	Second, Riker	June 1778.
Bowers, Isaac/Isick Private	Jan 1, 1777, Duration of War	Fourth, Walker	Dec 1777-April 1778 sick in hospital at Albany; May 1778 sick at Albany; June 18, 1778 deserted.
Bowls/Bolos, George Private	Three Years	Malcom's. Santford	Dec 1777 sick absent; Jan 1778 sick present; Feb 1778 tending on sick; March-April 1778; May 1778 in Regimental Hospital; June 1778 sick at Yellow Springs.
Bowman, Bacchus Private	Nine Months	Fourth, Titus	June 1, 1778 joined; June 1778 sick in Pennsylvania.

Boyce/Boice, Peter Private	Dec 17, 1776, Three Years	Second, Hallett	Dec 1777-Jan 1778; Feb 1778 payroll only; March-April 1778; May 1778 payroll only; June 1778.
Boyd/Boyde, George/Geo. Private	May 5, 1778, Nine Months	Second, Pelton	June 1778 sick in Pennsylvania.
Boyd, James Private	Three Years	Malcom's, Black	Dec 1777-Feb 1778 not joined.
Braden/Breeden, John Private	Jan 1, 1777, Duration of War	Second, Graham	Dec 1777 payroll only; Jan-June 1778.
Bradner, Andrew Private	March 1, 1777, Three Years	Second, Graham	Dec 1777 payroll only; Jan-Feb 1778 sick at Goshen, March 1778 on command lines; April-June 1778.
Bradner/Bradnor, Benoni Private	May 5, 1778	Second, Ten Eyck	June 1778 Payroll only.
Bradt/Braett, Andrew Private	March 10, 1777, Duration of War	Second, Pelton	Dec 1777-Feb 1778; March 1778 on command; April 1778 payroll only; May 1778 on command; June 1778.
Bradt/Bradtt, James Private	March 29, 1777, Duration of War	First, Ten Broeck	April-June 1778.
Brannon, Abraham Private	Three Years	Malcom's, Black	Dec 1777-Jan 1778 sick in quarters; Feb-March 1778; April 1778 sick present; May 1778.
Brannon, Michael/Michl Private	Three Years	Malcom's, Black	Dec 1777; Jan 1778 sick in quarters; Feb-May 1778.
Brannon, Ruben/ Rubin Private	Three Years	Malcom's, Black	Dec 1777; Jan 1778 sick in quarters; Feb-March 1778; April 1778 sick present; May 1778 sick in camp.
Bray, Thomas Private	Jan 4, 1777, Duration of War	First, Van Ness	April-June 1778.
Bray, William Corporal	Three Years	Malcom's, Black	Dec 1777-Jan 1778; Feb-April 1778 on command; May 1778.
Brink/Brinck, Cornelius Private	May 1, 1778, Nine Months	Second, Lounsbery	May 1778; June 1778 on guard.
Briton/Britton, John Private	Duration of War	Malcom's, Niven	Dec 1777; Jan-Feb 1778 furlough.
Broadbrook, Edward Private	Nov 16, 1776, Duration of War	First, Copp	April 6, 1778 deserted.

Brock, Robert/ Roberd Private	May 5, 1778, Nine Months	Fourth Strong	May-June 1778.
Bromagham, Thomas Private		First, Wendell	April 11, 1778 deserted.
Brooks, Joseph Private	May 5, 1778, Nine Months	Second, Wright	May-June 1778.
Brooks/Broocks, Robert/Robart Fifer	May 5, 1778	Fourth, Sacket	May 1778; June 1778 sick in Pennsylvania.
Brooks/Brook, Thomas Private	Jan 2, 1777, Three Years	Second, Wright	Dec 1777-Feb 1778; March 1778 on guard; April 1778 weeks command; May 1778 tending sick; June 1778 sick Corrells Ferry.
Broughton, Bartholomew Private	March 4, 1777, Duration of War	First, Copp	April-June 1778.
Brown, David Sergeant	Dec 15, 1776, Three Years	First, McCracken	April-June 1778.
Brown, Elisha Private	March 1, 1778, Duration of War	First, Copp	April 1778 sick in Schenectady. He appeared on the muster roll for May 1778, but the June 1778 muster roll shows he was "left sick in Schnectady April 6."
Brown, Francis Private	Dec 6, 1776, Duration of War	First, Hicks	April-June 1778.
Brown, George Private	March 10, 1777, Three Years	First, Finck	April-May 1778; June 1778 sick Cuckolds Town hospital.
Brown, James Private	June 2, 1777, Three Years	Second, Hallett	Dec 1777-Jan 1778; Feb 1778 payroll only; March-April 1778; May 1778 payroll only; June 1778 sick Pennsylvania; August 2, 1778 died.
Brown, John Private	Oct 28, 1777, Three Years	First, Graham	April-June 1778.
Brown, John Sergeant Major	Dec 16, 1776, Duration of War	Second	Dec 1777-April 1778; May-June 1778 on furlough.
Brown, John Private	Duration of War	Malcom's, Steel	Dec 16, 1777 deserted.
Brown, John/Jno Private	April 27, 1777, Duration of War	Malcom's, Lucas	Dec 1777-Feb 1778 wagoner; March-April 1778; May 1778 wagoner camp.
Brown/Browne, Jonas Private	Feb 1, 1777, Duration of War	Second, Graham	Dec 1777 payroll only; Jan-Feb 1778; March 1778 on command; April-June 1778.
Brown, Jonathan Ensign	Nov 21, 1776,	First, McCracken	April 29, 1778 resigned.

Brown, Joseph Private	March 11, 1777, Duration of War	First, Graham	April-June 1778.
Brown, Joseph Private	Feb 28, 1777, Duration of War	Fourth, Marvin	Dec 1777-June 1778.
Brown, Nicholas Private	March 16, 1777, Duration of War	First, Finck	April-May 1778; June 1778 on guard.
Brown, Samuel Private	Nov 21, 1776, Duration of War	Fourth, Davis	Dec 1777-May 1778; June 1778 sick Pennsylvania.
Brown, Samuel Private	Nov 21, 1776, Duration of War	Fourth, Titus	Dec 1777-March 1778 sick absent; April 1778 sick at Albany; May 26, 1778 deserted.
Brown, Samuel Private	April 30, 1777, Three Years	Malcom's, Niven	Dec 1777 sick nigh camp; Jan 1778.
Brown, Thomas Sergeant	Dec 13, 1776, Duration of War	First, Graham	April-June 1778.
Brownen, Samuel Private	Nov 18, 1776, Duration of War	First, Hicks	April 1778; May 1778 sick regimental hospital; June 1778 sick at hospital Cuckolds Town.
Bruce, Benjamin/Benjm Private	March 10, 1777, Duration of War	Second, Graham	April 1778; May 1778 on duty; June 1778.
Brumley, John Corporal	March 4, 1777, Duration of War	First, Van Ness	April 1778 on command at Saratoga State of New York; May 1778 on General Schuyler's guard; on command General Schuyler's guard.
Brumley, William Private	April 29, 1777, Duration of War	First, Van Ness	April 1778; May 1778 sick in Regimental hospital.
Brunsen, Samuel Private	May 5, 1778, Nine Months	Fourth, Smith	July 1778.
Brush, David Private	Three Years	Malcom's, Santford	May 24, 1778 joined; May-June 1778.
Brush, Selah Private/Corporal	Nov 21, 1776, Duration of War	Fourth, Titus	Dec 1777 on command; Jan-May 1778; May 15, 1778 promoted to Corporal; June 1778 on General Poor's guard.
Buchanan/ Buccannon, Robert/Robt Private	Duration of War	Malcom's, Kearsley	Dec 1777-Feb 1778; March 1778 sick present; April 1778.
Buchanan/ Buchannan, Robert Corporal	Nov 3, 1777, Three Years	Malcom's, Tom	Dec 1777-May 1778; June 1778 sick at Corryells Ferry.
Buchanan, Samuel/Saml Private	Nov 21, 1776, Duration of War	Fourth, Sacket	Dec 1777 on command waiting on P. Master; Jan-May 1778; June 1778 on furlough.
Buck, Enoch Private	May 5, 1778	Second, Ten Eyck	June 1778 payroll only.

Buckingham, Stephen Drummer	Dec 28, 1776, Duration of War	Fourth, Smith	Dec 1777-April 1778; May 1778 sick in camp; June 1778 sick in Pennsylvania; July 1778 muster roll shows he died on June 27, 1778.
Buckleman, Henry Private	April 13, 1777, Duration of War	Fourth, Titus	Dec 1777-April 1778; May 1778 sick in quarters; June 1778 sick in Pennsylvania; June 27, 1778 died.
Budin/Budine, Francis Private	Feb 1, 1777, Duration of War	Fourth, Walker	Dec 1777 sick in hospital at Fishkill; Jan-May 1778; June 1778 on General Lee's guard.
Bullock see Block			
Bunker/Bonker, William Private	April 12, 1777, Three Years	Fourth, Pearsee	Dec 1777-March 1778 sick at Nine Partners; April 21, 1778 discharged.
Bunting/Buntinge, Thomas Corporal	Jan 1, 1777, Three Years	Second, Lounsbery	Dec 1777-June 1778.
Burch, Henry Private	Nine Months	Fourth, Titus	June 1, 1778 joined; June 1778 sick in Pennsylvania.
Burch, Samuel Private	March 29, 1777, Duration of War	First, Ten Broeck	April-May 1778; June 1778 sick Prince Town.
Burck, John Private	Duration of War	First, Van Ness	April-June 1778.
Burdick, Elisha Private	May 5, 1778, Nine Months	Fourth, Walker	June 1778 sick Pennsylvania.
Burdick, Henry Private	May 27, 1777, Duration of War	Second, Wright	Dec 1777 sick absent; Jan 1778 sick at New City; Feb-March 1778 sick absent; April 1778 sick in camp; May 1778 sick present; June 1778 sick at Valley Forge.
Burdick/ Burdock, Moses Sergeant	Dec 19, 1776, Three Years	+ Second, Hallett	Dec 1777-Jan 1778 sick at Fishkill; Feb 1778 payroll only; April 1778 muster roll shows him as "Deserted 1 March 1778;" April 1778 payroll notes "Reported deserted in March & April Muster rolls, but since joined being sick absent;" May 1778 "returned deserted but was sick;" June-July 1778 sick at Valley Forge.
Burgadis/ Burgadus, Abraham Private	May 27, 1777, Duration of War	Second, Wright	Dec 1777 sick absent; Jan 1778 sick at Cats Keell, Feb-March 1778 sick absent.

Burgess, Archibald Sergeant	Jan 1, 1777, Duration of War	Second, Pell	Dec 1777 sick present; Jan-Feb 1778 on furlough; March 1778 sick absent; April-May 1778 sick at Kakiat.
Burlin/Burling, Lewis Private	May 10, 1777, Duration of War	Second, Pell	Dec 1777-June 1778.
Burnes/Burns, Robert Private	Dec 10, 1776, Three Years	Second, Hallett	Dec 1777-Jan 1778; Feb 1778 payroll only; March-April 1778; May 1778 payroll only; June 1778.
Burnham/ Bernham, William Private	Jan 1, 1777, Duration of War	Fourth, Walker	Dec 1777-Jan 1778; Feb 1778 sick in quarters; March-June 1778.
Burns, John Private	Duration of War	Malcom's, Kearsley	Dec 1777-April 1778.
Burr, Aaron Lt. Col.	June 27, 1777	Malcom's	Dec 1777-March 1778; April 1778 on furlough; May 1778. Oath at Valley Forge on June 8, 1778.
Burrage/Burrige, John Private	Duration of War	Malcom's, Irvine	Dec 1777 on commissary guard; Jan 1778; Feb-April 1778 on furlough; May 1778 on command Carlisle; June 1778 on command E. Town.
Burrol/Burroll, Zachariah/ Zachoriah Private	May 5, 1778, Nine Months	Second, Wright	May-June 1778. Muster roll shows "Time of Entry" as May 20, 1778.
Burrows/Burrow, Edward Sergeant Major		Malcom's	Dec 1777-Feb 1778; March 4, 1778 deserted.
Burve, Jacob Private	March 6, 1777, Three Years	First, McCracken	April-June 1778.
Burve, Matthew Private	March 3, 1777, Three Years	First, McCracken	April-May 1778; June 28, 1778 killed.
Bush, Peter Private	June 27, 1777, Duration of War	Second, Lounsbery	Dec 1777-Jan 1778 sick hospital in Albany; Feb-March 1778 sick in hospital; April 1778 sick Fishkill; May-June 1778 sick New York.
Bussing, John Private	May 12, 1778, Nine Months	Second, Pell	May 1778.
Butler, John Private	Dec 4, 1776, Three Years	First, Wendell	April-June 1778 sick in General Hospital Albany.

Name/Rank	Enlistment	Company	Service
Byers/Byars, Andrew/Adw Sergeant		Malcom's, Steel	Dec 1777 sick; Jan 1778 in hospital; Feb 1778 sick in hospital; March 1778 sick hospital; April-June 1778 sick in Reading Hospital.
Cable, George Private	May 5, 1778, Nine Months	Second, Hallett	First appears on rolls for July 1778.
Caen see Coan			
Cahel, Robert Private	Dec 5, 1776, Three Years	First, Wendell	April-May 1778; June 1778 sick at Englishtown State of New Jersey.
Cahil/Cahill, John Private	Nov 17, 1776, Duration of War	First, Copp	April 1778-May 1778; June 1778 on duty.
Cain, Abel Private	Dec 5, 1777, Duration of War	First, Copp	April-May 1778; June 1778 absent without leave and supposed to be sick.
Callahan/ Callaghan, John Private		Malcom's, Kearsley	Feb 1778 on on command; March 1778 on command to York Govt; April 1778.
Camby see Kamby			
Cameron/Camron, Alexander/Alexr Private	April 18, 1777, Duration of War	Malcom's, Lucas	Dec 1777-Jan 1778; Feb 4, 1778 deserted.
Cameron, Daniel/Danl Private	Nov 28, 1776, Duration of War	First, Graham	April-June 1778.
Cammell/Cambel, Andrew Private	Dec 7, 1776, Duration of War	Fourth, Marvin	Dec 1777-April 1778; May 1778 on command; June 1778.
Camp, Esau Private	May 5, 1778	Second, Ten Eyck	June-Sept 1778 sick at Valley Forge.
Campbell, John/Jno Private	Jan 2, 1777, Duration of War	Second, Ten Eyck	Dec 1777-Feb 1778 on furlough; March-April 1778 on furlough at furlough at Albany; May 1778 furlough; June 1778 muster roll shows he deserted on Jan 1, 1778.
Campbell, William Corporal	Jan 1, 1777, Three Years	Second, Pell	Sept 1777-March 1778 on command with his Excellency; April-May 1778 on command in the Forage Department; June 1778 furlough at Sing Sing.
Cane, Henry Private	Dec 19, 1777, Duration of War	First, Copp	April 1778 sick in quarters; May 1778 sick regimental hospital; June 1778 sick near Springfield.
Canfield, Amos Private	May 5, 1778, Nine Months	Fourth, Marvin	May 1778 in inoculation; June 1778.
Cannaday/ Canneday, John Private	Jan 1, 1777, Duration of War	Fourth, Strong	Dec 1777-June 1778.

Cannon, Thomas/Thos Private	Duration of War	Malcom's, Black	Dec 1777-Feb 1778; March 1778 sick present; April-May 1778.
Canterbury, Samuel Private	Duration of War	Malcom's Irvine	Dec 1777; Jan-March 1778 on command; April 12, 1778 deserted.
Carby/Carbey, Richard Private	Jan 5, 1777, Duration of War	Fourth, Sacket	Dec 1777; Jan-March 1778 on party; April 1778 on duty; May- June 1778.
Carman, Hendrick Private	Nov 28, 1776, Duration of War	First, Wendell	April 1778; May 1778 muster roll shows he died on June 1, 1778.
Carmen, John Private	May 5, 1778, Nine Months	Second, Pelton	June 1778 sick present.
Carney, Barnibus Private	May 5, 1778, Nine Months	Fourth, Walker	June 1778.
Carr/Car, Anthony Private	May 5, 1778, Nine Months	Fourth, Pearsee	May 1778; June 1778 sick in Jersey.
Carr, William Private	March 19, 1777, Three Years	First, Van Ness	April-June 1778.
Carrey, John Private	May 5, 1778, Nine Months	Fourth, Pearsee	June 1778.
Carson, James Sergeant	Jan 1, 1777, Duration of War	Second, Pell	Dec 1777-June 1778.
Carter, John Private	May 5, 1778	Second Ten Eyck	June 1778 payroll.
Casey, Robert Corporal	Feb 2, 1777, Duration of War	First, Ten Broeck	April 1778; May 1778 sick present; June 1778 Sick Valley Forge.
Cashin, William Private	Nov 21, 1776, Duration of War	Fourth, Titus	Dec 1777-March 1778 sick absent; April 1778 sick at Albany; May 1778 sick in Country.
Casady/Casidy, Peter Private	Jan 20, 1777, Duration of War	Second, Riker	Dec 1777 sick present; Jan-April 1778; May 1778 sick in camp; June-July 1778 sick at Valley Forge.
Casselman, Christian Private	Dec 13, 1776, Duration of War	First, Finck	April-June 1778.
Catch, John Musician/Private	May 1, 1777, Duration of War	Second, Ten Broeck	April-May 1778; May 1778 reduced to Private; June 1778.
Catchem see Ketcham			
Cator see Keator			

Cato Drummer	Jan 1, 1777, Duration of War	Fourth, Walker	Dec 1777; Jan 1778 sick present; Feb 1778 sick in quarters; March 1778 sick in camp; April-June 1778. As no last name is shown, Cato is assumed to have been a patriot of African descent.
Cavener/Cavoner, Moses Private	Jan 4, 1777, Three Years	Second, Wright	Dec 1777-May 1778; June 1778 sick at Kings Ferry.
Chambers, John Private	Duration of War	Malcom's, Santford	Dec 1777 at Commissarys; Jan-April 1778; May 1778 in Regimental Hospital; June 1778 at Valley Forge.
Chambers/ Cambers, John	Duration of War	Malcom's, Irvine	Dec 1777-Jan 1778 sick absent.
Chambers/ Chaimbers, Leonard Private	Nov 1, 1776, Duration of War	First, Finck	April 1778 on command General Schuyler's guard; May 1778 on command; June 1778 on command General Schuyler's guard.
Champlain, James Private	May 5, 1778, Nine Months	Second, Pell	May-June 1778.
Chappel/Chapel, Benjamin Armorer	Nov 21, 1776	Fourth, Sacket	Dec 1777; Jan-Feb 1778 Armorer for the Brigade; March 1778 for Genl. Poor's Brigade.
Chappel, Benjamin/Benjm Private	Nov 21, 1776, Duration of War	Fourth, Davis	Dec 1777-June 1778.
Chappel, Benjamin/ Benjm, Jr. Private	Duration of War	Fourth, Davis	April-June 1778.
Charles, Christeaen/ Christeden Private	Duration of War	First, Van Ness	April 1778 sick Fishkills State of New York; May-June 1778.
Charlesworth, John/John M. Fifer	Dec 1, 1776, Duration of War	Fourth, Strong	Dec 1777-May 1778; June 1778 sick Valley Forge "Pennsylvany."
Chase/Chace, Jacob Private	Jan 18, 1777, Three Years	First, Wendell	April-June 1778.
Chatfield, David Private	Feb 9, 1777, Duration of War	First, Copp	April-June 1778.
Chatfield, Samuel/Saml Private	March 27, 1778,	First, Ten Broeck	April 1778 sick at Fishkill; May 1778 sick at Fishkill Hospital; June 1778.

Cherry, John Private	May 5, 1778, Nine Months	Fourth, Pearsee	June 1778.
Chevalier see Shavalier			
Christian/Cristeon, Benjamin Private	March 1, 1777, Duration of War	Second, Wright	Dec 1777; Jan 1778 on command with Forage Master; Feb 1778 sick absent; March-April 1778; May 1778 sick present; June 15, 1778 died.
Christion/Cristin, Peter Private	Duration of War	Second, Wright	April 1778 sick present; May 29, 1778 died.
Church, John Private	Duration of War	Malcom's, Irvine	June 1778 joined.
Clark, Benjamin Fifer	Nov 1, 1777	First, Graham	April-June 1778.
Clark, David Sergeant	March 1, 1777, Duration of War	Fourth, Marvin	Dec 1777-Jan 1778; Feb 1778 on furlough; March-June 1778.
Clark, Ephraim Private	May 5, 1778, Nine Months	Fourth, Marvin	May 5 1778 joined; May-June 1778.
Clark, George Private	Aug 5, 1777, Duration of War	Malcom's, Lucas	Dec 13, 1777 deserted.
Clark/Clarke, John Private	Feb 14, 1777, Duration of War	Fourth, Sacket	Dec 1777-March 1778; April-May 1778 sick present; June 1778 sick in Pennsylvania.
Clark, Moses Private	March 15, 1777, Three Years	Malcom's, Tom	Dec 1777 sick absent; Jan 1778 sick quarters; Feb-April 1778 on furlough; May-June 1778 sick State of New York.
Clarke, Jeremiah 1st. Lt.	Nov 21, 1776	Second Lounsberry	December 17, 1777 resigned.
Clarke/Cleark, Samuel/Saml Private/Corporal	April 5, 1777, Three Years	Malcom's, Santford	Dec 1777-Jan 1778; Jan 1778 promoted to Corporal; Feb 1778 on furlough; March-June 1778.
Claxton/Claxon, George Private	Jan 1, 1777 Duration of War	Second, Graham	Dec 1777 payroll only; Jan 1778; Feb 1778 on a week's command; March-June 1778.
Clement, Nicholas Private	Nov 9, 1776, Duration of War	First, Copp	April-May 1778; June 1778 sick in hospital Cuckolds Town.
Clements/ Clamants, Jacob Private		First, Finck	April-May 1778; June 1778 on command Colonel Morgan
Cleveland, Josiah Private	May 5, 1778	Second, Hallett	June 26, 1778 deserted.
Clift, Joseph Private	Dec 18, 1776, Duration of War	Fourth, Sacket	Dec 1777-June 1778.
Cloese/Kloese, Adam Private	Duration of War	Malcom's, Kearsley	Dec 1777-Jan 1778; Feb 1778 deserted hospital.

Clopper, Peter Private	Feb 17, 1777, Three Years	First, Wendell	April-June 1778.
Close/Closs, Christopher Private	May 5, 1778, Nine Months	Fourth, Titus	June 1, 1778 joined; June 1778.
Clough, Benjamin Private	March 3, 1777, Three Years	First, Ten Broeck	April 1778; May 1778 sick present; June 1778 sick Valley Forge.
Coan/Caen, Edward/Edwd Private	Duration of War	Malcom's, Steel	Dec 1777-March 1778 sick hospital; April muster roll notes he was "sent to Phila. wounded after Battle of Brandywine not heard of since." April payroll shows him missing.
Coates/Coats, Joseph Private	Jan 1, 1777, Three Years	Fourth, Titus	Dec 1777-March 1778 sick absent; April 1778 sick at Albany; May 26, 1778 deserted.
Coblar, Conrad Private	April 14, 1778	Second, Hallett	May 1778.
Cockle, George Private	May 5, 1778, Nine Months	Second, Pell	June 1778 tending sick in the hospital.
Cockley, John Private	Feb 1, 1777, Three Years	First, Ten Broeck	April-June 1778 command with General Schuyler.
Cocks, George Private	Jan 31, 1777, Duration of War	First, Ten Broeck	April-May 1778 on command at hospital Schnectady; June 1778 on command Schenectady.
Codwise, Christopher, 1st. Lt.	Nov 21, 1776	Second, Hallett	Dec 1777-Jan 1778 on command Fishkill; Feb 1778 payroll only; March-April 1778 on command Fishkill; May 1778 payroll only; June 1778.
Cogden, John Private	Oct 16, 1777, Duration of War	First, Finck	April-May 1778; June 1778 wagoner to Artillery.
Cole see Kole			
Cole, Aaron/Aron Private	May 5, 1778, Nine Months	Fourth, Marvin	May 5, 1778 joined; May-June 1778.
Cole/Coall, Cornelous/ Cornelius Private	Three Years	Malcom's, Niven	Dec 1777-Jan 1778 not joined; Feb 1778 not joined deserted.
Cole, David Private	April 9, 1777 Duration of War	Second, Pelton	Dec 1777-March 1778; April 1778 payroll only; May-June 1778.
Cole, Oliver Private	Nine Months	Fourth, Marvin	June 1778 muster roll shows he joined on May 3, 1778; June 1778.
Cole, Samuel Private	May 5, 1778, Nine Months	Second, Pelton	May 1778; June 1778 on command.

Cole, Tunis Private	March 24, 1777, Duration of War	Second, Wright	Dec 1777; Jan 1778 on command at Pots Grove; Feb-March 1778 on command; April-June 1778.
Cole, William Private	May 5, 1778, Nine Months	Fourth, Strong	May 1778; June 1778 sick in "Pensilvany."
Coleman, Samuel Musician	May 5, 1778, Nine Months	Fourth, Davis	May-June 1778.
Colford, Matthew Fife Major		Malcom's	Dec 1777-April 1778; May 1778 sick present.
Collins, Edward Private	Jan 1, 1777, Duration of War	Fourth, Walker	Dec 1777; Jan 1778 on party; Feb-March 1778; April 1778 on command at Radnor; May 1778; June-July 1778 sick Pennsylvania.
Collins/Collans, John Private	Dec 23, 1776, Three Years	Second, Hallett	Dec 1777-Jan 1778; Feb 1778 payroll only; March-April 1778; May 1778 payroll only; June 1778.
Collord, Edward Fife	Sept 25, 1777, Duration of War	First, Van Ness	April 1778; May 1778 sick regimental hospital; June 1778 left sick at Cuckoldstown.
Colter/Coltar, Nathanael/Nathl Private	Duration of War	Malcom's, Steel	Dec 1777-Feb 1778; March 1778 sick present; April-May 1778; June 1778 command for Col. Morgan.
Commins/ Cummins, Cornelius, Private	March 19, 1777, Duration of War	First, Van Ness	April-June 1778.
Conaway/Conway, John Corporal	Jan 1, 1777, Three Years	Second, Lounsbery	Dec 1777-May 1778; June 1778 on guard.
Condo, William Private	March 2, 1777, Three Years	First, McCracken	April-May 1778; June 1778 waiter to the Captain.
Concklin/Conklin, Edmund/Edward Private	Dec 10, 1776, Duration of War	Fourth, Smith	Dec 1777; Jan-March 1778 sick in hospital; April-June 1778.
Conklin/Concklin, Danniel/Daniel Private	Dec 8, 1776, Duration of War	Fourth, Marvin	Dec 1777-June 1778.
Conklin, John Private	Nov 18, 1777, Three Years	Second, Hallett	Dec 1777; Jan 1778 sick at Fishkill; Feb 1778 payroll only; March 1778 sick at Fishkill; April 21, 1778 transferred.
Conklin/Conkling, Joseph Private	May 20, 1777, Duration of War	Second, Graham	Dec 1777 payroll only; Jan 1778 on command; Feb 1778 on command with the captain; March-June 1778.

Conkling, Silvanus 2nd. Lt./1st. Lt.	Nov 21, 1776	Fourth, Davis	Dec 1777-Jan 1778; Jan 22, 1778 promoted to First Lieutenant; Feb 1778; March 1778 on party; April-June 1778.
Conn, William/Wm Private	Nov 21, 1776, Duration of War	Fourth, Davis	Dec 1777-June 1778.
Conner, Daniel Private	May 1, 1778, Nine Months	Second, Lounsbery	May-June 1778.
Conner, John Corporal	Feb 4, 1777, Duration of War	First, Ten Broeck	April-May 1778; June 7, 1778 died.
Conner, John Private	Duration of War	Malcom's, Irvine	Dec 1777-Jan 1778; Feb-April 1778 on furlough; May 1778 on fatigue; June 1778.
Connolly/ Conolly, John Private	May 1, 1777, Three Years	First, Graham	April-June 1778.
Connoly/Conoly, James Corporal	June 20, 1777, Duration of War	Fourth, Pearsee	Sept 1777-March 1778 sick at Fishkill; April-June 1778.
Connor/Conner, John Corporal	May 5, 1778, Nine Months	Fourth, Marvin	May 5, 1778 joined; May-June 1778.
Connor/Conor, Patrick Private	Jan 1, 1777, Duration of War	Fourth, Walker	Dec 1777-June 1778.
Connor, William Corporal	May 7, 1778, Nine Months	Second, Pell	May 1778; June 1778 on Q M G Guard.
Constable, Gerrit/Garrett Private	May 1, 1778, Nine Months	Second, Lounsbery	May 1778; June-July 1778 sick Pennsylvania.
Conway/Conwey, Cornelius Private	May 1, 1778, Nine Months	Second, Lounsbery	May 1778 sick in camp; June 1778.
Conway, Henry/ Henerey Fife	Three Years	Malcom's, Black	Dec 1777-Feb 1778 sick in quarters; March 1778; April 16, 1778 died.
Conway, William Private	Nov 15, 1776, Duration of War	First, Hicks	April-June 1778.
Cook/Cooke, John Jr. Private	Nov 28, 1776, Duration of War	First, Copp	April-June 1778.
Cook/Cooke, John Sr. Private	July 23, 1777, Duration of War	First, Copp	April-June 1778.
Cook, Moses Private	April 25, 1777, Three Years	Fourth, Pearsee	Dec 1777; Jan 1778 on party; Feb-April 1778; May 1778 sick present; June 1778.

Cook, Nathan Private	Dec 10, 1776, Three Years	Fourth, Smith	Dec 1777 sick in quarters; Jan-Feb 1778; March 1778 guard; April 1778; May 1778 sick in camp; June 1778.
Cooke/Cook, George Private	Nov 21, 1776, Duration of War	Fourth, Titus	Dec 1777-March 1778; April-May 1778 sick in quarters; June 1778 sick in Pennsylvania.
Coole, Aron Private	May 1778	Fourth, Marvin	First appears on muster roll for September 1778.
Coon, Jacob Private	Dec 15, 1776, Duration of War	Fourth, Smith	Aug 25, 1777 deserted; March 10, 1778 joined; March-June 1778.
Cooper, John/Jno Private	Jan 1, 1777, Duration of War	Second, Graham	Dec 1777 payroll only; Jan-Feb 1778 wounded at Albany.
Cooper, Richard Private	One Year	Malcom's, Irvine	Dec 1777-Feb 1778.
Cooper, Thomas Private	Duration of War	First, Van Ness	April-May 1778; June 1778 left on the road sick at Spotswoods.
Copeland, William Private	Dec 16, 1776, Duration of War	First, Copp	April-June 1778.
Copp, John Captain	Nov 21, 1776	First, Copp	April-June 1778.
Corporal/Cobler, Conrad Private	April 14, 1778	Second, Hallett	April-June 1778.
Corrington/ Cornington, Joseph Private	April 29, 1777, Three Years	Malcom's, Tom	Dec 1777-Jan 1778.
Corter/Carter, John Private	May 5, 1778	Second, Ten Eyck	June 1778 payroll only.
Corter, Philip Private	June 29, 1777, Duration of War	Second, Graham	Dec 1777 payroll only; Jan 1778; Feb 1778 sick in smallpox; March-May 1778; June-August 1778 sick at Valley Forge.
Cortlandt/ Cortland, Philip Colonel	Nov 21, 1776	Second	Dec 1777 sick absent; Jan-Feb 1778; March 1778 on furlough; April-June 1778.
Cosier, Hezekiah Private	Oct 24, 1776, Duration of War	First, Hicks	April-June 1778.
Cotter, James Private	Nov 28, 1776, Duration of War	First, Graham	April-June 1778.
Cotton, George Private	Duration of War	Malcom's, Niven	Dec 1777-Feb 1778; April 1778; May 1778 fatigue.
Cottrill/Cottrell, Richard Private	Jan 1, 1777, Duration of War	Fourth, Walker	Dec 1777-May 1778; June 1778 with Baron Steuben.

Counts, Adam Private	Nov 5, 1777, Duration of War	First, Finck	April 1778 sick in quarters; May-June 1778.
Couray, Michael Private	May 5, 1778, Nine Months	Fourth, Pearsee	June 1778.
Courtney/ Courtenay, Francis Sergeant	Dec 24, 1776, Duration of War	Second, Hallett	Dec 1777-Jan 1778; Feb 1778 payroll only; March-April 1778; May 1778 payroll only; June 1778.
Cowan/Cowen, Thomas Private	Feb 1, 1777, Three Years	Second, Lounsbery	Dec 1777-Jan 1778 sick hospital Fishkill; Feb-March 1778 sick in hospital; April 19, 1778 deserted.
Cowdon, David Private	March 14, 1777, Duration of War	Second, Lounsbery	Dec 1777-Jan 1778 sick hospital Fishkill; Feb-March 1778 sick in hospital; April-May 1778; June 1778 sick in Pennsylvania.
Cox, John Private	Nov 21, 1776, Duration of War	Fourth, Sacket	Dec 1777; Jan sick in camp; Feb 1778 sick present; March-June 1778.
Cox, Robert Private	April 27, 1777, Duration of War	Second, Lounsbery	Dec 1777; Jan-Feb 1778 on command; March-June 1778.
Cox, Simon Private	Jan 1, 1777, Duration of War	Fourth, Walker	Dec 1777 sick in quarters; Jan-March 1778; April 1778 on main guard; May-June 1778.
Cox, William Private	April 20, 1777, Three Years	Malcom's, Tom	Dec 1777-April 1778; May 1778 sick Regimental Hospital; June 1778 sick Bucks County.
Craft, Nathaniel/Nathanl. Private	Jan 5, 1777, Duration of War	Fourth, Sacket	Dec 1777; Jan 1778 waggoner; Feb-June 1778.
Craig, John Private	Nov 28, 1776, Duration of War	First, Graham	April-May 1778; June 1778 on command Colonel Morgan.
Craig, John Private	Dec 12, 1776	Fourth, Smith	Dec 1777-Jan 1778; Feb 17, 1778 died.
Crandle/Crandell, Godfrey Private		First, Finck	April-May 1778; June 1778 on command Col. Morgan.
Crandle, Wilson, Private	Feb 22, 1777, Three Years	Second, Graham	Dec 1777 payroll only; Jan-May 1778 sick at 9 Partners; June 1778 9 Partners.
Crandle, Wright Private	May 5, 1778, Nine Months	Second, Ten Eyck	May-June 1778.
Crane, Stephen Private	Three Years	Malcom's, Santford	Dec 1777-April 1778; May 1778 on duty; June 1778.
Crannel, William Private	May 18, 1778, Nine Months	First, Hicks	April 1778 from the New York drafts for 9 months from May 1778; June 1778.
Crawford, John/Jno Private	May 5, 1778, Nine Months	Fourth, Smith	May-June 1778.

Crawford/Craford, William/Wm Private	Duration of War	Malcom's, Niven	Dec 1777-Jan 1778 not joined; Feb 1778 not joined deserted.
Cripes/Cripen, Frederick/ Fredrick C. Private	Three Years	First, Van Ness	April 1778 muster roll shows he deserted on March 5, 1778.
Crispel/Crispell, Abram/Abraham Private	May 1, 1778, Nine Months	Second, Lounsbery	May-June 1778.
Cristeon/Cristion, John Private	March 22, 1777, Duration of War	Second, Wright	Dec 1777-March 1778; April 1778 sick in camp; May 1778 sick present; June 1778.
Croft/Crofts, James Corporal	April 10, 1778	Second, Hallett	First appears on rolls for July 1778.
Crofot/Crowfut, Nehemiah Sergeant	Jan 1, 1777, Duration of War	Fourth, Titus	Dec 1777-March 1778 sick absent; April 1778 sick at Albany.
Crofot, Samuel Sergeant	Oct 24, 1776, Duration of War	First, Hicks	April-June 1778.
Cronck, John Private	Nov 13, 1776, Duration of War	First, Hicks	April-June 1778.
Cronin/Cronnon, Patrick Sergeant/ Quartermaster	Dec 20, 1777, Duration of War	Malcom's, Niven	Dec 1777; Dec 20, 1777 appointed Quartermaster; Jan 1778; Feb 1778-March 1778 on furlough; April-May 1778. Oath at Valley Forge on May 11, 1778 on which the last name appears as Cronen.
Cronkhite, Patrick Private	Jan 21, 1777, Three Years	First, Wendell	April-June 1778.
Crook/Krook, Martin Private	Three Years	Malcom's, Black	Dec 1777 attending sick; Jan-Feb 1778; March 1778 sick present; April-May 1778.
Crook, William Private	March 23, 1777, Three Years	Second, Wright	Dec 1777 prisoner of war.
Crosbey/ Crosby, Enos/Enoch Private	May 5, 1778, Nine Months	Fourth, Strong	May 1778; June 1778 sick in Pennsylvania.
Crossen, Samuel Private	Dec 12, 1776, Duration of War	First, Copp	April-June 1778.
Crossman, Daniel Private	May 5, 1778, Nine Months	Second, Graham	May 1778; June 1778 Brunswick.
Crowder, Anthony Private	Duration of War	First, Wendell	April-June 1778.
Crugar, William Private	May 5, 1778, Nine Months	Second, Riker	May-June 1778.

Crum, William Private	May 1, 1778	Second, Lounsbery	First appears on muster roll for October 1778.
Cuffman, John Private	Nov 13, 1777, Duration of War	First, Van Ness	May 2, 1778 died.
Cummers, Jonathan Private		Fourth, Sacket	Dec 1777 taken prisoner at White Plains July 30; Jan 1778 prisoner.
Cunningham, Archibald Private	Jan 1, 1777, Duration of War	Fourth, Titus	Dec 1777; Jan 1778 on command; Feb 1778; March 1778 on command; April 1778; May 1778 sick in quarters; June 1778.
Cunningham, Henry Private	May 5, 1778, Nine Months	Fourth, Strong	May 1778; June 1778 sick in Jerseys.
Cunningham, James Private	May 5, 1778, Nine Months	Second, Graham	May-June 1778.
Cunningham/ Cuningham, Shubel/Shubal Private	Jan 1, 1777, Three Years	Second, Pell	Dec 1777-June 1778.
Cure/Curd, William Private	May 5, 1778, Nine Months	Fourth, Sacket	May-June 1778.
Curtice/Curtise, Naniard/Niard Private	Dec 1, 1776, Duration of War	Fourth, Strong	Dec 1777; Jan-Feb 1778 on command; March-April 1778; May 1778 sick in hospital; June- Dec 1778 sick at Valley Forge; Jan 31, 1779 deserted.
Curwine/Curwin, Edward Private	March 1, 1777, Duration of War	Fourth, Sacket	Dec 1777-June 1778.
Curwine/Corwin, Gershom/Gersham Private	Nov 21, 1776, Duration of War	Fourth, Titus	Dec 1777-May 1778; June 1778 sick in Pennsylvania.
Dailly/Dayley, Silas Private	Three Years	Malcom's, Black	Dec 1777 sick in quarters; Jan 1778 attending sick; Feb-April 1778; May 1778 sick in camp.
Dane/Dean, Abraham Sergeant	May 5, 1778, Nine Months	Fourth, Smith	May-June 1778.
Daniels, Henry Private	Dec 23, 1776, Three Years	First, Van Ness	April-May 1778; June 1778 on guard.
Darby/Derby, Charles Fifer	July 7, 1777, Three Years	Second, Hallett	Dec 1777-Jan 1778 sick at Goshen; Feb 1778 payroll only; March-April 1778; May 1778 payroll only; June 1778.
Darling, Moses Private	Oct 24, 1776, Duration of War	First, Finck	April-June 1778.

Darrow, Jedediah Private	May 5, 1778	Second, Hallett	First appears on rolls for July 1778.
Daughaty/ Daughety, William Private	Nov 18, 1776, Duration of War	First, Hicks	April-June 1778.
Davidson, William Sergeant	Duration of War	Malcom's, Irvine	Dec 1777; Jan 1778 on furlough; Feb 1778; March-April 1778; May 1778 on furlough; June 24, 1778 reduced to private; June 1778 Princeton Hospital.
Davies/Davis, Chapman Private	Nov 21, 1776, Duration of War	Fourth, Sacket	Dec 1777-April 1778; on command guarding stores.
Davies/Davis, Joshua Private	Nov 21, 1776, Duration of War	Fourth, Sacket	Dec 1777-June 1778.
Davies/Davis, Richard Corporal	Nov 21, 1776, Duration of War	Fourth, Sacket	Dec 1777-Feb 1778; March 1778 sick in hutts; April 1778 sick present; May-June 1778.
Davis, Andries/Andrew Private	May 1, 1778, Nine Months	Second, Lounsbery	May 1778 sick in camp; June 1778.
Davis, Elias Private	Three Years	Malcom's, Black	Dec 1777 sick in quarters; Jan-Feb 1778; March 1778 sick present; April 1778; May 1778 on fatigue.
Davis, Herman Private	Jan 1, 1777, Duration of War	Second, Pell	Dec 1777; Jan 2, 1778 deserted; March 1778 under sentence of a Court Martial; March 21, 1778 enlisted; April-June 1778.
Davis, John Sergeant	May 1, 1778, Nine Months	Second, Lounsbery	May-June 1778.
Davis/Davice, John Captain	Nov 21, 1776	Fourth, Davis	Dec 1777-June 1778.
Davis, John Private	May 5, 1778, Nine Months	Fourth, Marvin	May-June 1778.
Davis/Davies, John Private	Duration of War	Malcom's, Niven	Dec 1777-Jan 1778; Feb 1778 on furlough; April-May 1778.
Davis, Joseph Private	May 5, 1778, Nine Months	Fourth, Strong	May 1778; June 1778 on Gen: Poors guard.
Davis, Patrick Private	May 5, 1778, Nine Months	Fourth, Marvin	May 1778 in inoculation; June 1778; July-Oct 1778 sick at Valley Forge.
Davis, Richard Private	March 13, 1777, Duration of War	Fourth, Marvin	Dec 1777-March 1778; April 1778 sick in quarters; May 1778 sick in camp; June 1778.

Davis, Thomas Private	May 5, 1778, Nine Months	Fourth, Marvin	May 1778 in inoculation; June 1778.
Davison, James Private	May 5, 1778, Nine Months	Second, Pelton	May 1778 smallpox; June 1778.
Dawson/Dauson, Thomas Musician	Duration of War	Malcom's, Niven	Dec 1777 sick nigh camp; Jan 1778 sick absent; Feb 1778 sick in quarters; April 1778 sick in camp; May 1778; July 1778 sick Yellow Springs.
Dayton/Daton, Bennet/ Benet Private	Nov 21, 1776, Duration of War	Fourth, Sacket	Dec 1777; Jan 1778 on party; Feb 1778; March 1778 sick in hutts; April-May 1778 sick present; June 1778 sick in Jersies.
Dayton/Daton, Ezekiel Private	Feb 10, 1777, Duration of War	Second, Wright	Dec 1777 on furlough; Jan 1778 sick at Wright's Mills; Feb 1778 sick absent; March 1778 on weeks command; April 1778 sick in camp; May 1778 sick present; June-July 1778 sick Valley Forge.
Dean, Isaac Private	June 2, 1777, Duration of War	Second, Wright	Dec 1777; Jan 1778 sick in quarters; Feb-April 1778; May 1778 on guard; June 1778.
Debois, Lewis Private	Nov 28, 1776, Duration of War	First, Graham	April-June 1778.
Decamp, Mathias Private	Feb 22, 1777, Duration of War	First, Finck	April-June 1778.
Decker/Deckor, George/Jerry Private	May 7, 1777, Three Years	Fourth, Pearsee	Dec 1777-March 1778; April 1778 sick in camp; May 1778 sick present; June 1778 sick Valley Forge.
Decker, Jacob Private	Three Years	Malcom's, Black	Dec 1777-Feb 1778; March-April 1778 on furlough; May 1778.
Decker, John Private	Jan 4, 1777, Three Years	First, Hicks	April 1778 sick at Fishkill; May-June 1778.
Decker, John Private	Jan 27, 1776, Three Years	First, Wendell	April-June 1778.
Defew/Defue, George Private	May 5, 1778, Nine Months	Fourth, Davis	June 1778; July-Sept 1778 sick in Pennsylvania.
DeFreest, Abraham Sergeant	Jan 1, 1777, Duration of War	First, Wendell	April-June 1778.
Delany, Dennis Private	May 5, 1778, Nine Months	Fourth, Davis	May-June 1778.
Demarist/Demaris, Nicholas Private/Corporal	May 5, 1778, Nine Months	Second, Riker	May-June 1778; June 1, 1778 promoted to Corporal.

Demerest/ Demoress, John Private	May 5, 1778, Nine Months	Fourth, Strong	May-June 1778.
Demott, Peter Private	Dec 10, 1776, Three Years	Fourth, Smith	Dec 1777 sick in quarters; Jan 9, 1778 died.
Dempsy, John Private	Duration of War	Malcom's, Niven	Dec 1777 on command; Jan-Feb 1778 on furlough; April 1778 in dispute with Captain Porterfield 11th Virginia Regiment. No man of this name appears in the 11th Virginia rolls.
Denney, John 2nd. Lt.	Nov 21, 1776	First, McCracken	April-June 1778.
Dennis, John Private	Jan 1, 1777, Duration of War	Second, Ten Eyck	Dec 1777 unfit for service; Jan 1, 1778 discharged.
Dennison/ Denison, Thomas Private	Jan 1, 1777, Duration of War	Fourth, Walker	Dec 1777-June 1778.
Denniston, Daniel/Danl "Voluntier"		First, Graham	April-June 1778.
Denny/Denney, Peter Private	Nov 21, 1776, Duration of War	Fourth, Sacket	Dec 1777-April 1778; May 1778 sick present; June-Sept 1778 sick in Pennsylvania.
Depew, Abraham Corporal	Jan 2, 1777, Duration of War	Second, Wright	Dec 1777; Jan-Feb 1778 sick in quarters; March 1778 sick present; April-May 1778; June 1778 tending sick Kings Ferry.
Depew, Francis Private	Jan 3, 1777, Three Years	Second, Wright	Dec 1777; Jan 1778 on guard; Feb-April 1778; May 1778 on guard; June 1778.
Depew, Henry Private	March 26, 1777, Duration of War	Second, Wright	Dec 1777-Jan 1778; Feb 1778 sick in quarters; March-May 1778; June-July 1778 sick at Valley Forge.
Depew, John Private	Feb 10, 1777, Duration of War	Second, Wright	Dec 1777-April 1778; May 1778 sick present; June-July 1778 sick at Valley Forge; Aug 1778 dead.
DeRushe/D Rushe, Anthony Private	Jan 1, 1777, Duration of War	Fourth, Walker	Dec 1777-June 1778.
Desert/Disert, John Private	Nov 29. 1777, Duration of War	Fourth, Sacket	Jan 1778; Feb 1778 on command at Fishkill; March 28, 1778 deserted; April 1778 "Muster'd Deserted Since Join'd"; May 18, 1778 deserted.
Devore, Andrew Private	Nine Months	Second, Graham	April 1778 joined; May 1778; June-Sept 1778 sick at Valley Forge.

Dewey, Elisha Private	March 13, 1778	Second, Hallett	April 1778; May 1, 1778 died.
DeWitt, Johannes Private	May 1, 1778, Nine Months	Second, Lounsbery	May-June 1778.
DeWitt, Levi Quartermaster	Nov 21, 1776	Second	Dec 1777-March 1778; April 17, 1778 resigned.
Dick Fifer	Jan 1, 1777, Duration of War	Fourth, Walker	Dec 1777-June 1778. As no last name is shown, Dick is assumed to have been a patriot of African descent.
Dick, Thomas Private	May 5, 1778, Nine Months	Fourth, Walker	June 1778.
Dickens/Dickins, James Private	April 15, 1777, Duration of War	Second, Pell	Dec 1777-May 1778; June 1778 sick at Coryells Ferry.
Dickens/Dickins, Thomas Private	Jan 10, 1777, Duration of War	Second, Graham	Dec 1777 payroll only; Jan-June 1778 sick at Danbury.
Dickens/Dikens, William/Willm Private	Dec 16, 1776, Duration of War	First, Graham	April-June 1778.
Dickerson, Abraham Corporal	Nov 21, 1776, Duration of War	Fourth, Davis	Dec 1777-June 1778.
Dickerson, Benjamin Private	May 5, 1778, Nine Months	Fourth, Sacket	May-June 1778.
Dickerson, David Corporal	Nov 21, 1776, Duration of War	Fourth, Sacket	Dec 1777-Feb 1778; March 1778 sick in hutts; April-June 1778.
Dickerson, Jeduthan Private	May 5, 1778, Duration of War	Fourth, Smith	June 1778.
Dickerson/ Dickersan, John Private	May 5, 1778, Nine Months	Fourth, Davis	May 1778; June 1778 sick Princeton.
Dimmick, Perius, Sergeant	June 1, 1777, Duration of War	Second, Pelton	Dec 1777 sick in hospital; Jan-Feb 1778 sick in Hospital at Albany; March 1778 sick in hospital; April 1778 payroll only; May 1778 dead.
Dingman, Abraham Private	April 6, 1777, Duration of War	First, Ten Broeck	April-June 1778.
Dixon, Andrew Private	Duration of War	Malcom's, Kearsley	Dec 1777-Jan 1778 sick in hospital; March 25, 1778 joined; March-April 1778.

Name	Enlisted	Company	Remarks
Dixon, Thomas Private	May 14, 1777, Three Years	Malcom's, Tom	Dec 1777; Jan-Feb 1778 sick in quarters; March-April 1778; May 1778 sick the State of N Y.; June 1778.
Doblin, George Private		Malcom's, Steel	March 1778 sick present; April 22, 1778 died.
Dodds, Joseph Private	Duration of War	Malcom's, Kearsley	Dec 1777; Jan 15, 1778 died.
Dodge, Samuel Sergeant	May 2, 1777, Duration of War	Fourth, Pearsee	Dec 1777-April 1778; April 1778 sick present; June 1778 on furlough.
Doleway/Dollivay, Jeremiah Private	May 5, 1778, Nine Months	Second, Pelton	May 1778; June 1778 on guard.
Dolph, Moses Private	May 5, 1778, Nine Months	Second, Graham	May-June 1778.
Dolson, Peter Ensign	Nov 21, 1776	Riker	Dec 1777; Jan 19, 1778 resigned
Dolton/Dalton Frederick/Fredk Private	Feb 1, 1777, Duration of War	Second, Wright	Dec 1777-June 1778.
Dolton, Thomas Corporal	April 1, 1777	Second, Wright	Dec 1777 sick absent; Jan 1778 wounded at Albany; Feb-March 1778 sick absent; April at Albany; May 1778 sick absent; June 1778 sick Fishkill.
Donaldson, Peter Private	Dec 16, 1776, Three Years	Second, Hallett	Dec 1777 on command pressing wagons; Jan 1778; Feb 1778 payroll only; March-April 1778; May 1778 payroll only; June 1778.
Donnalson/ Donalson, Thomas Corporal	Duration of War	Malcom's, Kearsley	Dec 1777 on furlough; Jan 1778; Feb 1778 on duty; March-April 1778.
Donnely, James Private	Jan 7, 1777, Duration of War	First, Copp	April-June 1778.
Doriss/Doris, James Private	April 28, 1777, Duration of War	Malcom's, Lucas	Dec 1777-April 1778; May 1778 sick in hutts.
Dorn, John Private	March 11, 1777, Duration of War	First, Finck	April-June 1778.
Doty, John Private	May 5, 1778, Nine Months	Fourth, Smith	June 1778.
Dougharty, John Private		First, Ten Broeck	April 26, 1778 deserted.

Dougherty/ Daugherty, John/Jno Private	Duration of War	Malcom's, Steel	Dec 1777-Feb 1778 wounded in hospital; March 1778; April 1778 "Sick in ye Hutt"; May 1778; June 1778 unfit for service.
Dougherty, Mark Private	Duration of War	Fourth, Walker	Dec 16, 1777 deserted.
Dougherty/ Dougharty, William Fife Major		First	April 1778; May 1778 sick present; June 1778.
Douglas/Douglass, George/Geo Sergeant	Jan 28, 1777, Duration of War	Second, Ten Eyck	Dec 1777; Jan-Feb 1778 sick in quarters; March-June 1778.
Douglas/Duglis, James Private	March 24, 1777, Duration of War	First, McCracken	April-May 1778; June 1778 nurse to hospital.
Douglass, Rice Private	May 6, 1777, Duration of War	Malcom's, Lucas	Dec 21, 1777 deserted.
Dow, Alexander/Alexr 1st. Lt.	April 18, 1777	Malcom's, Lucas/ Steel	Dec 1777-June 1778. In March he transferred to, and took command of Steel's Company as all the officers had resigned on March 8, 1778. Oath at Valley Forge on May 11, 1778.
Downing, Richard/Richd Private	Nov 12, 1777, Three Years	First, Graham	April-June 1778.
Downs/Douns, James Corporal	Duration of War	Malcom's, Black	Dec 1, 1777 promoted to Corporal; Dec 1777-April 1778 sick in hospital; May 1778.
Doyle/Doyll, Patrick Private	May 13, 1777, Duration of War	Malcom's, Lucas	Dec 1777; Jan 1778 on commissary guard; Feb 18, 1778 deserted.
Drake, Joshua 2nd. Lt.	March 25, 1777	Malcom's, Santford	Dec 1777-Jan 1778 on furlough; Feb-June 1778. Oath at Valley Forge on May 11, 1778.
Drincks, Andrew Private	Jan 9, 1778, Duration of War	First, Van Ness	April-June 1778.
Dublin/Doublin, George/Geo Private	Duration of War	Malcom's, Steel	Dec 1777-Feb 1778; March 1778 sick present; April 1778 muster roll shows he died on April 29, while the April 1778 payroll shows he died on April 22.
Ducher/Duchere, Adam/Addam Private	May 5, 1778, Nine Months	Fourth, Strong	May 1778; June-July 1778 sick Pennsylvania.
Duff, Peter Private	May 5, 1778, Nine Months	Fourth, Smith	May 1778.

Duguid/Dogat, John Private	May 5, 1778	Fourth, Pearsee	May 1778; June 1778 on General Lee's guard.
Duncan, John Sergeant	Dec 10, 1776, Duration of War	First, Wendell	May-June 1778 prisoner on parole in Albany.
Dunavan/ Dunnavun, Peter Private	Dec 7, 1776, Duration of War	Fourth, Marvin	Dec 1777-Jan 1778; Feb 1778 sick in quarters; March-June 1778.
Duncan, Thomas Corporal	April 1, 1777, Three Years	Second, Hallett	Dec 1777-Jan 1778 sick at Albany; Feb 1778 payroll only; March-April 1778 sick at Albany; May 1778 payroll only; June 1778.
Dunham, Andrew/Andris Private	March 2, 1777, Three Years	First, McCracken	April-June 1778.
Dunham/Dunhem, Israel Fifer	Jan 1, 1777, Three Years	First, McCracken	April-May 1778; June 1778 on guard.
Dunham/Durham, Stephen Private	Jan 27, 1777, Three Years	First, Hicks	April-June 1778 sick at "Livingston Manner."
Dunlap, Andrew Sergeant	May 19, 1777, Duration of War	Second, Wright	Dec 1777 sick absent; Jan 1778 on command Cats Kell; Feb-March 1778 on command; April 1778; May 1778 sick present; June 1778 sick Valley Forge.
Dunlap, James Corporal	Feb 28, 1777, Duration of War	First, Ten Broeck	April-June 1778.
Dunlap, John Sergeant	Jan 28, 1777, Duration of War	First, Ten Broeck	April-June 1778.
Dunlap, John Private	Duration of War	Malcom's, Irvine	Dec 1777-March 1778; April 1778 on command; May-June 1778 on command Carlisle.
Dunlap, Thomas/Thos Private	Three Years	Malcom's, Black	Dec 1777 sick in hospital; Jan-Feb 1778 sick in quarters; March 1778 on guard; April-May 1778.
Dunmore, Caesar/ Cesar Private	May 5, 1778, Nine Months	Fourth, Marvin	May-June 1778.
Dunn, Alexander Sergeant/ Quartermaster Sergeant	Dec 19, 1776, Three Years	Second, Hallett	Dec 1777; Jan 1, 1778 promoted to Quartermaster Sergeant; Jan-June 1778.
Dunnavon/ Dunnivan, John Private	Jan 1, 1777, Duration of War	Fourth, Walker	Dec 1777-June 1778 with General McDougall.

Dunnivan/ Dunivan, John Private	Dec 23, 1776, Duration of War	First, Hicks	April 1778 sick at Schnectady; May-June 1778 sick General Hospital Schnectady.
Dunscomb, Edward Drummer		First, Graham	April-June 1778.
Dunscomb, Edward 1st. Lt.	Nov 21, 1776	Fourth, Smith	Sept 1777; prisoner, New York; Dec 1777 lately exchanged not yet joined; Jan-June 1778.
Durham, Stephen ppp	Jan 27, 1777, Three Years	First, Hicks	April-June 1778 sick at Livingstons Manner.
Eagleston, Eli Private	May 5, 1778	Second, Ten Eyck	June 1778 sick Valley Forge.
Eaken/Aikin, Solomon/Solamon Private	Duration of War	Malcom's, Irvine	Dec 1777-Jan 1778.
Eastwood, Benjamin Private	May 5, 1778, Nine Months	Fourth, Walker	June-July 1778 sick in Pennsylvania.
Eckler/Ecklar, John Private	Duration of War	First, Finck	May 1, 1778 returned from desertion; May 1778 sick in quarters.
Edget/Idget, George Private	May 20, 1777, Three Years	Fourth, Sacket	Dec 1777-March 1778; April 1778 on duty; May 22, 1778 dead.
Edwards, David Private	Nov 21, 1776, Duration of War	Fourth, Davis	Dec 1777; Jan-Feb 1778 sick in camp; March 16, 1778 died.
Edwards, William Private	May 5, 1778, Nine Months	Second, Riker	May-June 1778.
Elder/Ealder, Joseph Private	May 5, 1778	Second, Graham	May-June 1778.
Eldridge, Jonathan Private	Jan 11, 1776, Three Years	First, Hicks	April-June 1778.
Elker/Elkir, Emmer Private	May 5, 1778, Nine Months	Fourth, Strong	May-June 1778.
Ellerton/Elerton, Joseph Private	Duration of War	Malcom's, Niven	Dec 1777 sick Pennsylvania; Jan 1778 sick in quarters; Feb 1778 roll shows he deserted on March 3, 1778.
Elliott/Elliot, Archibald Private	Jan 1, 1777, Duration of War	Fourth, Titus	Dec 1777 sick absent; Jan-April 1778; June 1778 sick in Pennsylvania.
Elliot, John Private	May 5, 1778	Second, Wright	June 1778 on furlough.
Elliott/Eliot, Henry Corporal/Private	Feb 2, 1777, Duration of War	Second, Riker	Dec 1777; Jan 1778 sick in camp; Feb-June 1778; June 1 reduced to private.

Ellis, Benjamin Private	May 12, 1777, Duration of War	First, Graham	April-June 1778.
Ellis, Daniel Private	Feb 15, 1777, Three Years	First, McCracken	April-May 1778; June 1778 sick at Cuckoldstown.
Ellis/Allis, John Private	Dec 15, 1776, Duration of War	Fourth, Strong	Dec 1777-June 1778.
Ellison, Benjamin Private		Malcom's, Tom	April 24, 1778 joined; April-June 1778.
Ellison, Isaac Private	May 5, 1778, Nine Months	Fourth, Strong	May-June 1778.
Ellison, James Private	Sept 18, 1777, Three Years	Malcom's, Tom	Dec 1777-Feb 1778; March 1778 sick present; April 1778 on command; May-June 1778.
Ellison, Joseph Private	April 20, 1777, Three Years	Malcom's, Tom	Dec 1777-June 1778.
Ellison, Richard Private	May 5, 1778, Nine Months	Fourth, Smith	May-June 1778.
Ellison, Robert/Robart Private	Feb 4, 1777, Duration of War	Second, Pell	Dec 1777-April 1778; May 1778 on Main Guard; June 1778.
Elmendorph/ Elmindorph, Peter/Petrus Ensign	April 4, 1777	Malcom's, Black	Dec 1777 sick in quarters; Jan 1, 1778 resigned.
Elsworth, John Private	May 7, 1778, Nine Months	Second, Pell	May 1778.
Elsworth, John Private	Jan 1, 1777, Duration of War	Fourth, Marvin	August 1, 1777 deserted; May 4, 1778 joined; May-June 1778.
Elsworth, Peter 2nd. Lt./1st. Lt.	Nov 25, 1776	Fourth, Strong, Marvin	Dec 1777; Jan 9, 1778 promoted to First Lieutenant and transferred to Marvin's Company; Jan-March 1778; April-May 1778 on command; June 1778.
Elwiston/Elviston, William Private	Feb 22, 1777, Duration of War	First, Van Ness	April-June 1778.
English see Inglish			
Enslin, Gotthold Frederick Lt.	March 4, 1777	Malcom's, Kearsley	Dec 1777-Feb 1778; March 14, 1778 cashiered.
Epton, Benjamin Private		Fourth, Marvin	June 1778.

Erket/Ersket, Anthony Sergeant		Malcom's, Steel	May 1778 roll shows him as Absent from the regiment Oct 20, 1777, joined again May 27, 1778; May 30, 1778 reduced to private; May 1778 sick in Regimental Hospital; June 16th deserted; retaken 19th confined in Philadelphia.
Erwin, John Private	Feb 28, 1777, Duration of War	Fourth, Smith	Dec 1777-April 1778 sick at Fishkill; May 1778 sick in camp.
Esmond, Isiah Private	May 5, 1778, Nine Months	Fourth, Marvin	June 1778 muster roll shows he joined on May 5, 1778; June 1778.
Etkerson see Atkinson			
Evans/Evens, John Private	May 1, 1778, Nine Months	Second, Lounsbery	May 1778 on command Easton; June 1778.
Evans, John Private	May 5, 1778, Nine Months	Second, Riker	May 1778; June 1778 wagoner.
Evans, Israel Chaplain, Brigade Chaplain		Second	Dec 1777 on furlough; Jan 5, 1778 promoted to Brigade Chaplain.
Evolt/Avout, Philip Private	May 5, 1778	Fourth, Pearsee	May-June 1778.
Ezeler/Ezelar, Jacob Musician	April 1, 1777, Three Years	Malcom's, Santford	Dec 1777-March 1778; April 1778 sick present; May-June 1778.
Fairley see McFairley			
Farguson, James Private	Feb 3, 1777, Duration of War	First, Ten Broeck	April-June 1778.
Farguson, William Sergeant	Jan 20, 1777, Three Years	First, Ten Broeck	April-May 1778; June 1778 on duty.
Fairchild, Jesse Private	Nov 20, 1776, Duration of War	First, Hicks	April-June 1778.
Fairlie/Fairle, James 2nd. Lt	Nov 21, 1776	Second, Graham	Dec 1777 payroll only; Jan-Feb 1778 on furlough; March 1778; April 1778 on command for clothing for the regiment; May 1778; June 1778 absent with leave.
Fashee/Fishee, David Corporal	March 21, 1777, Duration of War	Second, Wright	Dec 1777-Feb 1778; March 1778 sick present; April-May 1778; June 1778 on furlough.
Feltman, Henry/Henery Private	April 2, 1777, Three Years	Malcom's, Santford	Dec 1777; Jan 1778 sick present; Feb 25, 1778 died.

Felty/Feltee, Augustus Private	April 9, 1778	First, Finck	May-June 1778.
Fergason, Samuel Private	May 5, 1778, Nine Months	Fourth, Titus	May 1778 sick in quarters; June 1778.
Ferguson/ Forgerson, Samuel Private	June 1, 1778	Second, Ten Eyck	First appears on the rolls for August 1778.
Ferris, Ludowick/ Lodwick Private	May 5, 1778	Fourth, Marvin	May 1778 in innoculation; June 1778.
Field/Fields, Philip Private	April 17, 1777, Duration of War	Second, Pelton	Dec 1777 sick in hospital; Jan-Feb 1778 sick at Albany; March 1778 sick in hospital; April 1778 payroll only; May-June 1778 sick at Albany.
Finck, Andrew, Jr. Captain	Nov 21, 1776	First, Finck	April-June 1778.
Fish, Abner/Ebner Private	May 5, 1778	Fourth, Marvin	May 1778 in innoculation; June 1778.
Fish, Caleb Private	May 5, 1778, Nine Months	Second, Ten Eyck	May-June 1778.
Fish, Moses Private	May 5, 1778, Nine Months	Second, Ten Eyck	May-June 1778.
Fish, Nicholas Major	November 21, 1776	Second	Dec 1777 sick absent; Jan-June 1778.
Fitzgerald, Christopher Miller/Christr. M. Private	Jan 1, 1777, Three Years	Fourth, Titus	Dec 1777-April 1778; May 1778 sick in quarters; June-August 1778 sick in Pennsylvania.
Flagg, Ebenezer Private	Dec 19, 1776	Second, Hallett	Dec 1777-Jan 1778 in the laboratory Springfield; Feb 1778 payroll only; March 1778 in the laboratory Springfield.
Flemming/ Flemmin, Michael Sergeant	Nov 28, 1776, Duration of War	First, Van Ness	April-June 1778.
Fletchner, Laurence/Laurentz Drum Major	Aug 12, 1777, Duration of War	Fourth	Dec 1777-March 1778; April 26, 1778 died.
Flick, Martin Private	Nov 25, 1776, Duration of War	First, Finck	April-June 1778.
Flinn, John Ensign	April 29, 1777	Malcom's, Lucas	Dec 1777-Jan 1778 on furlough; Feb-March 1778; April 9, 1778 resigned.

Flood, Francis, Private	Jan 1, 1777, Duration of War	Second, Pelton	Dec 1777 sick in hospital; Jan-Feb 1778 sick in hospital at Albany; March 1778 sick in hospital; April 1778 payroll only; May 1778 sick Albany; June 1778 sick Fishkill.
Forbush, Bartholomew, Private	Jan 20, 1777, Three Years	First, Finck	April-June 1778.
Ford, Timothy, Private	Jan 1, 1777	Second, Hallett	Dec 1777-Jan 1778 sick at Albany; Feb 1778 payroll only; March 1778 sick at Albany.
Ford, William/Wm Private	May 5, 1778, Nine Months	Fourth, Davis	May 1778; June-Dec 1778 sick in Pennsylvania.
Forde, George Private	May 5, 1778, Nine Months	Second, Pelton	June 1778.
Foreman, Christeon Private	Oct 26, 1777, Duration of War	First, Ten Broeck	April-June 1778.
Foster, Benoni Private	Mary 5, 1778	Second, Wright	First appears on the muster roll for July 1778.
Foster, John Private	March 3, 1777, Duration of War	First, Ten Broeck	April-May 1778; June 1778 command Valley Forge.
Foster, John Private	Dec 2, 1776	Second, Hallett	Dec 1777-Jan 1778 sick at Albany; Feb 1778; March-April 1778 sick at Albany.
Foster, John Private		Malcom's, Niven	Dec 1777-Feb 1778; April 1778 on guard; May 1778.
Foster, Nathaniel Private	May 5, 1778	Second, Ten Eyck	June 1778 payroll only.
Foulstron/ Fowlstron, Henry Private	May 9, 1778	First, Finck	May-June 1778.
Fowler, Theodosius 1st. Lt.	Nov 21, 1776	Fourth, Walker	Dec 1777; Jan-Feb 1778 on furlough; March-June 1778.
Foy, Edward Sergeant	Nov 28, 1776, Duration of War	First, Graham	April-June 1778.
Franks, John Paymaster	April 10, 1777	Fourth	Dec 1777 sick at New Haven; Jan 1778 on command; Feb-April 1778; May-June 1778 on command at Hartford.
Franks/Frank, Michael/Michal Private	Nov 1, 1777, Duration of War	Fourth, Sacket/ Smith	Dec 1777-Feb 1778; March 1, 1778 transferred to Smith's Company; March-June 1778.
Franks/ Francks, Peter Private	Dec 7, 1776, Duration of War	Fourth, Marvin	Dec 1777-April 1778; May 26, 1778 died.

Fransee, John Private	Dec 17, 1776, Duration of War	Fourth, Marvin	Dec 1777-March 1778; April 1778 sick in quarters; May 3, 1778 died.
Frazier/Fraser, Daniel/Danl Private	April 24, 1777, Duration of War	Malcom's, Lucas	Dec 1777-Feb 1778 sick in hospital; March 1778 confined Brig[ ]; April-May 1778.
Frazier/Frasier, Duncan Private	Nov 5, 1776, Duration of War	First, Copp	April-June 1778.
Frazier, Jeremiah Private	Dec 3, 1776, Three Years	First, Graham	April-June 1778.
Frederick, Johannis Private	June 7, 1778	Second, Pelton	First appears on muster roll for Oct 1778.
Free, John Private	Three Years	Malcom's, Steel	Dec 1777-Jan 1778 sick absent; Feb 1778 absent.
Freebush, Matthew/Mathw Private	Nov 1, 1777, Duration of War	Second, Ten Eyck	Dec 1777; Jan 1778 sick in quarters; Feb-April 1778; May 1778 tending Lt. Livingston; June 1778.
Freer/Frear, Peter Corporal	Aug 11, 1777, Three Years3	Second, Lounsbery	Dec 1777-March 1778 sick absent; April-June 1778.
French, Abner 1st. Lt.	Nov 21, 1776	Second, Pelton	Dec 1777-Feb 1778; March 1778 on command; April 1778 payroll only; May 1778; June 1778 absent with leave. French commanded the company after Captain Pelton resigned on March 18, 1778.
Fredenburgh/ Vredenburgh, James Private	Jan 8, 1777, Duration of War	Fourth, Marvin	Dec 1777-March 1778; April 1778 sick in quarters; April 1778 sick in camp; June 1778.
Freyenschner/ Frienseiner, George Private	April 9, 1778	First, Finck	May-June 1778.
Frilock/Frelock, Joseph Ensign/2nd. Lt.	Nov 21, 1776	Fourth, Marvin, Strong	Dec 1777; on Jan 9, 1778, he was promoted Second Lieutenant "but Rank from 2nd. Sepr. 1777", and transferred to Strong's Company; Jan-June 1778.
Frink, Elisha Private	Nov 4, 1776, Duration of War	First, McCracken	April-June 1778.
Fry/Frey, Laurence/ Lourentz Drummer	Duration of War	Malcom's, Kearsley	Dec 1777-Jan 1778; Feb 1778 sick at hospital; March 1778; April 1778 sick Yellow Springs;

Name, Rank	Enlistment	Company	Service
Fry/Frey, Michael, Private	Duration of War	Malcom's Kearsley	Dec 1777-Jan 1778; Feb 1778 on duty; March 1778 sick in hospital; April 1778 sick Yellow Springs; August 1778 sick Yellow Springs.
Fuller, Josiah, Private	May 5, 1778	Second, Ten Eyck	June 1778 sick Valley Forge.
Fullerton, John, Private	Dec 2, 1776, Duration of War	First, Wendell	April-June 1778.
Fulton, Alexander, Sergeant	Feb 1, 1777, Three Years	Second, Graham	Dec 1777 payroll only; Jan-Feb 1778 sick at Goshen; March 1778; April 1778 on weeks command; May 1778 sick in camp; June-Sept 1778 sick Valley Forge.
Fulmer/Fulmor, George, Private	March 20, 1777, Duration of War	First, Wendell	April-June 1778.
Gaites, Michael, Private	Nov 6, 1776, Duration of War	First, McCracken	April 1778 sick regimental hospital; May-June 1778.
Gardener/Gardineer, Peter, Private	Oct 16, 1777, Three Years	First, Wendell	April-June 1778.
Gardner, George, Sergeant	Three Years	Malcom's, Black	Dec 1777-Jan 1778; Feb-April 1778 on furlough; May 1778.
Gareheart, Matthew, Private	May 5, 1778	Second, Ten Eyck	June 1778 payroll only.
Garrett/Garret, Samuel, Private	Duration of War	First, Wendell	April-May 1778; June 1778 sick at Spotswood in State of New Jersey.
Garman/Germin, James, Private	May 5, 1778, Nine Months	Second, Riker	May-June 1778.
Garrison/Garreson, John, Private	March 6, 1777, Duration of War	Second, Pell	Dec 1777; Jan 1778 on command; Feb-June 1778.
Garway/Garraway, William, Private	Sept 12, 1777 Three Years	Malcom's, Santford	Dec 1777 sick absent; Jan 1778 sick present; Feb 1778 sick in quarters; April 1778 sick in quarters; May 6, 1778 joined the Invalid Corps.
Gasper, Peter, Corporal/Sergeant	Jan 3, 1777, Duration of War	First, Wendell	April 1778. May 1778 muster roll shows him promoted to Sergeant on May 15, but the May 1778 payroll shows the promotion date as May 10. May-June 1778.

Gebin see Jebine

Gee, David Private	Jan 1, 1777, Duration of War	Fourth, Titus	Dec 1777-Jan 1778 on command; Feb-March 1778; April-May 1778 sick in quarters; June 1778 sick in Pennsylvania.
Gee, Ezekiel Private	Jan 1, 1777, Duration of War	Fourth, Titus	Dec 1777-Jan 1778 on command; Feb 1778 sick absent; March 1778 sick in hospital; April-June 1778.
Geers, Benjamin Private	May 5, 1778	Fourth, Marvin	May 1778 in inoculation; June 1778.
George, Joshua Private	May 27, 1778, Three Years	Second, Ten Eyck	May 1778; June 1778 payroll only.
Gibson, John Private	May 5, 1778, Nine Months	Fourth, Strong	June 1778.
Gibson, Robert Private	Nov 12, 1776, Duration of War	Fourth, Marvin	Dec 1777-March 1778; April 1778 sick in quarters; May 10, 1778 died.
Gilbert, Benjamin Ensign	Nov 21, 1776	First, Copp	April-June 1778.
Gilbert, John Casper Private	Nov 19, 1777, Duration of War	First, Wendell	April-June 1778.
Gilbert, William Private	Dec 7, 1776, Three Years	Second, Hallett	Dec 1777-April 1778; May 1778 payroll only; June 1778.
Gilbert/Gibert, William Corporal/ Sergeant	Duration of War	Malcom's, Kearsley	Dec 1777 sick in the country; Jan 1778 sick in hospital; Feb 1778 on duty; March 24, 1778 promoted to Sergeant; March-April 1778.
Gilchrist/Gillcrist, John Private	Dec 28, 1776, Duration of War	Fourth, Smith	Dec 1777 sick absent Fishkill; Jan-April 1778 sick Fishkill; April 1778 left sick Fishkill; June 1778 left sick at Fishkll; July 22, 1778 deserted.
Gildersleeve/ Gildersliv, Daniel/Danl Corporal/ Quartermaster Sergeant	Duration of War	Malcom's, Santford	Dec 1777 promoted to Quartermaster Sergeant; Dec 1777-Jan 1778. The muster roll for February 1778 shows he died on March 13, 1778, the muster roll for March, 1778 shows he died on March 5.
Gildersleeve/ Gildersleve, Finch Ensign	Dec 20, 1777	Malcom's, Tom	Jan-June 1778. Oath at Valley Forge in May, 1778.
Giles, Richard Private	June 4, 1777, Duration of War	Second, Lounsbery	Dec 1777-Jan 1778 sick in hospital at Albany; Feb-March 1778 sick in hospital; April-May 1778 sick Albany; June 1778 sick New York.

Gillchrist/Gillcrist, William/Wm Drummer	May 28, 1777, Three Years	Fourth, Pearsee	Dec 1777; Jan 1778 sick in quarters; Feb-May 1778; June 1778 sick Valley Forge.
Gimblet, Peter Private	May 7, 1778	Second, Hallett	June 22, 1778 died
Glasby/Gilaspie James Private	Feb 1, 1777, Duration of War	Fourth, Walker	Dec 1777-April 1778; May 1778 sick present; June-October 1778 sick in Pennsylvania.
Glenny, William Ensign	Nov 21, 1776	Second, Ten Eyck	Dec 1777-May 1778; June 1778 payroll only.
Glexton, see Claxton			
Godwin, William Corporal	March 4, 1777, Duration of War	First, Van Ness	April-June 1778.
Goldsmith, Azra/Ezra Private/Sergeant	Nov 21, 1776, Duration of War	Fourth, Sacket	October 21, 1777 promoted to Sergeant; Dec 1777; Jan 1778 on party; Feb 1778; March 1778 sick in hutts; April 1778 sick present; May-June 1778.
Gones/Jones, John Private	May 5, 1778, Nine Months	Second, Wright	June 1778 sick at Valley Forge.
Goodale/ Goodales, Benjamin/Benjm Private	Nov 28, 1776, Duration of War	First, Wendell	April-June 1778 on command General Schuyler's guard.
Goodin/Goodwin, George Private	Jan 14, 1777, Duration of War	Fourth, Smith	Dec 1777-Jan 1778; Feb 1778 sick in camp; March-April 1778; May 1778 sick in camp; June 1778.
Goold, Joseph Private	April 6, 1777, Duration of War	Malcom's, Santford	Dec 1777-April 1778; May 1778 in Regimental hospital; June 1778.
Gordineer/ Gordennear, Gilbert Private	Oct 25, 1776, Duration of War	First, McCracken	April-June 1778.
Gordon/Gorden, Charles/Charls Private	Duration of War	Malcom's, Irvine	Dec 1777-March 1778; April 1778 on command; May 1778 on command Carlisle; June 1778 attending [ ] officers.
Gorham, Jabus Private	May 5, 1778	Second, Hallett	May-June 1778 sick in Pennsylvania.
Gorman, Richard/Richd Private	Dec 1, 1776, Duration of War	First, Graham	April-June 1778.

Name/Rank	Date	Company	Notes
Gould/Gold, John/Jno Private	July 13, 1777, Duration of War	Second, Graham	Dec 1777 payroll only; Jan 1778 on command; Feb 1778 sick in smallpox; March-May 1778; June-October 1778 sick at Valley Forge; Oct 1778 died.
Gowdey, John Private		Malcom's, Steel	October 20, 1777 deserted; June 4, 1778 joined; June 1778.
Graham, Charles Captain	Nov 21, 1776	Second, Graham	Dec 1777 payroll only; Jan 1778 on command; Feb 1778 sick absent; March-April 1778; May 1778 on command at Easton; June 1778.
Graham, John Captain	Nov 21, 1776	First, Graham	April-May 1778; June 1778 on furlough.
Grahams/ Grahames, Jacob/Jacobus Private	Duration of War	Malcom's, Black	Dec 1777-Jan 1778 sick in quarters; Feb 1778; March 1778 sick present; April-May 1778 sick in camp.
Granger/ Grainger, John Private	Jan 1, 1777, Duration of War	Fourth, Titus	Dec 1777-Feb 1778 sick absent; March 1778; April 1778 on command at Germantown; May 1778 sick in quarters; June 1778 sick in Pennsylvania.
Graves, Josiah Private	May 5, 1778	Fourth, Walker	First appears on the muster roll for September 1778.
Graves, Lennis/Lewis Private	May 5, 1778, Nine Months	Second, Pelton	June 1778.
Graves, Seldon Private	May 5, 1778, Nine Months	Fourth, Walker	June 1778 sick in Pennsylvania.
Gray, Benjamin Private	May 5, 1778, Nine Months	Fourth, Walker	May 1778; June 1778 muster roll shows he died at Brunswick on July 5, 1778.
Gray, Philip Corporal	Oct 24, 1776, Duration of War	First, Finck	April-June 1778.
Gray, Silas 2nd. Lt./1st. Lt.	Nov 21, 1776	Fourth, Walker, Pearsee	Dec 1777-March 1778; March 13, 1778 promoted to First Lieutenant and transferred to Pearsee's Company; April 1778; May 1778 on command Easton; June 1778. After Captain Pearsee resigned on April 23, Gray commanded this company for the rest of Valley Forge Encampment.

Gray, Thomas Corporal	Feb 26, 1777, Duration of War	Second, Pelton	Dec 1777-March 1778; April 1778 sick absent; May 1778; June 1778 sick in Jersey; July 1778 "Sick on the road to Valley Forge."
Gray, Thomas/Thos Private	May 11, 1777, Duration of War	Malcom's, Lucas	Dec 1777-Jan 1778; Feb 4, 1778 deserted.
Green, Charles Private	July 20, 1777, Three Years	First, McCracken	April-June 1778.
Green, Isaac Private	April 30, 1777, Three Years	Malcom's, Niven	Dec 1777; Jan 1778 sick in quarters; Feb 1778.
Green, Lort/Lord Private	Duration of War	Malcom's, Steel	Dec 1777-March 1778; April 1, 1778 died.
Green, Silas Private	March 18, 1777, Three Years	First, Graham	April-May 1778 on command General Schuyler's guard; June 1778 on command General Schuyler's guard Saratoga.
Grew, Michael Private	Duration of War	Malcom's, Niven	May 1, 1778 joined; May 1778.
Grier/Greer, David Private	Feb 14, 1777. Duration of War	Fourth, Sacket	Dec 1777-March 1778; April 1778 sick present; May-June 1778.
Griffen/Griffin, Barney Private	May 23, 1777, Duration of War	Fourth, Pearsee	Dec 1777; Jan 1778 not fit for service; Feb 21, 1778 discharged.
Griffin, Benjamin/Benjm Private	Feb 4, 1777, Duration of War	Second, Wright	Dec 1777; Jan 1778 on command with General Greene; Feb 1778 sick in quarters; March-June 1778.
Griffin, John Private	May 5, 1778, Nine Months	Second, Riker	May-June 1778.
Griffin, Joseph Private	May 5, 1778, Nine Months	Second, Riker	May-June 1778.
Griffin/Griffen, Stephen Sergeant	Feb 6, 1777, Duration of War	Fourth, Sacket	Dec 1777; Jan 1778 on party; Feb 1778; March 1778 sick in hutts; April-May 1778 sick present; June 1778 sick Pennsylvania.
Griffith/Griffiths, Abraham Corporal/ Sergeant	Feb 26, 1777, Duration of War	Second, Pelton	Dec 1777-Jan 1778 on command; Feb-March 1778; April 1778 payroll only; May 1778; May 24, 1778 promoted to Sergeant; June 1778 on furlough.
Griffiths/Griffis, James Private	Feb 4, 1777, Duration of War	Second, Wright	Dec 1777-March 1778; April 1778 on guard; May 1778; June 1778 on guard.

Griffiths/Griffith, Samuel Corporal/Private	Dec 8, 1776, Three Years	Second, Hallett	Dec 1777; Jan 1778 on command; Jan 18, 1778 reduced to Private; Feb 1778 payroll only; March-April 1778; May 1778 payroll only; June-July 1778 sick at Valley Forge.
Griggs/Greggs, Jeremiah/Jeremh Private	Jan 1, 1777, Duration of War	Second, Ten Eyck	Sept 1777 roll shows he deserted on May 23, 1777; Muster roll dated Jan 2, 1778 shows he "Returned from the Enemy & joined Nov 13, 1777"; Jan-Feb 1778; March 1778 on duty; April-May 1778; June 1778 payroll only.
Grissel/Grissil, Jabus/Jabos Private	May 5, 1778, Nine Months	Second, Pelton	June 1778 sick in Pennsylvania.
Grogan, John Private	Jan 1, 1777, Duration of War	Second, Graham	Dec 1777 payroll only; Jan-June 1778.
Gross, John Private	Sept 30, 1777, Duration of War	First, Copp	April-June 1778.
Groundhart, George Private	March 12, 1777, Three Years	First, Finck	April-June 1778.
Gullion, John Private	July 16, 1777, Duration of War	Second, Ten Eyck	Dec 1777; Jan 1, 1778 deserted.
Gutlick, Christain Private	Oct 25, 1777, Duration of War	First, Copp	April 1778; May 1778 sick in regimental hospital; June 1778 sick in hospital Cuckolds Town.
Hadden/Heddon, Jonathan Private	April 28, 1777, Duration of War	Malcom's, Lucas	Dec 1777-Jan 1778; Feb 1778 "Killed or Taking".
Hadley, Joseph Sergeant	Feb 6, 1777, Three Years	Second, Pell	Dec 1777-Jan 1778; Feb 1778 on weeks command; March 1778 on fatigue; April 1778 on command with General Poor; May 1778; June 1778 payroll only.
Hadlock, Robert/Robt Private	Duration of War	Malcom's, Steel	Jan 1778 "who was taken Prisoner Sept 17th joined his Company after his escape from ye Enemy, 25th Jan"; Feb-April 1778; May 1778 on fatigue; June 16, 1778 deserted.
Hagerman/ Hagermane, Nicholas Private		First, Ten Broeck	April-May 1778 on command at Albany as an evidence by order of the Co[uncil]; June 1778 on command as an evidence Albany.

Haight/Height, Thomas K./ Thos Sergeant	Jan 1, 1777, Duration of War	Second, Wright	Dec 1777; Jan 1778 sick in quarters; Feb 1778; March 1778 on guard; April-May 1778; June 1778 on furlough.
Hall, Isaac Private	May 5, 1778, Nine Months	Fourth, Davis	May-June 1778.
Hall, James Private	Jan 15, 1777, Duration of War	First, Finck	April-June 1778 on command General Schuyler's guard.
Hall, John Private	May 5, 1778, Nine Months	Second, Riker	May-June 1778.
Hally/Heally, Daniel/Danl Private	Duration of War	Malcom's, Niven	Dec 1777-Jan 1778; Feb 11, 1778 deserted.
Hallenbee/ Halanbee, Jacob Private	June 6, 1777, Duration of War	Second, Wright	Dec 1777; Jan-March 1778 on furlough; April 1778; May 1778 sick present; June sick Valley Forge.
Hallanbee/ Halanbee, Jacob T. Private	June 6, 1777, Duration of War	Second, Wright	Dec 1777-Jan 1778; Feb 1778 sick in quarters; March 1778; April 1778 sick in camp; May 1778 sick present; June 1778 sick Valley Forge.
Hallett, Jonah 2nd. Lt.	July 17, 1777	Malcom's, Irvine	Dec 1777-Jan 1778; Feb-March 1778 on command; April 1778 on furlough; May 1778; June 1778 on command on the lines. Oath at Valley Forge on June 8, 1778.
Hallett, Jonathan Captain	Nov 21, 1776	Second, Hallett	Dec 1777-Jan 1778 sick at Fishkill; Feb 1778 payroll only; March 1778 sick at Fishkill; April 1778; May 1778 payroll only; June 1778.
Halsey/Holsey, Abraham Private	Nov 21, 1776, Duration of War	Fourth, Davis	Dec 1777; Jan 1778-June 1778.
Hammer, William Private	May 5, 1778, Nine Months	Second, Pelton	June 1778 muster roll shows he deserted on July 14, 1778.
Hammon, J. Chason/Chasson Private	May 5, 1778, Nine Months	Fourth, Pearsee	June-July 1778. This man and the individual below may be the same person.
Hammon/ Hammond, Isaac Private	May 5, 1778, Nine Months	Fourth, Pearsee	May 1778.
Handell/Handler, John Private	Duration of War	First, Finck	April 24, 1778 deserted; May 24, 1778 returned from desertion; May-June 1778.
Hanford/Henford, Obadiah/Obediah Private	Nov 1, 1776, Duration of War	First, Hicks	April-June 1778.

Hankee/Henkee, John Corporal/Private	March 1, 1777, Three Years	First, Van Ness	April-May 1778; May 22, 1778 reduced to Private; June 1778 left sick at Cuckoldstown.
Hanley, James Private	Jan 1, 1777, Duration of War	Fourth, Smith	Dec 1777-April 1778; May 1778 sick in camp; June 1778.
Hanly/Hanley, John Private	Duration of War	Malcom's, Irvine	Dec 1777-April 1778; May 1778 on weeks command; June 1778 on command on the lines.
Hanmore, Jabez. Private	May 5, 1778, Nine Months	Fourth, Walker	May-June 1778.
Hannis/Hinnis, William Private	April 5, 1777, Three Years	Malcom's, Tom	Dec 1777 sick absent; Jan-April 1778; May 1778 on duty camp; June 1778 on command tending sick.
Hanyon/Henyon, Garret/Gerret Private	May 5, 1778, Nine Months	Second, Graham	May 1778; June 1778 sick at Valley Forge.
Hardenbergh, Abraham 2nd. Lt.	Nov 21, 1776	First, Van Ness	April-June 1778.
Hardenbergh/ Hardenberg, John L./Jno 2nd. Lt	Nov 21, 1776	Second, Hallett	Dec 1777-Jan 1778; Feb 1778 payroll only; March-June 1778.
Harding, Henry Private	April 25, 1778	Second, Hallett	First appears on rolls for July 1778.
Harper, Joseph, Ensign	Nov 21, 1776	Second, Hallett	Dec 1777 sick at Albany; Jan on command Fishkill; Feb 1778 payroll only; March 1778 on command Fishkill; April 1778 sick at Fishkill; May 1778 payroll only; June 1778.
Harrington, Alexander/Alexd Private	Three Years	Malcom's, Black	Dec 1777; Jan-Feb 1778 sick in quarters; March-May 1778.
Harrington, John/Jno Private	Three Years	Malcom's, Black	Dec 1777-May 1778.
Harris, David Sergeant	May 5, 1778, Nine Months	Second, Graham	May 1778; June 1778 on furlough.
Harris/Harriss, Evans Private	Dec 15, 1776, Duration of War	Fourth, Smith	Dec 1777; Jan-Feb 1778 sick in hospital; March 4, 1778 died.
Harris, George Private	March 2, 1777, Duration of War	First, Copp	April sick in Schnectady; May 1778 sick in General Hospital Schnectady; June 1778.
Harris, George Private	Three Years	Malcom's, Black	Dec 1777-Feb 1778 not joined.

Name, Rank	Enlisted	Regiment, Company	Service
Harris, Michael Private	Dec 22, 1776, Duration of War	First, Graham	April-June 1778.
Harris, Moses/Mosis Sergeant	March 20, 1777, Three Years	Second, Wright	Dec 1777 sick absent; Jan-Feb 1778; March 1778 sick in quarters; April-May 1778; June 1778 absent with leave.
Harris, William Corporal	Jan 24, 1777, Duration of War	First, Hicks	April 1778; May-June 1778 General Schuyler's guard.
Harris, Zach Private	Jan 1, 1777, Duration of War	Fourth, Walker	Dec 1777-Jan 1778 on command with whale boats; Feb-March 1778 in whale boats on N. River; April 30, 1778 deserted.
Harrison/Harison, Jacob Private	Three Years	Malcom's, Black	Dec 1777-Feb 1778; March 1778 sick present; April 1778; May 1778 sick in camp.
Hart, Thomas Private	Feb 2, 1777, Three Years	First, Van Ness	April-May 1778; June 1778 left sick at Cuckoldstown.
Hartness, Andrew Quartermaster Sergeant	Jan 21, 1777, Duration of War	Fourth, Sacket	Dec 1777 sick present; Jan-March 1778 on furlough; April 1778 sick in camp; May-June 1778.
Harvey, David Private	May 5, 1778, Nine Months	Fourth, Davis	May-June 1778.
Hattis, Thomas Private	Duration of War	First, Wendell	April-June 1778.
Havens, William/Wm 1st. Lt.	Nov 21, 1776	Fourth, Davis	Nov 7, 1777 resigned.
Haviland, Ebenezer Surgeon	Nov 21, 1776	Second	Dec 1777 on furlough; Jan-Feb 1778; March 1778 on furlough; April-May 1778; June 28, 1778 died.
Havilish, Melcher/Michel Private	April 15, 1778, Duration of War	Second, Hallett	April 1778; May 1778 payroll only; June 1778 sick in Pennsylvania.
Hawkins, David Sergeant	Nov 21, 1776, Duration of War	Fourth, Titus	Dec 1777 sick absent; Jan-March 1778 on furlough; April 1778 on furlough at the State of New York; May 31, deserted.
Hawkins, Isaac Private	Dec 14, 1776, Duration of War	First, Hicks	April-June 1778 on command General Schuyler's guard.
Hawkins, Nowah/Noah Private	May 5, 1778, Nine Months	Fourth, Marvin	June 1778.
Hawkins, Zachariah Private	Nov 21, 1776, Three Years	Fourth, Titus	Dec 1777; Jan 1778 on command; Feb-March 1778; April 1778 on General Poor's guard; May 1778 sick in quarters; June 1778 sick in Pennsylvania.

Name	Enlisted	Company	Service
Hawkins, Loper/Lophar Private	Nov 21, 1776, Duration of War	Fourth, Sacket	Dec 1777; Jan 1778 on party; Feb 1778 on duty; March 1778 sick in hutts; April-May 1778; June-July 1778 sick in Pennsylvania.
Hawthorn, William Private/ Corporal/ Private	Duration of War	Malcom's, Steel	Dec 1777 sick in hospital; Jan 1778 in hospital; Feb 1778 sick in hospital; March-April 1778; April 1778 promoted to Corporal; May 1778 sick Regimental hospital; June 1, 1778 reduced to Private; June 1778 sick Yellow Springs.
Hay, James Private	May 5, 1778, Nine Months	Second, Graham	May-June 1778.
Haycock, John Private	Nov 28, 1776, Duration of War	First, Graham	April-June 1778.
Hayes/Haise, Thomas Private	March 28, 1777, Duration of War	First, Ten Broeck	April-June 1778.
Hazard/Hazerd, James Private	Dec 13, 1776, Three Years	Second, Hallett	Nov 23, 1777 deserted; Jan 1778 at Fishkill; Feb 1778 payroll only; March 1778 sick at Fishkill; April 1778; May 17, 1778 died.
Hazard, Raymond Private	March 23, 1777, Three Years	First, Copp	Nov 1, 1777 deserted; March 9, 1778 returned; April-June 1778.
Heavens/Havens, Joseph Corporal	Aug 7, 1777, Duration of War	First, McCracken	April-June 1778.
Hebbard/ Hebbar, Abel Sergeant	Jan 1, 1777, Three Years	Fourth, Titus	Dec 1777-Jan 1778; Feb 1778 sick in camp; March-April 1778 sick in quarters; May 1778; June 26, 1778 died.
Heddon/Hadden, Jonathan Private		Malcom's, Lucas	Dec 1777-Jan 1778; Feb 1778 taken or killed.
Height, Stephen Private	Feb 1, 1778, Three Years	First, Van Ness	April-May 1778; June 1778 on command with Colonel Morgan.
Helmer, John Corporal	Oct 25, 1776, Duration of War	First, Finck	April-June 1778.
Helmer, John, Jr, Private	Nov 25, 1776, Duration of War	First, Finck	April-June 1778.
Helmer, Philip Private	Jan 22, 1777, Three Years	First, Finck	April-June 1778.
Hempson/ Hampson, Caleb/Calob Private	April 5, 1777, Duration of War	Malcom's, Santford	Dec 1777; Jan 1778 on the Commissary Guard; Feb-March 1778; April 26, 1778 discharged.
Henderson, James Corporal	July 1, 1777	Malcom's, Lucas	Dec 1777-Jan 1778; Feb 4, 1778 deserted.

Henderson, Samuel Sergeant	Nov 28, 1776, Duration of War	First, Graham	April-June 1778.
Henderson, William Private	Oct 25, 1776, Duration of War	First, McCracken	April 1778 sick on furlough; May-June 1778 sick in Albany.
Hendricksen, Cornelius Private		First, Finck	April-June 1778.
Henly, David Private	Nov 19, 1776, Duration of War	First, Hicks	April-June 1778.
Hennesey/ Hanaysee, John Private	May 5, 1778, Nine Months	Fourth, Pearsee	May-June 1778.
Henry, Nathaniel 2nd. Lt.	Nov 21, 1776	First, Graham	April-June 1778.
Herington/ Herrington, Benjamin Private	May 5, 1778	Second, Hallett	June 1778 sick in Pennsylvania; Aug 20, 1778 deserted.
Herington/ Herrington, Isaac Private	May 5, 1778	Second, Hallett	June 1778 sick in Pennsylvania, Aug 20, 1778 deserted.
Hermans/Herman, Edward Private	May 7, 1778, Nine Months	Second, Pell	May-June 1778.
Herrick, William/Wm Private	May 5, 1778, Nine Months	Fourth, Smith	May 1778.
Hewit/Howot, Benjamin Private	May 18, 1778, Nine Months	Second, Wright	May 1778; June 1778 tending sick at Kings Ferry.
Hichcock/ Hitchcock, Samuel/Saml Private	Feb 1, 1777, Duration of War	Second, Wright	Dec 1777; Jan 1778 on command; Feb-May 1778; June 1778 absent with leave.
Hicks, Benjamin Captain	Nov 21, 1776	First, Hicks	April-June 1778.
Hicks, Jacob Corporal	Nov 21, 1776, Duration of War	Fourth, Davis	Dec 1777; Jan 1778 on command with General Greene; Feb 1778; March 1778 on party; April 1778 on fortnight command; May-June 1778.
Hifman/Hufman, Gabriel Private	May 5, 1778, Nine Months	Fourth, Strong	June 1778 on command at Tarrytown.

Higby, Samuel Corporal	Dec 18, 1776, Duration of War	Fourth, Smith	Dec 1777-Jan 1778 sick in quarters; Feb-March 1778; April 1778 sick in quarters; May 1778 sick in camp; June 1778.
Higgins, Thomas Private	May 5, 1778	Second, Ten Eyck	June-Sept sick at Valley Forge.
Hill, Matthew Private	March 21, 1777, Duration of War	Malcom's, Lucas	Dec 1777-April 1778.
Hill, Thomas Private	Jan 1, 1777, Duration of War	Fourth, Titus	Dec 1777-March 1778 sick absent; April 1778 sick at Albany; May-June 1778 sick in the country.
Hill, William Private	Jan 31, 1777, Duration of War	Fourth, Strong	Dec 1777; Jan 1778 on command; Feb-June 1778.
Hilley, Isaac Private	May 5, 1778, Duration of War	Fourth, Strong	May 1778.
Hilts, Frederick Private	March 29, 1777, Duration of War	First, Ten Broeck	April-May 1778; June 1778 sick at Princeton.
Himalon/ Himileon, Adam Private	March 3, 1778, Duration of War	Second, Hallett	April 1778; May 1778 payroll only.
Hitchcock/ Hichcock, John Private	Jan 1, 1777, Duration of War	Second, Pell	Dec 1777; Jan 2, 1778 deserted; March 1778 under sentence of a Court Martial; March 21, 1778 enlisted; April-June 1778.
Hix/Hicks, Joseph Drummer		Malcom's, Tom	Dec 1777 sick absent; Jan-Feb 1778 sick in quarters; March 1778; April 1778 sick present; May 1778 sick Regimental hospital.
Hodge, Abraham Private	Feb 2, 1777, Duration of War	First, Ten Broeck	April 1778; May 1778 sick present; June 1778.
Hodge, David Private	Feb 2, 1777, Duration of War	First, Ten Broeck	April 1778; May 1778 sick present; June 1778.
Hoff/Huff, William Private	May 9, 1777, Three Years	Fourth, Pearsee	Dec 1777-Jan 1778 sick at Livingston Manor; Feb-May 1778 sick at Albany; June 13, 1778 deserted.
Hoffman/ Huffman, Andrew Private	Oct 25, 1777, Duration of War	First, Finck	April-June 1778.
Hogan, Patrick Private	Oct 30, 1776, Duration of War	First, Copp	April 1778; May 1778 sick regimental hospital; June 1778 sick in hospital Cuckolds Town.
Holdon/Holden, Thomas Private	May 8, 1777, Duration of War	Malcom's, Lucas	Dec 1777; Jan 1778 sick in quarters; Feb 1778 roll dated March 4 reads "Returned Back from Desertion & Deserted 4 Inst."

Holdridge, Amasa Private	May 4, 1778	Second, Wright	June 1778.
Holly/Holley, John Private/Corporal	Jan 1, 1777, Duration of War	Fourth, Titus	Dec 1777-Feb 1778; March 1778 on command; April 1778; April 15, 1778 promoted to Corporal; May 1778 sick in quarters; June 1778 sick in Pennsylvania.
Holley/Holly, William/Wm Private	March 11, 1777, Three Years	Malcom's, Tom	Dec 1777-March 1778; April 1778 sick present; May 1778 command Radnor; June 1778 sick Kingstown.
Holmes/Holms, Ezekiah/Hezekiah Private	May 5, 1778, Nine Months	Second, Graham	May-June 1778.
Holmes/Holms, Thomas Private	Feb 1, 1777, Duration of War	Fourth, Walker	Dec 1777; Jan 1778 sick present; Feb-May 1778; June 1778 sick Crab Orchard.
Holmes/Holms, William/Wm Private	March 22, 1777, Duration of War	Malcom's, Lucas	Dec 1777-Jan 1778; Feb 11, 1778 deserted.
Holms/Holoms, Daniel Private	April 19, 1777, Duration of War	Second, Pell	Dec 1777-Feb 1778; March 1778 on main guard; April 1778; May 1778 on General Poor's Guard; June 1778.
Holsey/Halsey, Thomas Private	Nov 21, 1776, Duration of War	Fourth, Davis	Dec 1777; Jan 1778 on command with General Greene; Feb 1778; March 1778 on command; April-June 1778.
Homan, John Private	May 5, 1778, Nine Months	Fourth, Walker	May 1778; June 1778 on furlough New Windsor.
Homes, John Private	May 5, 1778, Nine Months	Fourth, Strong	June 1778.
Homes/Hoolmes, John Private	Dec 8, 1776, Duration of War	Fourth, Marvin	Dec 1777 sick Fishkill; Jan-June 1778.
Honoven/ Hanoven, Rice Private	May 5, 1778, Nine Months	Fourth, Davis	June 1778.
Hooghkirk/ Hooghkerk, John 1st. Lt.	Nov 21, 1776	First, Van Ness	April 1778; May 1778 on guard; June 1778.
Hope, Thomas Private	Nov 19, 1776, Duration of War	First, Hicks	April-June 1778.
Hopkins, Noah Fifer	Feb 1, 1777, Three Years	Second Graham	Dec 1777 payroll only; Jan-June 1778.

Hopper, John Sergeant/Private	Jan 1, 1777, Duration of War	Second, Pell	Dec 1777; Jan 2, 1778 deserted; March 1778 under sentence of a court martial; March 21, 1778 enlisted; April 1778 on main guard; June-July 1778 tending sick at Valley Forge.
Hoppole/Hoppoll, John Musician	July 5, 1777, Duration of War	First, Finck	April-June 1778.
Hornbeck, Epharim/ Ephraim Private	May 5, 1778, Nine Months	Second, Riker	May 1778 sick in camp; June 1778.
Horsford, Jesse Private	March 23, 1777, Duration of War	First, Copp	April 1778; May 1778 sick regimental hospital; June 1778 sick in hospital Cuckolds Town.
Horton, Christopher Private	April 15, 1777, Three Years	Second, Pell	Dec 1777-Jan 1778; Feb-March 1778 on command; April 1778 payroll only; May-June 1778.
Horton, Frederick Private	May 5, 1778, Nine Months	Fourth, Smith	May 1778; June 1778 sick Pennsylvania.
Horton/Horten, John Private	Three Years	Malcom's, Black	Dec 1777-Jan 1778; Feb 1778 on command; March-May 1778.
Hosford, Ithamor/Ithamer Private	May 5, 1778, Nine Months	Fourth, Davis	June 1778.
Hotchkiss/ Hotskill, William/Willm Private	Dec 4, 1777 Duration of War	Second, Wright	Dec 1777; Jan 1778 on weeks command; Feb 1778 sick in quarters; March 1778 on guard; April 1778 weeks command; May 1778 sick present; June 25, 1778 died.
Houff, John Private	Duration of War	First, Van Ness	April-June 1778.
House, Anthony Private	Dec 13, 1777, Three Years	Second, Hallett	Dec 1777-April 1778; Feb 1778 on command; March-April 1778; May 1778 unfit for service.
House, Christian Private	April 6, 1777, Duration of War	First, Ten Broeck	April 1778; May 1778 sick present; June 1778.
House, Jacob Private	May 14, 1777, Duration of War	First, Ten Broeck	April 1778; May 1778 sick present; June 1778 sick Valley Forge.
House, John Private	Jan 26, 1777, Duration of War	First, Finck	April-June 1778.
House/Howse, Zachariah/Zach Private	Jan 1, 1777, Duration of War	Fourth, Titus	Dec 1777-Feb 1778 sick absent; March 1778 on furlough; April 1778 sick at Albany; May 26, 1778 deserted.

Howe/How, John Private	Jan 1, 1777, Duration of War	Fourth, Titus	Dec 1777-March 1778 sick absent; April 1778 sick at Albany; May-June 1778 sick in the country.
Howel/Howell, William/Wm Private	Duration of War	Malcom's, Niven	Dec 1777-Feb 1778; April 1778 on command at the lines; May 1778 sick [ ].
Howell/Howel, George Sergeant	Nov 21, 1776, Duration of War	Fourth, Davis	Dec 1777-Feb 1778; March 1778 on furlough; April 1778 on furlough in Connecticut; May 1778; June 1778.
Howell/Howel, Jehiel Sergeant	Jan 30, 1777, Duration of War	Fourth, Strong	Dec 1777-May 1778; June 26, 1778 died.
Howell/Howel, Seth Private	Nov 21, 1776, Duration of War	Fourth, Davis	Dec 1777-June 1778.
Hoyt/Hoit, Cesar Private	May 5, 1778, Nine Months	Second, Wright	June-Aug 1778 sick at Valley Forge. August 1778 muster roll shows he was discharged on August 9, but the Sept 1778 muster roll shows he was discharged on July 9.
Hubbell/Hubble, Isaac Private	Nov 28, 1776, Duration of War	First, Graham	April-June 1778.
Hubbert/Hubert, John Private	May 21, 1777, Duration of War	Fourth, Pearsee	Dec 1777; Jan 1778 on guard; Feb-May 1778; June-July 1778 sick Valley Forge.
Hudsal/Hudsler, Nicholas Private	Nov 29, 1777	Second, Pelton	Jan-Feb 1778 sick at Fishkill; March 1778; April 1778 payroll only; May-June 1778.
Hughes, Thomas Private	Nov 30, 1776, Duration of War	First, Copp	April-June 1778.
Hughs, James Sergeant	June 1, 1777	Malcom's, Lucas	Dec 1777.
Hughson/Huson, William Private	May 18, 1777, Duration of War	Fourth, Pearsee	Dec 1777-May 1778 sick Fishkill; June 1, 1778 deserted.
Huldler/Hudlor, Solomon, Private	Three Years	Malcom's, Black	Dec 1777-Feb 1778 sick quarters; March-May 1778.
Humphry/ Humphrey, Samuel/Saml Private	May 5, 1778, Nine Months	Fourth, Smith	May-June 1778.
Hunt, David Private	May 5, 1778, Nine Months	Second, Riker	May-June 1778.

Hunt, John Private	May 1, 1777, Duration of War	Second, Pell	Dec 1777; Jan-Feb 1778 on command with the Surgeon; March 1778 on command with the Doctor; April-May 1778; June 12, 1778 died.
Hunt, Solomon Private	May 5, 1778, Nine Months	Fourth, Strong	June 1778 tending sick Pennsylvania.
Hunt, Thomas 2nd. Lt.	Nov 21, 1776	Fourth, Smith	Dec 1777 sick absent Fishkill; Jan 1778 sick absent; Feb-June 1778.
Hunt, William Private	Jan 1, 1777, Duration of War	Second, Graham	Dec 1777 payroll only; Jan-March 1778; April 1778 on duty; May-June 1778.
Hunter, Benjamin Private	Jan 1, 1777, Duration of War	Fourth, Titus	Dec 1777; Jan 1778 on guard; Feb-June 1778.
Hunter, Ezekiel/ Ezekil Private	May 5, 1778, Nine Months	Fourth, Smith	May-June 1778.
Hunter, James Sergeant	Duration of War	Malcom's, Niven	Dec 1777 sick absent nigh camp; Jan 1778 sick in quarters; Feb 1778 sick present; April-May 1778.
Hunter, John Captain	April 11, 1777	Malcom's, Hunter/ Lucas	Dec 22, 1777 resigned. Captain Lucas succeeded in the command of this company.
Hunter/Junter, Jonathan Private	May 5, 1778, Nine Months	Fourth, Pearsee	June 1778.
Hunter, Robert, Ensign	July 1, 1777	Malcom's, Black	Dec 1777-Feb 1778; April-May 1778. Oath at Valley Forge on May 11, 1778.
Hunter, William/Wm Private	Duration of War	Malcom's, Steel	Dec 1777; Jan-Feb 1778 on furlough; March-June 1778.
Hurley/Halay, James Private	May 5, 1778, Nine Months	Second, Riker	May 1778; June 1778 on General Poor's guard.
Hurtigh, John Private	Jan 22, 1777, Three Years	First, Finck	April-June 1778.
Huston, Jeremiah/Jerh Private	Jan 30, 1777	Second, Hallett	Dec 1777-Jan 1778 sick at Peekskill; Feb 1778 payroll only; March 1778 Peekskill; April 1778 sick at Peekskill; May 1778 payroll only.
Huston, William Private		Fourth Pearsee	June 1, 1778 deserted.

Name, Rank	Enlistment	Company	Service Record
Hutchins, William Private	April 9, 1777, Three Years	Second, Pelton	Dec 1777 sick in hospital; Jan-March 1778 sick absent; April 1778 payroll only; May-June 1778 sick at Danbury.
Hutchinson/ Hutchison, Richard/Richd Private	Duration of War	Malcom's, Niven	Dec 1777; Jan 1778 sick in camp; Feb 1778; April-May 1778.
Hyatt, Abraham 2nd. Lt.	Nov 21, 1776	Fourth, Titus	Dec 1777 sick in quarters; Jan 1778 on command; Feb 1778; March 1778 on guard; May 1778; April 1778 on furlough; June 1778.
Hyatt/Hyett, Abraham/Abrm Private	Oct 28, 1776, Three Years	Fourth, Pearsee	Dec 1777-March 1778; April 1778 sick in camp; May 1778 sick present; June-July 1778 sick Valley Forge.
Hyer, Jacob Private	Nov 28, 1776, Duration of War	First, Graham	April-June 1778.
Hymes, Joseph Private	May 5, 1778, Nine Months	Fourth, Davis	June 1778.
Hynes/Hines, Thomas Private	Oct 29, 1776, Duration of War	First, Van Ness	April-June 1778 on command General Schuyler's guard.
Idget see Edget			
Inglish/English, John Private	Jan 1, 1777, Duration of War	Fourth, Sacket	Dec 1777-Feb 1778; March 1778 sick in hutts; April 1778 muster roll shows he died on May 1, 1778.
Irvine, Matthew Captain	May 12, 1777	Malcom's, Irvine	Dec 1777; Jan 20, 1778 resigned. Jonah Hallett commanded the company for the rest of the Valley Forge Encampment.
Isaacs, Isaac Sergeant	July 4, 1777, Three Years	First, Wendell	April-June 1778.
Ivory, Jacobus Private	Jan 1, 1777, Duration of War	Second, Lounsbery	Dec 1777-Jan 1778 sick in hospital at Fishkill; Feb-March 1778 sick in hospital; April-June 1778.
Jacklin, Samuel Private	May 5, 1778, Nine Months	Fourth, Marvin	May-June 1778.
Jackson, Thomas Private	March 4, 1777, Duration of War	Fourth, Smith	May-June 1778.
Jacobs, David Fifer	May 4, 1778	Malcom's, Black	May 1778.
Jacobs, Joseph Private	April 13, 1778, Duration of War	Malcom's, Niven	April 1778 sick in quarters; May 1778.

Name/Rank	Enlistment	Company	Service Record
Jaquish/Jaquich, John Corporal/ Sergeant	Feb 20, 1777, Duration of War	Second, Pelton	Dec 1777; Jan 1778 on command; Feb 1778 on guard; March 1778; April 1778 payroll only; May 1778; May 22, 1778 promoted to Sergeant; June 1778.
James, Ebenezer Private	Nov 21, 1776, Duration of War	Fourth, Titus	Dec 1777; Jan 1778 on command; Feb-April 1778; June 1778 Gen. Poors guard.
James, Henry Sergeant	One Year	Malcom's, Irvine	Dec 1777-Feb 1778.
James, Mordecai Sergeant	Three Years	Malcom's, Black	Dec 1777 sick in hospital; Jan 1778 sick quarters; Feb 1778 roll shows he died Jan 13, 1778.
Jane/Jaine, Jotham Private	May 5, 1778, Nine Months	Fourth, Marvin	May 5, 1778 joined; May-June 1778.
Jarvis/Jervis, Nathaniel Corporal	Nov 21, 1776, Duration of War	Fourth, Titus	Dec 1777-March 1778; April 1778 sick in quarters; May-June 1778.
Jebine/Gebin, John/Jno Drummer	Dec 2, 1776, Duration of War	Second, Riker	Dec 1777-June 1778.
Jeffers, John Private	Dec 7, 1776, Duration of War	Fourth, Marvin	Dec 1777-April 1778; May 1778 sick in camp; June 1778.
Jemison, Alexander Private	Duration of War	First, Wendell	April 20, 1778 deserted.
Jenkins/Jonkins, James Corporal	May 5, 1777, Three Years	Malcom's, Tom	Dec 1777-Feb 1778; March-April 1778 sick present; May-June 1778.
Jillet/Jillitt, James Private	May 5, 1778, Nine Months	Fourth, Strong	May-June 1778.
John/Johns, Francis Private	Oct 28, 1776, Duration of War	First, Van Ness	April-May 1778; June 1778 on guard
Johns, Henry/Henery Private	August 30, 1777, Three Years	Malcom's, Lucas	Dec 1777-April 1778; May 1778 on command at Radnor.
John/Johns, Silas Drummer	Jan 1, 1777, Three Years	Fourth, Titus	Dec 1777-Jan 1778; Feb 15, 1778 died.
Johnson, Abraham/Abrm Corporal	March 2, 1777, Three Years	First, Graham	April-May 1778; June 1778 on command Colonel Morgan.
Johnson/Johnston, George 2nd. Lt	Nov 21, 1776	Second, Pell	Nov-Jan 1778 on furlough; Feb 1778; March 1778 on furlough; April 9, 1778 resigned.
Johnson, James Private	May 5, 1778, Nine Months	Second, Riker	May-June 1778.
Johnson, Peter Private	May 1, 1778, Nine Months	Second, Lounsbery	May 1778; June 1778 on guard.

Name/Rank	Enlisted/Term	Regiment/Company	Service Record
Johnson/Jonson, Samuel/Saml Private	Jan 1, 1777, Duration of War	Fourth, Walker	Dec 1777; Jan 1778 unfit to parade; Feb-May 1778; June 1778 on furlough Newark.
Johnson, Uriah Corporal	Dec 28, 1776, Three Years	Fourth, Smith	Dec 1777; Jan 1778 sick in hospital; Feb 7, 1778 died.
Johnson/Jonson, William Private	March 10, 1777, Duration of War	Fourth, Walker	Dec 1777-June 1778.
Johnston/Jonston, James Private	Duration of War	Malcom's, Kearsley	Dec 1777-Jan 1778 sick in hospital; Feb-March 1778 hospital Jerseys; April 1778 sick Jerseys.
Jones see Gones			
Jones, Evan Corporal	April 1, 1777, Three Years	Second, Graham	Dec 1777 payroll only; Jan-June 1778.
Jones, Ezra Private		First, Hicks	April-June 1778.
Jones, James Corporal	Nov 29, 1777, Duration of War	First, Graham	April-June 1778.
Jones, Jacob Fifer	May 9, 1777, Duration of War	Second, Pell	Dec 1777-May 1778; June-Aug 1778 sick at Valley Forge.
Jones, John Private	Jan 1, 1777, Duration of War	Fourth, Titus	Dec 1777-March 1778 sick absent; April 1778 sick at Albany; May 26, 1778 deserted.
Jones, William Private	Nov 11, 1776, Duration of War	First, Copp	April-June 1778.
Jordan, Thomas Volunteer/Private	May 18, 1778	First, McCracken	April 1778 on furlough; May-June 1778. He appears as a Volunteer on the April 1778 and earlier rolls, enlisted as a Private on May 18, 1778.
Joy, Samuel Private	May 5, 1778, Nine Months	Fourth, Sacket	June 1778 on duty.
Joyce/Joice, James Private	Feb 14, 1777, Duration of War	Second, Pell	Dec 1777-Jan 1778 on command; Feb 1778 sick smallpox; March 1778; April 1778 payroll only; May 1778; June 1778 sick Pennsylvania.
Jupiter/Juberter, Silas/Silias Private	June 3, 1777, Duration of War	Second, Pell	Dec 1777 sick present; Jan 1778; Feb 1778 sick in smallpox; March-June 1778.
Kamby/Camby, James Private	Aug 24, 1777, Duration of War	Fourth, Sacket	Dec 1777; Jan 1778 on duty; Feb-March 1778; April 1778 on duty; May 1778; June 1778 sick in Jersies.
Kearish, Frederick Private	Nov 7, 1777, Duration of War	First, Hicks	April-May 1778; June 20, 1778 deserted.

Name	Enlistment	Regiment, Company	Service
Kearsley, Samuel/Saml Captain	Feb 28, 1777	Malcom's, Kearsley	Dec 1777-Jan 1778 on furlough; March 1778; April 1778 on command.
Keator/Cator William Private	Three Years	Malcom's, Black	Dec 1777 on command; Jan-Feb 1778; March 1778 sick absent; April-May 1778.
Keef/Keefe, Arthur Private	Feb 1, 1777, Duration of War	Fourth, Walker	Dec 1777; Jan 1778 unfit to parade; Feb 1778 in quarters—too naked to parade; March-April 1778; April 1778 turned over to First New York Regiment by Court Martial. See Kief, Arthur.
Keeler/Keeller, Edward Private	Three Years	Malcom's, Black	Dec 1777-Feb 1778; March 1778 fit for duty; April-May 1778.
Keevin, Jacob Private	Feb 5, 1778, Duration of War	First, Copp	April-May 1778; June 1778 on command with Colonel Morgan.
Keller, John Private	Dec 13, 1776, Duration of War	First, Finck	April-June 1778.
Keller, Nicholas Private	March 12, 1777, Three Years	First, Van Ness	April-June 1778.
Kellerman/ Kellerhan, John Private	Duration of War	Malcom's, Irvine	Dec 1777-Jan 1778 sick absent.
Kelley/Killey, Denis/Dennis Private	May 5, 1778, Nine Months	Fourth, Strong	May-June 1778.
Kelley/Kelly, Isaac Private	May 5, 1778, Nine Months	Fourth, Strong	May 1778-June 1778.
Kelley/Kelly, Maurice/Morris Private	Dec 1, 1776, Duration of War	Fourth, Sacket	Dec 1777-June 1778.
Kelly/Kelley, David Private	April 8, 1777, Duration of War	Malcom's, Santford	Dec 1777-June 1778.
Kelly/Kelley, John Private	May 5, 1778, Nine Months	Second, Riker	May-June 1778.
Kelly, Patrick Private	Duration of War	First, Van Ness	April-May 1778; June 1778 on command with Colonel Morgan.
Kelly/Kelley, Robert Private	Nov 21, 1776, Duration of War	Fourth, Titus	Dec 1777; Jan 1778 on command; Feb 1778; March 1778 on command; April-June 1778.
Kelly, Zephaniah Private		Malcom's, Tom	April 24, 1778 joined; April-June 1778.
Kelsh, John Private	March 12, 1777, Three Years	First, Finck	April 1778 sick in quarters; May-June 1778.

Kelson, Phineas, Private	May 7, 1778	Second, Hallett	June 14, 1778 died.
Kenney/Kenny, Charles Private	Nov 21, 1776, Duration of War	Fourth, Davis	Dec 1777-May 1778; June-August 1778 sick in Pennsylvania.
Ketcham/ Catchem, John Private	May 9, 1777, Three Years	Fourth, Sacket	Dec 1777-March 1778; April-May 1778 sick present; June-August 1778 sick in Pennsylvania.
Ketcham/Kitcham, Joseph Private	Jan 14, 1777, Duration of War	Second, Hallett	Dec 1777-April 1778; May 1778 payroll only.
Keyser/Keyzer, Henry Drum Major	Oct 29, 1776, Duration of War	First	April-June 1778.
Kidd, Alexander Sergeant	Aug 7, 1777, Duration of War	First, McCracken	April-May 1778; June 1778 sick at Corryell's Ferry.
Kider/Kiddair, Wilder/Wildair Sergeant/Private	April 1, 1777, Three Years	Malcom's, Santford	Dec 1777-June 1778; June 1778 reduced to Private.
Kief/Keef, Arthur Private		First, Ten Broeck	May 26, 1778 joined; May-June 1778. See Keef, Arthur.
Kieft/Kieff, Arther/Arthur Private	May 5, 1778, Nine Months	Fourth, Davis	June 1778 sick at Hopewell Jersey.
Kincaid, William Private	March 19, 1777, Duration of War	First, Wendell	April-June 1778.
Kinch/Kench, Jacob Private	Duration of War	Malcom's, Steel	Dec 1777-Feb 1778; March 1778 sick in hospital; April 1778 sick Yellow Springs; May-June 1778 wagoner.
King, John Private	Oct 25, 1776, Duration of War	First, Hicks	April-June 1778.
King, William Private	Oct 23, 1776, Duration of War	First, Van Ness	April-June 1778.
King, William Private	May 5, 1778, Nine Months	Second, Pelton	May 1778; June 1778 sick in Jersey.
Kinner, Jonathan Private	Nov 21, 1776, Duration of War	Fourth, Davis	Dec 1777-April 1778; April 1778 sick present; June 1778 sick in Pennsylvania.
Kinter, Nicholas Private	March 12, 1777, Three Years	First, Finck	April-June 1778.
Kipp/Kip, James Private	Feb 6, 1777, Duration of War	Second, Riker	Dec 1777; Jan 1778 sick present; Feb 1778; March 1778 sick absent; April-May 1778; June 1778 on furlough.
Kipp/Kip, Matthew Private	Nov 26, 1776, Duration of War	Fourth, Pearsee	Dec 1777-March 1778; April 1778 sick present; June-July 1778 sick Valley Forge.

Kipple, Frederick Private		Malcom's, Kearsley	Jan 1778 sick in hospital; Feb 1778 deserted from hospital.
Kirk, George Musician	Oct 26, 1776, Duration of War	First, Finck	April-June 1778.
Kirk, James Private	Duration of War	Malcom's, Kearsley	Dec 1777 sick in camp; Jan 1778 sick Eastown; Feb 1778 in hospital; March 1778 on command to Bethlehem; April 1778 on command Bethlehem.
Kirk, Joseph Private	May 5, 1778, Nine Months	Fourth, Davis	May-June 1778.
Kirkpatrick, Kirckpatrick, David Ensign	April 24, 1777	Malcom's, Kearsley	Dec 1777 on furlough; Jan-March 1778; April 1778 on furlough. Oath at Valley Forge on May 23, 1778.
Kitcham/Ketcham, Samuel Private	May 5, 1778, Nine Months	Fourth, Marvin	May-June 1778.
Klock, Jacob Ensign	Nov 21, 1776	First, Finck	April-May 1778; June 14, 1778 on command Johnstown.
Kloese see Cloese			
Knapp/Knap, Caleb Private	March 17, 1777, Duration of War	Second, Pelton	Dec 1777; Jan 1778 on command; Feb-March 1778; April 1778 payroll only; May 1778; June 1778 sick Peekskill.
Knapp, Isaac Private	March 22, 1777, Duration of War	Second, Pelton	Dec 1777-March 1778; April 1778 payroll only; May 1778 on guard; June 1778.
Knapp/Knap, James Drummer	Feb 26, 1777, Duration of War	Second, Pelton	Dec 1777 sick in hospital; Jan-Feb 1778 sick absent; March 1778; April 1778 payroll only; May-June 1778.
Knapping, Jeremiah Private	May 5, 1778, Nine Months	Fourth, Davis	June 1778.
Knepple/Knipple, Frederick/Fredk Private	Duration of War	Malcom's, Kearsley	Dec 1777; Jan 1778 sick in hospital; Feb 1778 deserted hospital.
Knickabocker/ Knickabauer, Andrew Private	June 1, 1777, Three Years	Second, Graham	Dec 1777 payroll only; Jan-Feb 1778; March 1778 on guard; April-May 1778; June 1778 Valley Forge.
Knight, William Private	Jan 10, 1777, Duration of War	Second, Riker	Dec 1777; Jan 1778 sick present; Feb-May 1778; June-July 1778 sick at Valley Forge.
Knight, John Jacob Private/Corporal	Oct 29, 1776, Duration of War	First, Van Ness	April-May 1778; May 22, 1778 promoted to Corporal; June 1778.

Kole/Koole, Philip, Private	Feb 28, 1777 Three Years	Second, Lounsbery	Dec 1777-Jan 1778 sick in the hospital at Albany; Feb-March 1778 sick in hospital; April 1778 on guard; May-June 1778.
Krook see Crook			
Lacky/Lackey, Hugh Sergeant	March 10, 1777	First, Finck	April-June 1778.
Lamb, John Private	May 5, 1778, Nine Months	Second, Ten Eyck	May 1778; June 1778 payroll only.
Lambertson, Simon Corporal	Dec 7, 1776, Three Years	Second, Hallett	Dec 1777; Jan 1778 on command; Feb 1778 payroll only; March-April 1778; May 1778 payroll only; June 1778.
Landon/Landing, Laben Private	April 27, 1777, Three Years	Malcom's, Tom	Dec 1777-Jan 1778.
Lane, William Private	Aug 1, 1777, Three Years	Malcom's, Tom	Dec 1777-Jan 1778; Feb 1778 on command; March-June 1778.
Langley, William H. Private		Malcom's, Steel	April 1778 sick in Regimental Hospital
Lansing, John Private	May 5, 1778, Nine Months	Fourth, Strong	June 1778 on guard.
Lathan, John Private	March 1, 1777, Duration of War	Fourth, Davis	Dec 1777; Jan 1778 on command with General Greene; Feb 1778; March 1778 on party; April-June 1778.
Laverty, John Private	Nov 18, 1776, Duration of War	First, Hicks	April-June 1778.
Lawrance/ Lawrence, Jonathan 2nd. Lt.	March 11, 1777	Malcom's, Tom	Dec 1777; Jan 1778 on furlough; Feb-June 1778. Oath at Valley Forge on May 23, 1778.
Leary, Kady Private	Jan 1, 1777, Duration of War	Second, Graham	Dec 1777 payroll only; Jan-March 1778; April 1778 fortnights command; May 1778; June 1778 sick Brunswick.
Leathers, Ezekiel Private	March 8, 1777, Duration of War	First, Ten Broeck	April-June 1778.
Ledyard, Benjamin Major	Nov 21, 1776	Fourth/ First	Dec 1777; Jan-Feb 1778 on furlough; March-April 1778; May 1, 1778 transferred from Fourth New York; May 1778; June 1778 "on furlough since 29th June by his Excellency."
Lee, Daniel/Danl Private	Nov 28, 1776, Duration of War	First, Graham	April-June 1778.

Lee, Japath Private	May 5, 1778, Nine Months	Fourth, Walker	May-June 1778.
Lee, Seth Private	May 5, 1778, Nine Months	Fourth, Smith	May-June 1778.
Lenny/Lanee, Philip, Private	Jan 1, 1777, Duration of War	Second, Graham	Dec 1777 payroll only; Jan-May 1778; June 1778 sick at Spotswood.
Leonard/ Leonnard, Edward Private	Jan 1, 1777, Duration of War	Fourth, Walker	Dec 1777-Jan 1778; Feb 1778 in quarters, too naked to parade; March 1778 sick in camp; April-June 1778.
Lent, Abraham/ Abram Private	Feb 10, 1777	Second, Hallett	March 23, 1778 joined; April 1778 sick in camp; May 1778 payroll only; June-July 1778 sick Valley Forge; Aug 4, 1778 died.
Lent/Lint, Elias Private	Jan 1, 1777, Duration of War	Second, Wright	Dec 1777 sick absent; Jan 1778 sick at Peekskill; Feb 1778 sick absent; March-April 1778; May 1778 sick present; June-July 1778 sick at Valley Forge.
Lent, Hendrick Private	Dec 25, 1776, Duration of War	Second, Hallett	Dec 1777-Jan 1778 on furlough; Feb 1778; March 1778 on furlough; April 1778; May 1778 payroll only; June-July 1778 sick at Valley Forge; July 10, 1778 died.
Lester, John Sergeant	July 1, 1777, Duration of War	Second, Wright	Dec 1777-March 1778; April 1778 sick in camp; May-June 1778.
Levins/Levines, Thomas Private	Duration of War	Malcom's, Niven	Dec 20, 1777 deserted.
Lewis, Henry Sergeant/Private	March 19, 1777, Duration of War	First, Van Ness	April-May 1778; May 21, 1778 reduced to Private; June 1778.
Lewis/Lewiss, Jabish/Jabez, Private	May 5, 1778, Nine Months	Fourth, Davis	May-June 1778.
Lewis, James Private	Feb 28, 1777, Three Years	Second, Lounsbery	Dec 1777-June 1778.
Lewis, Joseph Private	Dec 25, 1776, Duration of War	First, Graham	April-May 1778 on command General Schuyler's guard; June 1778 on command General Schuyler's guard Saratoga.
Lewis, Leonard Corporal	May 5, 1778	Second, Riker	May-June 1778.
Lewis, Richard Sergeant	May 5, 1778	Second, Riker	May-June 1778.

Lewis, Samuel/Saml Private	Nov 28, 1776, Duration of War	First, Graham	April-May 1778; June 17, 1778 deserted.
Lewis, William Private	Feb 18, 1778, Duration of War	First, Ten Broeck	April 17, 1778 deserted.
Lidle/Little, William/Wm Private	May 5, 1778, Nine Months	Fourth, Smith	May 1778; June 1778 sick Rocky Hill.
Light, John Private	Feb 26, 1777, Duration of War	Fourth, Pearsee	Dec 1777-May 1778 sick Fishkill; June 1, 1778 deserted.
Lighthal/Lighthall, John Private	Dec 5, 1776, Duration of War	First, Copp	April-May 1778; June 1778 sick in hospital Cuckolds Town.
Lighthall, Abaham/Abraham Corporal	July 5, 1777	First, Finck	April-May 1778; June 18, 1778 sick Cuckolds Town.
Lincamore/ Lingamore, John Private	Duration of War	Malcom's, Kearsley	Dec 1777-April 1778; August 1778 sick Yellow Springs.
Linch, John Private	May 5, 1778, Nine Months	Fourth, Strong	June 1778 sick in "Pensilvany"; August 1, 1778 deserted.
Linch, Larance/ Laurence Private	Jan 1, 1777, Duration of War	Fourth, Strong	Dec 1777-May 1778; June-July 1778 sick Pennsylvania.
Linch, Owen Private	Nov 13, 1776, Duration of War	First, Hicks	April-June 1778.
Lindsey/Linsey, Abraham Private	Jan 1, 1777, Three Years	First, McCracken	April-June 1778 sick at Albany.
Linegar, John Private	Nov 18, 1776, Duration of War	First, Hicks	April-June 1778.
Lines, Hosea Private	Nov 21, 1776, Duration of War	Fourth, Titus	Dec 1777-March 1778; April-May 1778 sick in quarters; June 1778 sick in Pennsylvania.
Livingston, Gilbert J. 2nd. Lt.	Nov 21, 1776	Second, Ten Eyck	Dec 1777 sick at Poughkeepsie; Jan-April 1778; May 1778 sick in camp; June 1778 payroll only.
Livingston, Henry Beekman/ Henry B. Colonel	Nov 21, 1776	Fourth	Dec 1777; Jan 1778 sick absent; Feb 1778 absent in the country; March 1778; April 1778 on command at Radnor; May 1778 on duty; June 1778 on furlough.
Lloyd, James Fifer	April 1, 1777, Duration of War	Fourth, Davis	Dec 1777-Feb 1778; March 27, 1778 discharged.
Lloyd, John 1st. Lt.	Nov 21, 1776	Fourth, Titus	Dec 1777-Feb 1778; March 24, 1778 discharged.
Lochry/Louihry, Daniel Private	Duration of War	Malcom's, Kearsley	Dec 1777 sick in country; Jan 1778 sick in hospital; Feb 1778 deserted from hospital.

Lock, John Private	May 5, 1778, Nine Months	Fourth, Strong	May-June 1778.
Long, Andrew Private	Nov 24, 1777, Duration of War	First, McCracken	April-May 1778; June 1778 sick at Brunswick.
Longley/Longly, William H./Wm Private	Duration of War	Malcom's, Steel	Dec 1777-April 1778; May 1778 sick Regimental hospital; June 16, 1778 deserted.
Loofborrow/ Loofbarron, Isaac Sergeant	Jan 1, 1777, Duration of War	Second, Ten Eyck	Dec 1777; Jan-Feb 1778 on furlough; March 1778 on furlough at Peekskill; April-May 1778 on command at Peekskill; June 1778 payroll only.
Loomis/Lomis, Jacob Private	Aug 19, 1777	Second, Lounsbery	Dec 1777-Jan 1778 sick hospital Albany; Feb 1778 sick in hospital; March-April 1778; May 1778 tending sick; June 1778 sick in Pennsylvania.
Loper, Abraham Sergeant	Nov 21, 1776, Duration of War	Fourth, Davis	Dec 1777-March 1778 sick absent; April 1778 sick at Stonington, Connecticut; May 28, 1778 discharged.
Lord, Benjamin Private	May 5, 1778	Second, Ten Eyck	June 1778 payroll only; August 1778 died Valley Forge.
Lord, Timothy Private		Second, Hallett	April 1778 died.
Lossey/Loosey, Jacob Private	May 5, 1778, Nine Months	Second, Pelton	May-June 1778.
Louis/Lovis, John Private	Nov 28, 1776, Duration of War	First, Graham	April-June 1778.
Louke/Logue, Abraham Private	Duration of War	Malcom's, Kearsley	Dec 1777; Jan-Feb 1778 on command; March 1778 on command at the Forge; April 1778 at the Valley Forge; August 1778 on command at Valley Forge.
Lounsbery/ Lounsberry, Edward Captain	Nov 21, 1776	Second, Lounsbery	Dec 1777; Jan-March 1778 on furlough; April-May 1778; June 1778 on furlough.
Lovejoy, John Private	Jan 10, 1777, Duration of War	First, McCracken	April-June 1778 sick at Schnectady.
Lovejoy, Nathan Private	May 5, 1778, Nine Months	Second, Wright	June 1778.
Low, John Private	May 5, 1778, Nine Months	Second, Pelton	May 1778 tending sick; June 1778.
Lowry, John Private	May 5, 1778	Second, Hallett	First appears on rolls for July 1778.

Lucas, Thomas/Thos 1st. Lt./Captain	Dec 22, 1777	Malcom's, Niven Lucas	On December 22, 1777 he was promoted to Captain and assumed command of Hunter's former company; Dec 1777; Jan 1778 on furlough; March-April 1778; May 12, 1778 cashiered.
Ludlow/Ludlum, Daniel/Danniel Sergeant/Private	Dec 7, 1776, Duration of War	Fourth, Marvin	Dec 25, 1777 reduced to Private; Dec 1777-March 1778; April-May 1778 sick in quarters; June 1778.
Ludlum, John Private	March 18, 1777, Duration of War	Fourth, Strong	Dec 1777-May 1778; June 1778 sick Pennsylvania.
Lusk, John Private	May 5, 1778	Second, Ten Eyck	June 1778 sick Valley Forge.
Lutts/Luts, Coonrod/Conraid Private	May 5, 1778, Nine Months	Second, Riker	May-June 1778.
Lynch, William/Willm Corporal/Private	Nov 30, 1776, Duration of War	First, Graham	April-June 1778; June 15, 1778 reduced to Private.
Lyons, Michael Private	April 12, 1777, Three Years	Second, Lounsbery	Dec 1777-May 1778; June 1778 on furlough.
Lyonson/Lyons, William Private	May 5, 1778, Nine Months	Second, Riker	May 1778; June 1778 sick in camp.
Lytle, William Private/Sergeant	Oct 30, 1776, Duration of War	First, Copp	April 4, 1778 promoted to Sergeant; April-June 1778.
McArthur, John Private	Jan 26, 1777, Three Years	First, Finck	April-June 1778.
McBride, William Private	May 5, 1778, Nine Months	Second, Riker	May-June 1778.
M'Cain see McLeane			
McCalley, Charles Private	May 5, 1778, Nine Months	Fourth, Sacket	June 1778.
McCalum, James Private		Malcom's, Niven	Jan 1778 only record.
McCarty, Charles Private	Duration of War	Malcom's, Kearsley	Dec 1777 wounded hospital.
McCarty/ McCartney, Isaac Private	May 5, 1778, Nine Months	Second, Riker	May-June 1778.
McCarty, Thomas Private	March 11, 1777, Three Years	Malcom's, Tom	Dec 1777 missing at Fort Montgomery.
McCauley/ McCawley, James Private	March 4, 1777, Duration of War	First, Copp	April-June 1778.

McCay/McCoy, William 1st. Lt.		Malcom's, Steel	Dec 1777-Jan 1778 on furlough; March 8, 1778 resigned.
McCine, Daniel Private	May 6, 1778, Nine Months	Second, Graham	May-June 1778.
McClane/McLean, Allen/Allan Corporal/ Sergeant	August 4, 1777	Malcom's, Lucas	Dec 1777; Jan 21, 1778 promoted to Sergeant; Jan-Feb 1778; March 1778 quarters guard; April 1778; May 1778 sick in huts.
McClarin, David Musician	Duration of War	Fourth, Davis	May 1778; June 1778 sick in Pennsylvania; July 1778 muster roll shows he died on June 28, 1778.
McClean, John Sergeant	July 23, 1777, Duration of War	First, Copp	April-June 1778.
McClean, Neal Drummer	Dec 7, 1776, Duration of War	Fourth, Marvin	Dec 1777-April 1778; May 1778 sick in camp; June 1778.
McClelan/ McCleland, John Private	Duration of War	Malcom's, Steel	Dec 16, 1777 deserted; Jan-Feb 1778; March 1778 sick hospital; April 1778 sick Yellow Springs; May 1778; June 15, 1778 joined ; June 1778.
McCloskey/ McCosky, Arthur Private	Duration of War	Malcom's, Steel	Dec 1777-March 1778 sick in hospital; April 1778 sick Bethlehem; May-June 1778 sick Schaefferstown Hospital.
McClow, Joseph Private	Nov 22, 1776, Duration of War	First, Hicks	April-May 1778; June 1778 on command Colonel Morgan; July 2, 1778 deserted.
McClure/McCluer, William Private	May 5, 1778, Nine Months	Second, Graham	May 1778; June 1778 command Valley Forge.
McCluskey/ McClusky, Peter Fife Major	Dec 5, 1776, Duration of War	Second	Dec 1777-April 1778; May 1778 sick present; June 1778 sick at Valley Forge.
McCollister/ McCollester, William Sergeant	May 8, 1777, Three Years	Fourth, Pearsee	Dec 1777-Jan 1778; Feb 1778 on party; March-June 1778.
McCollom/ McCalum, James Private	Duration of War	Malcom's, Niven	Dec 1777-Feb 1778; April-May 1778 sick in camp.
McCollum, John/Jno Private	Nov 21, 1776, Duration of War	Fourth, Davis	Dec 1777-June 1778.
McConnel/ McConnell, William Private	Dec 12, 1776, Duration of War	First, Copp	April-June 1778.

McCormic, John Private	April 3, 1777, Duration of War	First, Ten Broeck	April-May 1778; June 1778 command with Colonel Morgan.
McCormick/ McCormack, James Private	Feb 1, 1777, Three Years	First, Van Ness	April 21, 1778 deserted.
McCoy/McKoy, William Private	Nov 26, 1777, Duration of War	First, Copp	April-June 1778.
McCracken/ McCraken, Joseph Captain	Nov 21, 1776	First, McCracken	April-May 1778; June 28, 1778 wounded in battle.
McCraken/ McCracken, William Private	Jan 1, 1777, Three Years	First, McCracken	April-May 1778; June 1778 waiter to the Captain.
McCullough/ McCulough, Andrew Private	Jan 1, 1777, Three Years	Fourth, Titus	Dec 1777-March 1778; April 1778 sick in quarters; May 1778 muster roll shows he died on June 1, 1778.
McCune, John Sergeant	April 1, 1777, Three Years	Malcom's, Tom	Dec 1777-Feb 1778; March 1778 sick hospital; April 1778 sick Yellow Springs; May-June 1778 on command Yellow Springs.
McDaniel, Daniel Private	March 12, 1777, Duration of War	First, Copp	April-May 1778; June 1778 sick in hospital Cuckolds Town.
McDavid, Henry Private	Nov 14, 1776, Duration of War	First, Hicks	April-May 1778; June 1778 driving Artillery wagon.
McDole/Mc.Dole, John Private	March 10, 1777, Duration of War	Fourth, Strong	Dec 1777-March 1778; April 1778 sick in quarters; May 1778 sick in hospital; June 1778 sick Pennsylvania.
McDonald, Reynold/Ranold Private	May 1, 1778, Duration of War	Second, Lounsbery	June 1778.
McDougle, John Corporal	Jan 21, 1777, Three Years	First, Ten Broeck	April 1778; May 1778 sick present; June 1778 sick Valley Forge.
McEvers, Daniel Private	May 6, 1778, Nine Months	Second, Graham	May 1778; June 1778 sick at Valley Forge.
McEvers, John Sergeant	Dec 28, 1776, Duration of War	Fourth, Smith	Dec 1777 sick absent Fishkill; June 1778 sick in hospital; Feb 6, 1778 died.
McFairley/Fairley, William Private	May 5, 1778, Nine Months	Fourth, Strong	May-June 1778.
McFall, Paul Private	Nov 28, 1776, Duration of War	First, Graham	April-June 1778.

McFarlan, Hosea Private	Duration of War	First, Wendell	April-June 1778,
McGowan/ McGown, Jeremiah Private	Jan 1, 1777, Three Years	Second, Hallett	Dec 1777-Jan 1778; Feb 1778 payroll only; March 23, 1778 joined; March 1778 on command; April 1778; May 1778 payroll only; June 1778.
McGowin, Dunkin/Duncan Private	May 5, 1778, Nine Months	Fourth, Smith	May-June 1778.
M'Gowen/ M'Gowin, James Private	Duration of War	Malcom's, Irvine	Dec 1777-Jan 1778 sick absent.
McGuigan, Michael Sergeant	Nov 5, 1776, Duration of War	First, Finck	April-May 1778; June 1778 sick at Englishtown.
McGuire, Archibald/Archd 2nd. Lt.		Malcom's, Steel	Dec 1777 on furlough.
McHenry/ McHenery, Edward Sergeant/ Private/Corporal	Duration of War	Malcom's, Steel	Dec 1777; Jan-Feb 1778 on furlough; March 1778; April 1, 1778 reduced to Private; April 1778 sick in camp; April 1778; June 1, 1778 promoted to Corporal; June 1778.
McIntire, Barney Private	Nov 26, 1776, Duration of War	First, Copp	April-June 1778.
McKee/McKey, Thomas Private	April 5, 1777, Duration of War	Malcom's, Santford	Dec 1777-Jan 1778 sick absent; Feb-April 1778; June 1778 sick Princeton Hospital.
McKelvie/ McKelvey, Thomas/Thos Private		Malcom's, Steel	Dec 16, 1777 deserted; March 16, 1778 rejoined; March 1778 sick present; April 1778 sick in camp; May 1778; June 18, 1778 deserted.
McKenny/ McKinney, Charles Sergeant	Dec 3, 1776, Three Years	Second, Hallett	Nov 1777-Feb 1778 sick at Peekskill; March 1778; April 1778 recruiting; May 1778 payroll only; June 1778.
McKiel, Adam Private	Nov 26, 1777, Duration of War	Fourth, Sacket	Dec 1777-Feb 1778 sick absent; March 1, 1778 deserted.
McKillip/ McKillup, Alexander Drummer	Oct 30, 1776, Duration of War	First, Copp	April-June 1778.
McKim, John Private	May 27, 1777	Second, Hallett	Dec 1777; Jan 1778 sick at Schenectady; Feb 1778 payroll only; March 1778 sick at Schenectady.

McKinley, Archibald Private	Nov 29, 1776, Duration of War	First, Finck	April 1778 on command at Albany; May-June 1778.
McKinney/ McKenny, James Private	Feb 14, 1777, Duration of War	Second, Wright	Dec 1777-June 1778.
McKinsey/ McKinsy, Malcom Private	Duration of War	Malcom's, Niven	Dec 1777-Feb 1778; April 1778 guard Pottsgrove; May 1778.
McLaughlin, Bernard Sergeant/Private	Oct 26, 1776, Duration of War	First, Van Ness	April 1778; May 1778 sick in quarters; June 1778; June 23, 1778 reduced to Private.
McLean/McClean, Angus Private	Duration of War	Malcom's, Niven	Dec 1777-Jan 1778; Feb 1778 on furlough; April-May 1778.
McLean/McLain, Anthony Private	Oct 27, 1777, Duration of War	First, Finck	April-June 1778.
McLeane/ McClain, Patrick Private	Duration of War	Malcom's, Kearsley	Dec 1777-Jan 1778; Feb 1778 on duty; March-April 1778.
McManus, William Private	April 30, 1777, Three Years	First, Wendell	April-May 1778; June 1778 on duty.
McMaster/ MachMaster, John Private	June 16, 1777, Three Years	Malcom's, Tom	Dec 1777; Jan 1778 on furlough; Feb 1778; March 1778 on guard; April-June 1778.
McMasters, Alexander/Alexr Private	Dec 1, 1776, Duration of War	First, Graham	April 1778; May 1778 on duty; June 1778.
McMasters, James Private	May 6, 1778, Nine Months	Second, Graham	May-June 1778.
McMicke/ McMiken, Ebenezer Private	May 5, 1778, Nine Months	Fourth, Strong	May 1778; June 1778 sick New Jersey.
McMullen/ M'mullen, Michael/Michl Private	Duration of War	Malcom's, Kearsley	Dec 1777-Jan 1778; Feb 1778 on guard; March 1778; April 1778 on guard.
McPike/M'Pike, John Corporal	One Year	Malcom's, Irvine	Dec 1777-Feb 1778.
McQown, William Sergeant		Malcom's, Steel	Dec 17, 1777 deserted.
McQuinn, Philip Private	Nov 19, 1777, Duration of War	First, Hicks	Nov 20, 1777 deserted; May 7, 1778 returned from desertion and joined; May-June 1778.

Name/Rank	Enlistment	Company	Service
McWhorter/ McWhorster, John Private	May 5, 1778, Nine Months	Fourth, Marvin	May-June 1778.
Mackey/Macky, John Private	Duration of War	Malcom's, Niven	Dec 1777-Feb 1778; April 1778; May 1778 on Commissary Guard.
Mackraback, Dycke Private	May 5, 1778, Nine Months	Fourth, Titus	May 1778; June 1778 sick at Peekskill.
Mahew/Mahu, Peter Private	June 26, 1777, Three Years	Second, Graham	Dec 1777 payroll only; Jan 1778; Feb 1778 sick in smallpox; March-May 1778; June 1778 on guard.
Malcom, John Lt.	April 29, 1777	Malcom's, Lucas	Dec 1777 sick absent.
Malcom, William Colonel	March 13, 1776	Malcom's	Dec 1777. Malcom left camp in January 1778 and did not return, though he remained in the army.
Maloy, James Private	May 5, 1778, Nine Months	Second, Riker	May-June 1778.
Manning/Mannin, Samuel/Saml Private	May 20, 1777, Three Years	Malcom's, Tom	Dec 1777 sick absent; Jan-Feb 1778 sick in quarters; March 1778 Lord Stirling's guard; April 1778 on command; May-June 1778 sick Yellow Springs.
Mapes, John Corporal/Private	Dec 15, 1776	Fourth, Strong	November 1777 reduced to Private; Dec 1777-April 1778; May 1778 sick in hospital; June 1778 sick Pennsylvania; July 1778 rolls show he died on June 27, 1778.
Mapes/Maps, Phineas Private	Duration of War	Malcom's, Santford	Dec 1777-Feb 1778; March-April 1778 Lord Stirling's guard; May 1778 in Regimental hospital; June 1778 Valley Forge.
Marks, Holiab/ Ahaliab Corporal/Private	April 25, 1777, Three Years	Fourth, Pearsee	Dec 1777-March 1778; April 22, 1778 reduced to Private; April 1778 sick in quarters; May 1778 sick present; June 1778 sick Peekskill.
Marlin, Isaac Private	Jan 15, 1777, Duration of War	Second, Wright	Dec 1777-April 1778; May 1778 sick present; June-July 1778 sick at Valley Forge.
Maroni, Florence Sergeant	Nov 28, 1776, Duration of War	First, Graham	April-June 1778 on command General Schuyler's guard.
Marricle/Marcell, Anthony Private	Feb 8, 1777, Three Years	First, McCracken	April-June 1778.

Marricle/Marcell, Henry Private	Feb 8, 1777, Three Years	First, McCracken	April-June 1778.
Marsden/Marsdon, Humphry/ Humphrey Private	Nov 28, 1776, Three Years	First, McCracken	April-June 1778.
Marsh, John Sergeant	Dec 15, 1776, Duration of War	First, Hicks	April-June 1778.
Marshall/Marshal, Elihu Adjutant/ Brigade Major	Nov 21, 1776	Second	Dec 1777 sick absent; Jan-Feb 1778 absent without leave; March-April 1778; April 26, 1778 appointed Brigade Major; May-June 1778.
Marshall, James Private	Jan 18, 1777, Duration of War	Fourth, Sacket	Dec 1777 wounded at Albany; Jan-March 1778 wounded left at Albany; April-May 1778 sick present; June 1778.
Martin/Marton, Archibald Sergeant	May 5, 1778, Nine Months	Fourth, Pearsee	May 1778; June 1778 sick in Jersey.
Marvin/Mervin, Benjamin/ Benjm 1st. Lt./Captain	Nov 21, 1776	Fourth, Marvin	Dec 1777; January 9, 1778 promoted to Captain to rank from September 2, 1777; Jan-Feb 1778 on furlough; March 1778; April 23, 1778 resigned. This company was then commanded by Peter Elsworth.
Marvin, Matthew Private	May 5, 1778, Nine Months	Second, Wright	June 1778.
Marvin, Stephen/Stephan Private	May 5, 1778	Fourth, Marvin	June 1778 muster roll shows he joined on May 8, 1778; June 1778.
Mason, Thomas/Thos Drummer	Jan 1, 1777, Duration of War	Second, Ten Eyck	Dec 1777-May 1778; June 1778 payroll only.
Mason, Thomas Private	Dec 8, 1776, Duration of War	Fourth, Marvin	Dec 1777; Jan-April 1778 sick in quarters; May 1778 sick in camp; June 1778.
Master, George Peter Private	March 2, 1778,	First, Wendell	April-June 1778,
Masters, Jonathan Private	Nov 20, 1776, Duration of War	First, Hicks	April-June 1778 on command General Schuyler's guard.
Mastin, Daniel Private	May 7, 1778, 1777	Second, Pell	May 1778 in small pox; June 1778.
Mathers, James Private	May 6, 1778, 1777	Second, Graham	May-June 1778.

Mathews, James Sergeant	April 1, 1777, Three Years	Second, Lounsbery	Dec 6, 1777 deserted.
Maxam/Maxim, Adonijah Private	May 5, 1778, 1777	Second, Riker	May-June 1778.
Maxwell, Anthony, Ensign	July 1, 1777	Malcom's, Santford	Dec 1777-June 1778. Oath at Valley Forge on May 11, 1778.
May, Daniel/ Danl Private	May 14, 1778, 1777	Second, Ten Eyck	May-June 1778.
Maybee/Mabey, Tobias Private	May 5, 1778, Nine Months	Fourth, Pearsee	May-June 1778.
Mead, Jehiel Private	May 5, 1778, 1777	Second, Ten Eyck	May 1778 small pox; June 1778.
Mead/Meed, Nathan Private	April 19, 1777, Three Years	Second, Pelton	Dec 1777 on command; Jan 1778 on command wagons; Feb 1778; March 1778 on guard; April 1778 payroll only; May 25, 1778 deserted.
Mead/Meed, William Surgeon	Nov 21, 1776	First	April-June 1778.
Meaker/Meker, Daniel Private	May 5, 1778, Nine Months	Fourth, Strong	May-June 1778.
Meloy/Maloy, John Private	May 5, 1778, Nine Months	Fourth, Pearsee	May-June 1778.
Merril, John Private	Sept 30, 1777, Three Years	First, McCracken	April 1, 1778 deserted.
Merrit, Ebenezer/ Ebenezard Private	May 5, 1778, Nine Months	Fourth, Pearsee	May-June 1778.
Merselus/ Merselious, Garret Private	Jan 27, 1777, Duration of War	First, Finck	April-June 1778.
Mical, Samuel Private	May 5, 1778, Duration of War	Fourth, Pearsee	June 1778 on guard.
Mildon, Daniel Private	May 5, 1778, Nine Months	Second, Riker	May-June 1778.
Miles/Mills, William/Wm Private/Corporal	May 25, 1777, Three Years	Malcom's, Lucas	Dec 1777-March 1778; March 5, 1778 promoted to Corporal; April 1778; May 1778 on Commissary guard.

Name	Enlistment	Regiment/Company	Service Record
Millar/Miller, Justus Private	Jan 1, 1777, Duration of War	Fourth, Sacket	Dec 1777-Jan 1778 sick absent.
Miller, Benjamin/Benjm Private	Nov 21, 1776, Duration of War	Fourth, Davis	Dec 1777-April 1778; May 1778 sick in hospital; June 1778 sick Pennsylvania.
Miller, David Corporal	Nov 7, 1776, Duration of War	First, Van Ness	April 1778 sick quarters; May 27, 1778 died.
Miller, George Private	Duration of War	Malcom's, Irvine	Dec 1777-Feb 1778; March-April 1778 on command; May 1778; June 1778 sick Valley Forge.
Miller, George Private	Duration of War	Malcom's. Kearsley	Dec 1777-Feb 1778; March 1778 sick at hospital; April 1778 sick at Yellow Springs.
Miller, George Private		Malcom's, Santford	July 1778 sick at Valley Forge.
Miller, Jacob Private	July 12, 1777	Second, Graham	Dec 1777 payroll only; Jan 1778 sick absent; Feb 1778 sick at 9 Partners; March 1778; April 1778 weeks command; May 1778; June 1778 sick at Valley Forge.
Miller, James 1st. Lt.	Nov 21, 1776	Second, Graham	Dec 1777 payroll only; Jan-Feb 1778 on command; March 1778; April 7, 1778 resigned.
Miller/Millor, Jesse/Jessee Corporal	Jan 1, 1777	Fourth, Marvin	Dec 1777-June 1778.
Miller, John Private	Duration of War	Malcom's, Kearsley	Dec 1777-Jan 1778 sick in hospital; August 1778 sick Yellow Springs.
Miller, William Private	Three Years	Malcom's, Black	Dec 1777-Feb 1778; March 1778 on command; April 1778 on guard; May 1778.
Mills see Miles			
Mills, Andrew Private	Dec 5, 1777, Duration of War	Fourth, Sacket	Dec 1777-Feb 1778; March 1778 sick in hutts; April-May 1778 sick present; June 1778 sick in Pennsylvania.
Mills, Alexander Private	Feb 2, 1777, Duration of War	First, Ten Broeck	April-June 1778.
Mills, Samuel Private	May 5, 1778, Nine Months	Second, Wright	First appears on the rolls for Aug 1778.
Milspaugh/Milspugh, Christopher Private	Three Years	Malcom's, Black	Dec 1777-April 1778; May 1778 on guard.
Minges/Mingus, Moses Private	Duration of War	Malcom's, Black	Dec 1777-March 1778; April 1778 sick in camp; May 1778.

Mingos/Minjoss, Harmonius/ Haromus Private	May 5, 1778, Nine Months	Fourth, Smith	May-June 1778.
Minks/Mink, John Private	May 7, 1777, Three Years	Fourth, Pearsee	Dec 1777 muster roll reads "in place of Michel Plass deserted—"; Jan 1778 on party; Feb-April 1778; May 1778 on guard; June 1778. Plass had deserted on August 1, 1777.
Mitchell/Mitchel, David Drummer/ Drum Major	June 19, 1777, Duration of War	Second, Lounsbery	Dec 1777; Jan 1, 1778 promoted to Drum Major; Jan-May 1778; June 1778 sick at Peekskill.
Mitchell/Mitchel, Edward Private	Oct 25, 1776, Duration of War	First, Hicks	April-June 1778.
Mitchell, George Private	Oct 25, 1776, Duration of War	First, McCracken	April 1778; May 1778 teamster; June 1778.
Mitchell, Martin Private	April 11, 1777, Three Years	Second, Hallett	Dec 1777 in the artillery; Jan 1778 sick at Fishkill; Feb 1778 payroll only; March-April 1778; May 1778 payroll only; June 1778.
Monell/Monnell, James 1st. Lt.	March 20, 1777	Malcom's, Black	Dec 1777-Feb 1778 on command; March-May 1778. Oath at Valley Forge on May 23, 1778.
Monhort/Manhart, John Private	May 26, 1777, Three Years	Malcom's, Santford	Dec 1777-Feb 1778; March 1778 sick present; April 1778; May 1778 in Regimental hospital; June 1778 Yellow Springs.
Montanye/ Montaye, Peter Private	May 12, 1778, Nine Months	Second, Graham	May-June 1778.
Montanye/ Mantaoney, Isaac Drummer	June 12, 1777, Duration of War	Malcom's, Santford	Dec 1777-Jan 1778; Feb 1778 absent without leave; March-June 1778.
Montgomery, James Sergeant	May 5, 1778	Second, Riker	May-June 1778.
Moody, James Private	Feb 21, 1777, Duration of War	Fourth, Walker	Dec 1777; Jan 1778 unfit to parade; Feb-March 1778; April 1778 sick in camp; May 1778 sick present; June 1778 sick Pennsylvania.
Moore, Charles Private	Dec 6, 1776, Three Years	Second, Hallett	Dec 1777-Jan 1778; Feb 1778 on command; March-April 1778; May 1778 payroll only; June 1778.

Moore/More, John Private	April 1, 1777, Duration of War	First, Ten Broeck	April-June 1778.
Moot/Moat, Ezekiel Private	Duration of War	Malcom's, Niven	Dec 3, 1777 deserted; April 1778 returned deserted Dec 3, apprehended tryd, and punished; April-May 1778.
More, Philip Private	March 12, 1778, Duration of War	First, Graham	March 22, 1778 deserted.
More/Moore, Richard Private	April 3, 1777, Duration of War	First, Ten Broeck	April-June 1778.
Morgan, David Corporal	March 25, 1777, Three Years	Malcom's, Tom	Dec 1777 sick at Cakiat; Jan-Feb 1778 sick absent; March-April 1778; May-June 1778 sick State of New York.
Morley, Abner Private	May 5, 1778	Second, Ten Eyck	June 1778 sick White Plains.
Morpeth/Morpath, William Private	Nov 21, 1776, Duration of War	Fourth, Davis	Dec 1777-March 1778; April 1778 on command at Radnor; May 1778; June 1778 on command with Colonel Livngston.
Morrell/Morral, Isaac Drummer	Dec 2, 1776, Three Years	Second, Hallett	Dec 1777-June 1778
Morrell, John Private	Dec 7, 1776, Duration of War	Second, Hallett	Dec 1777-Jan 1778; Feb 1778 payroll only; March-April 1778; May 1778 payroll only; June 1778.
Morrill/Morrell, Joseph Sergeant	Dec 10, 1776, Duration of War	Fourth, Smith	Dec 1777-May 1778; June 1778 on furlough by General Clinton.
Morris/Mooris, Isaac Private	April 21, 1777, Three Years	First, Wendell	April-June 1778 on command General Schuyler's guard.
Morris, Matthew Private	May 5, 1778, Nine Months	Second, Wright	June 1778.
Morrison, David Private	May 5, 1778, Nine Months	Second, Riker	May-June 1778.
Morrison, Dunkin/Duncan Private	May 5, 1778, Nine Months	Fourth, Smith	May-June 1778.
Morrison, Edward Sergeant Major		First	April-June 1778.
Mosier/Mosure, John Private	April 9, 1777, Duration of War	Malcom's, Santford	Dec 1777-June 1778.

Moss, Ebenezer, Private	March 20, 1777, Duration of War	First, Copp	July 18, 1777 missing on scout; March 9, 1778 joined; March-June 1778.
Moss, Stephen Private	March 18, 1777, Duration of War	First, Graham	April-June 1778.
Mott, Isaac Private	May 5, 1778	Second	First appears on muster roll forOctober 1778.
Mott, Noah Private	Feb 1, 1777, Duration of War	Second, Pell	Dec 1777-Jan 1778; Feb 1778 on week's command; March 1778 on command; April-June 1778.
Mount, Richard Volunteer		First, Copp	April-June 1778. Though listed as a volunteer, he receives pay for these months as a private.
Mullen, John Private	Oct 24, 1776, Duration of War	First, Finck	April-June 1778.
Muller, Christopher 2nd. Lt.	Nov 21, 1776	First, Wendell	April-June 1778.
Muller, Jeremiah C. Ensign	Nov 21, 1776	First, Wendell	April 1778 on furlough; May-June 1778.
Muller/Multer, Peter Private	Sept 22, 1777, Duration of War	First, Finck	April-May 1778; June 1778 sick at Amswell.
Mulliner, Moses Private	Dec 7, 1776, Three Years	Second, Hallett	Dec 1777-Jan 1778; Feb 1778 payroll only; March-April 1778; May 1778 payroll only; June 1778.
Mulvaney/ Mulvoney, John Private	Duration of War	Malcom's, Irvine	Dec 1777; Jan-April 1778 on furlough; May-June 1778 on command Newton.
Munday, David Private	Duration of War	First, Van Ness	April-June 1778.
Munday/Monday, James Corporal	Nov 25, 1776, Duration of War	Fourth, Strong	Dec 1777 on duty; Jan-June 1778.
Munday, William 2nd. Lt.	Nov 21, 1776	Second, Riker	Dec 1777 wounded at Albany; Jan-March 1778 on furlough; April 1778; May 1778 Acting Quartermaster; June 1778.
Munroe, Peter Private	Nov 21, 1776, Duration of War	Fourth, Titus	Dec 1777-March 1778 sick absent; April 1778 sick at Albany; May 26, 1778 deserted.
Munsey, Nathaniel Private	Sept 30, 1777, Three Years	First, McCracken	April-May 1778; June 1778 left with Sergeant Kidd. (Kidd was left sick at Corryell's Ferry.)

Murphy, Daniel Private	March 26, 1777, Duration of War	Fourth, Sacket	Nov 20, 1777 deserted; Jan 1778 "Muster'd last deserted but was sick absent & since Join'd."; Feb-May 1778; June 20, 1778 died.
Murray/Murry, George Private	March 12, 1777, Duration of War	First, Finck	April-June 1778.
Murray, Isaac Private	May 5, 1778, Nine Months	Second, Riker	May 1778 sick in camp; June 1778.
Murray/Murry, William Sergeant	Aug 8, 1777, Three Years	First, Ten Broeck	April-June 1778.
Myers, Zackaria Private	May 5, 1778, Nine Months	Fourth, Smith	May-June 1778.
Nafee/Naffee, Garrett Private	Oct 27, 1777, Duration of War	First, Ten Broeck	April-June 1778.
Neas/Nease, George Private	May 5, 1778, Nine Months	Second, Wright	May 1778; May 1778 shows time of entry as May 19, 1778; June 1778 on furlough.
Neely/Neily, Abraham 1st. Lt.	March 25, 1777	Malcom's, Santford, Lucas	Dec 1777-Jan 1778; Feb-March 1778 on furlough; April 1778; May 1778 transferred to Lucas' Company; May 1778. Oath at Valley Forge on May 23, 1778.
Nelm/Nelme, Lemuel Jones Private	July 18, 1777, Duration of War	First, Copp	April 1778 sick at Fishkill; May 1778 sick in General Hospital Fishkill; June 1778 attending G. Hospital Fishkill.
Nesbit, Joseph Corporal/Private	Oct 18, 1777, Duration of War	First, Copp	April-June 1778; June 15, 1778 reduced to Private.
Newcomb, James Private	Jan 1, 1777, Three Years	Second, Ten Eyck	Dec 1777; Jan-Feb 1778 sick in quarters; March 1778 on command; April-May 1778; June 1778 payroll only.
Newkerk/Nukerck, Charles 1st. Lt.	Nov 21, 1776	Second, Lounsbery	Dec 1777-Feb 1778; March 1778 on guard; April-June 1778.
Newkirk/Nukirk, Myndert Private	May 1, 1778, Nine Months	Second, Lounsbery	May-June 1778.
Newman, Abraham Private	May 5, 1778, Nine Months	Fourth, Marvin	May-June 1778.
Nickobacker see Knickabocker			

Nickerson/ Nickeson, Thomas Drummer	Feb 17, 1777, Duration of War	Second, Pelton	Dec 1777; Jan-Feb 1778 on furlough; March 1778; April 1778 sick absent; May-June 1778.
Nicol/Nicoll, Simon Private	May 5, 1778, Nine Months	Fourth, Smith	May-June 1778.
Nisbet/Nesbett, Alexander/Alexr Drummer	Duration of War	Malcom's, Steel	Dec 1777-Feb 1778; March 1778 on furlough; April-May 1778; June 1778 sick near Corryells Ferry.
Niven/Nivon, Daniel Captain	July 2, 1777	Malcom's, Niven	Dec 1777 on command; Jan-Feb 1778; April-May 1778. Oath at Valley Forge on May 11, 1778.
Noise/Nowes, Lewis Private	Dec 17, 1776, Three Years	Second, Hallett	Dec 1777-Jan 1778
Norrant, George Private	May 5, 1777, Duration of War	Fourth, Pearsee	On record is his name and date of enlistment on a roll dated September 14, 1778, at White Plains, New York.
Norton, George Private	Nov 21, 1776, Duration of War	Fourth, Sacket	Dec 1777; Jan 1778 on party; Feb 1778 sick present; March-June 1778.
Norton, Henry Private	Jan 1, 1777, Three Years	First, McCracken	April-June 1778.
Norton, Nathaniel 1st. Lt.	Nov 21, 1776	Fourth, Sacket	Dec 1777; Jan 1778 on command; Feb-June 1778.
Nostrant, George Private	May 5, 1778, Nine Months	Fourth, Pearsee	May-June 1778.
Nottingham, Thomas Private	May 1, 1778, Nine Months	Second, Lounsbery	May-June 1778.
Nottingham, William Ensign	Nov 21, 1776	Second, Lounsbery	Dec 1777-Jan 1778; Feb 1778 on command; March-April 1778; May 1778 on furlough; June 1778.
Oakley, John Private	March 1, 1778	Second, Hallett	March 23, 1778 joined; April 1778 sick in camp; May 1778 payroll only; June 1778 sick in Pennsylvania.
O'Brian, John Private	Jan 20, 1777, Three Years	First, Ten Broeck	April-June 1778.
O'Brian, Thomas Drummer	Jan 20, 1777, Duration of War	First, Ten Broeck	April-June 1778.
O'Bryen/O'Bryan, Thomas Private	Nov 18, 1776, Duration of War	First, Hicks	April-June 1778.

Occurman,
William/Wm
  Sergeant/
  Private/Sergeant
	Jan 1, 1777,
	Duration of War
		Second,
		Ten Eyck
			Dec 1777; Jan 3, 1778 deserted; March 21, 1778 returned from desertion; March 1778 under sentence of a Court Martial; April 10, 1778 reduced to private; April-May 1778; June 1778 payroll only; June 21, 1778 promoted to Sergeant.

O'Donaghy, Patrick Private	Dec 3, 1776, Three Years	First, Hicks	April-June 1778.
Ogden/Ogdon, Daniel Private	April 4, 1777, Duration of War	First, Ten Broeck	April-June 1778.
Oliphant, William/Willm Private	Dec 14, 1776, Duration of War	First, Graham	April-June 1778.
Oliver, Richard 2nd. Lt.	March 11, 1777	Malcom's, Black	Dec 1777 sick in quarters; Jan 1778; Feb 1778 appointed Paymaster pro tem; Feb-May 1778. Oath at Valley Forge on May 11, 1778.
Olmsted/ Olmstead, John Private	March 6, 1777, Duration of War	Second, Pelton	Dec 1777 sick in camp; Jan-March 1778; April 1778 payroll only; May-June 1778.
Onbehand, John Fifer	May 12, 1777	Malcom's, Lucas	Jan-April 1778; May 1778 sick in hutts.
O'Neal/O'Neel, Nicholas Private	Duration of War	Malcom's, Steel	Dec 1777-Jan 1778; Feb-March 1778 on furlough; April 1778 on furlough at Carlisle; May 1778 Lord Stirling's guard; June 1778 sick Brunswick
O'Neil, James Private	March 4, 1777, Duration of War	First, Copp	April-June 1778.
Oosterheut, Gilbert, Private	May 5, 1778, Nine Months	Second, Wright	June 1778.
Oosterhoudt/ Osterhout, Henry/Hendrick Private	May 1, 1778, Nine Months	Second, Lounsbery	May-June 1778.
Oosterhoudt/ Osterhout, Peter/Petrus Private	May 1, 1778, Nine Months	Second, Lounsbery	May-June 1778.
Orr, William Sergeant/Private	Dec 23, 1776, Duration of War	First, Wendell	April-May 1778; May 8, 1778 "reduced to a Sentinel"; June 1778 left sick at Brunswick.

Osterhoudt, Cornelius Private	May 5, 1778	Second	First appears on the muster roll for October 1778.
Ostrander, Adam Private	May 5, 1778, Nine Months	Second, Hallett	First appears on rolls for July 1778.
Oudenkirke/ Ouderkirke, Myndert/Mindirt Private	Feb 24, 1777, Three Years	First, Finck	April-June 1778.
Ousterhout/ Oustorhout, Peter Private	May 27, 1777, Duration of War	Second, Wright	Dec 1777-March 1778; April 1778 sick in camp; May-June 1778.
Owens, Amiziah/ Ameziah Private	Dec 8, 1776, Duration of War	Fourth, Marvin	Dec 1777-Jan 1778 sick absent; Feb-April 1778 sick at Fishkill; May 1778 sick Nine Partners; June 1778.
Packal/Pickle, John H./John Henry Private	May 5, 1778, Nine Months	Fourth, Pearsee	May-June 1778.
Padder/Pedder, John Private	Jan 2, 1777, Three Years	Second, Hallett	Dec 1777; Jan 1778 on command; Feb 1778 on guard; March 1778 on command; April 1778; May 1778 payroll only; June 1778 sick at Valley Forge.
Paddock, John Private	Dec 15, 1776, Duration of War	First, Hicks	April-May 1778; June 1778 left sick on the road from Pennsylvania.
Pain, Silas Private	Nov 21, 1776, Duration of War	Fourth, Davis	Dec 1777-May 1778; June 1778 sick Pennsylvania.
Pagett, John Corporal	Duration of War	Malcom's, Irvine	Dec 1777-March 1778; April 1778 on guard; May-June 1778.
Palmer, Amaziah Private	May 5, 1778, Nine Months	Fourth, Titus	June 1, 1778 joined; June 1778 sick in Pennsylvania.
Palmer/Palmor Jonathan Private	June 6, 1777, Duration of War	Second, Wright	Dec 1777-Jan 1778; Feb 1778 sick in quarters; March 1778; April 1778 on guard; May 1778 sick present; June-Aug 1778 sick at Valley Forge.
Palmetier/ Palmeter, Joseph Private	March 10, 1777, Duration of War	Second, Pelton	Dec 1777-Feb 1778; March 1778 on guard; April 1778 payroll only; May 1778 sick present; June 6, 1778 died.
Parker, Elisha Fifer	April 16, 1778, Duration of War	First, Copp	April-June 1778.
Parker, James Corporal	Jan 13, 1777, Duration of War	First, Wendell	April-June 1778.

Parker, Richard James Drummer	Nov 1, 1777, Duration of War	First, Wendell	April-June 1778.
Parkins/Pirkins, Thomas Private	May 5, 1778, Nine Months	Fourth, Pearsee	May 1778 tending sick in hospital; June 1778 sick Valley Forge.
Parks, William/Wm Corporal	May 5, 1778	Fourth, Walker	May-June 1778.
Parry/Pary, John Private	May 5, 1778, Nine Months	Second, Ten Eyck	June 1778 payroll only.
Parshall/Pershall, James Sergeant	June 1, 1777, Duration of War	Fourth, Walker	Dec 1777; Jan-March 1778 on furlough; April-June 1778.
Parshall, John Private	May 5, 1778, Nine Months	Fourth, Walker	May 1778; June 1778 sick Crab Orchard.
Parsons/Parssons, Charles 1st. Lt.	Nov 21, 1776	First, Hicks	April-June 1778.
Paterson, Thomas McC. Private	Nov 28, 1777. Duration of War	First, Hicks	April 1778; May 27, 1778 deserted.
Patterson/Pattison, Michael Private	May 1, 1778, Nine Months	Second, Lounsbery	May-June 1778.
Pawling, Albert Major	Jan 27, 1777	Malcom's	Dec 1777-May 1778. Oath at Valley Forge on June 8, 1778.
Peacock, Hugh 2nd. Lt.	July 9, 1777	Malcom's, Niven	Dec 1777-Jan 1778; Feb 1778 on furlough; April-May 1778. Oath at Valley Forge on May 11, 1778.
Pearsee, Jonathan Captain	Nov 21, 1776	Fourth, Pearsee	Dec 1777; Jan-Feb 1778 on furlough; March 1778; April 23, 1778 resigned. Lieutenant Silas Gray commanded this company for the rest of Valley Forge Encampment.
Pease, Cunradt/Conreat Private	Feb 14, 1777, Duration of War	First, Finck	April-June 1778.
Pease, Hanyost Private	Jan 27, 1777, Duration of War	First, Finck	April-June 1778.
Peck, William/Willm Drummer	Duration of War	Malcom's, Black	Dec 1777-Jan 1778; Feb 1778 sick in quarters; March-May 1778.
Peek/Peck, William/Wm Corporal	Three Years	Malcom's, Niven	Dec 1777 sick nigh camp; Jan-Feb 1778 sick in quarters; April-May 1778.
Peers/Pierce, John Private	Nov 19, 1776, Duration of War	First, Hicks	April-May 1778; June 1778 on command Colonel Morgan.

Peirce, Thomas/Thos Private	May 5, 1778, Nine Months	Fourth, Davis	June 1778.
Pell, Samuel T./ Saml Captain	Nov 21, 1776	Second, Pell	Dec 1777-May 1778; June 1778 on furlough at Fredericksburg.
Pellam/Pelham, Francis Private	May 5, 1778, Nine Months	Second, Riker	May-June 1778.
Pelton, Benjamin Captain	Nov 21, 1777	Second, Pell	Dec 1777; Jan 1778 on command; Feb 1778 absent without leave; March 18, 1778 resigned. Abner French commanded this company for the rest of the Vally Forge Encampment.
Pennoyer/Penoyer, Jesse Fifer	Jan 1, 1777, Three Years	Fourth, Titus	Dec 1777-Jan 1778 sick absent; Feb-April 1778; May 1778 sick in quarters; June-September 1778 sick in Pennsylvania.
Penoyer, Israel Private	May 5, 1778, Nine Months	Fourth, Marvin	May-June 1778.
Perkins, James Private	Aug 27, 1777, Three Years	First, Van Ness	April-May 1778; June 1778 left sick on the march near Spotswood.
Perkins, Joseph Private	June 5, 1778	First, Van Ness	Recruit, June 5, 1778 joined; June 1778.
Perkins, Thomas Private	May 5, 1778	Fourth, Pearsee	May 1778 tending sick in hospital; June 1778 sick Valley Forge.
Peter, Samuel Private	May 4, 1778	Fourth, Sacket	First listed on muster roll dated September 10, 1778, at White Plains, New York.
Peters, John Corporal	Oct 23, 1777, Duration of War	First, Hicks	April-June 1778.
Peters, John Private	March 21, 1777, Three Years	Second, Pell	Nov 1777-Feb 1778 on furlough; March-June 1778.
Peterson, John Private	May 5, 1778	Second, Ten Eyck	June 1778 sick Peekskill.
Peterson/ Petterson, John Private	March 25, 1777, Three Years	Second, Pell	Dec 1777-Feb 1778 on furlough; March-May 1778; June 1778 payroll only.
Peterson, Simon/Simeon Private	Dec 1, 1777, Duration of War	Fourth, Sacket	Dec 1777-June 1778.
Petted/Pettet, Samuel Private	May 5, 1778, Nine Months	Fourth, Sacket	June 1778 sick in Pennsylvania.

Name, Rank	Enlisted	Company	Service
Pettit, Samuel Private	Nov 28, 1777, Duration of War	First, McCracken	April-June 1778.
Phelps, Ebenezer/ Ebenesor Private	May 26, 1778, Nine Months	Second, Graham	June 1778 small pox Valley Forge; July 1778 sick at Valley Forge.
Phenix, Mathew/Matthew Private	April 8, 1777, Duration of War	Second, Lounsbery	Dec 1777-March 1778 on furlough; April-May 1778 sick State of New York; June 1778 sick New York.
Philip, Christian, Jr. Private	Feb 24, 1777, Duration of War	First, Graham	April-June 1778.
Phillips, Samuel Private		Second, Hallett	Dec 1777 payroll only.
Pier, John Earnest, Sergeant	Oct 25, 1776, Duration of War	First, Finck	April-June 1778.
Plass, Peter Private	May 9, 1777, Three Years	Fourth, Pearsee	Dec 1777-Jan 1778 sick at Livingston Manor; Feb-May 1778 sick at Albany; June 1, 1778 deserted.
Platner, John Private	Duration of War	First, Finck	April-June 1778.
Plowman, Christopher Private		First, Ten Broeck	April 26, 1778 deserted.
Plumb/Plum, Stephen Private	Dec 13, 1776, Duration of War	Fourth, Sacket	Dec 1777-June 1778.
Pollard, Thomas Corporal	Jan 1, 1777, Duration of War	Fourth, Walker	Dec 1777 on command with the waggons; Jan-March 1778; April 1778 sick in camp; May-June 1778.
Polman, Samuel Private	May 5, 1778	Fourth,	First listed on muster roll dated September 10, 1778, at White Plains, NewYork.
Post, Cornelius Private	May 7, 1778, Nine Months	Second, Pell	May-June 1778.
Post, Samuel Private	April 19, 1777, Duration of War	Fourth, Pearsee	Dec 1777-March 1778 sick at Fishkill; April-May 1778; June 28, 1778 missing.
Potter, Isaac Private	Jan 29, 1777, Duration of War	Second, Wright	Dec 1777-Jan 1778; Feb 1778 on guard; March 20, 1778 died.
Potter, Samuel Corporal	Dec 13, 1776, Duration of War	First, Graham	April-June 1778.
Potter, William Private	Nov 13, 1776, Duration of War	First, Hicks	April-June 1778.

Powell/Powel, Stephen Private	Jan 1, 1777	Second, Pell	Dec 1777; Jan 1778 absent with leave; Feb 1778; March 1778 absent with leave; April-May 1778; June 1778 on furlough Sing Sing.
Powers, Charles Sergeant	May 26, 1777, Duration of War	Second, Pell	December 17, 1777 deserted.
Powers, Charles Private	May 1, 1778, Duration of War	Second, Pell	May 1778 sick present; June 1778 sick at Kakiat.
Preston, Benjamin/Benjm Private	May 5, 1778, Nine Months	Fourth, Smith	May-June 1778.
Preston, Jonathan Corporal	Oct 1, 1777, Duration of War	First, Copp	April 1778; May 1778 sick regimental hospital; June 1778 sick in General Hospital Cuckolds Town.
Prier, Peter Private	Duration of War	Malcom's, Irvine	Dec 1777 on command; Jan 1778 sick absent. February 1778 rolls show he died on March 2, 1778.
Prince, Kemble/Kimble Sergeant	June 19, 1777, Three Years	Second, Graham	Dec 1777 payroll only Jan 1778; Feb 1778 sick in smallpox; March-June 1778.
Prindle, Jotham Private	Duration of War	First, Wendell	April-May 1778; June 1778 on duty.
Pritchard, Thomas/Thos Private	Dec 21, 1776, Three Years	Second, Hallett	Dec 1777; Jan 1778 sick in camp; Feb 1778 payroll only; March 24, 1778 died.
Proper, Frederick Private	Feb 9, 1777, Three Years	First, Wendell	April-May 1778; June 1778 on duty.
Provoost/Provost, Robert Jr. Pay Master	Nov 21, 1776	Second	Dec 1777-Feb 1778; March-April 1778 on furlough; May 1778; June 1778 on furlough.
Pudney/Putney, James Private	May 1, 1778, Nine Months	Second, Lounsbery	May 1778; June 1778 sick in Jersey.
Puhle, John Henry Private	May 5, 1778	Fourth, Pearsee	First listed on muster roll dated September 10, 1778, at White Plains, NewYork.
Pulman, Salter Private	Feb 20, 1777, Duration of War	Second, Pelton	Dec 1777; Jan 1778 on command; Feb 1778; March 1778 on command; April 1778; May 1778 payroll only; June 1778 tending sick.
Punderson, John Ensign	Nov 21, 1776	Fourth, Titus	Dec 1777 sick absent.
Pumshin/ Pumpshin, Daniel Private	June 1, 1777, Duration of War	Second, Hallett	Dec 1777-Jan 1778; Feb 1778 payroll only; March-April 1778; May 1, 1778, died.

Putman/Putnam, William Private	Feb 9, 1777, Duration of War	Fourth, Smith	Dec 1777 sick absent Albany; Jan 1778 sick at Albany; Feb 1778; March-April 1778 sick in quarters; May 1778 sick in camp; June 1778.
Quackenbush, Jacob Private	Feb 18, 1777, Three Years	First, Van Ness	April 1, 1778 deserted.
Quant, Henry Private	Three Years	Fourth, Pearsee	June 1778 muster roll shows he deserted on July 13, 1778.
Rady/Redey, James Private	Dec 2, 1776, Duration of War	Second, Riker	Dec 1777-Jan 1778; Feb 1778 on fatigue; March 1778 absent with leave; April-May 1778; June 1778 on guard.
Ramsey, Adam Private	Feb 20, 1777, Three Years	First, McCracken	April-June 1778.
Ramson/Ramsom, Henry Private	May 7, 1778, Nine Months	Second, Pell	May-June 1778.
Randall, Moses Private	May 5, 1778, Nine Months	Fourth, Smith	May 1778; June 1778 sick Princeton.
Randall, Nathaniel/Nathl Private	May 5, 1778, Nine Months	Fourth, Smith	May-June 1778.
Randle/Randel, John Private	May 5, 1778, Nine Months	Second, Riker	May-June 1778.
Randles/Rannels, John Ensign		Malcom's, Steel	Dec 1777; Jan 1778 on furlough; March 8, 1778 resigned.
Ranier, George Private	May 5, 1778, Nine Months	Fourth, Titus	June 18, 1778 joined; June 1778 sick in Jersies.
Ranken/Rankin, Daniel Private	Jan 13, 1777, Duration of War	First, Wendell	April-May 1778; June 1778 on command with Colonel Morgan.
Rankins, James Private	March 10, 1777, Duration of War	First, Finck	April-June 1778.
Ransier, John Private	Jan 12, 1777, Duration of War	First, Finck	April-June 1778.
Rapp, George Private	May 5, 1778, Nine Months	Second, Pelton	May-June 1778.
Rough/Ruff, Conrade/Conrad Private	May 5, 1778, Nine Months	Fourth, Walker	June 1778.
Ray, Isaac Private	May 5, 1778, Nine Months	Second, Ten Eyck	May-June 1778.
Ray, James Drummer	Jan 2, 1777, Duration of War	First, McCracken	April-June 1778.

Ray/Reay, John Private	Duration of War	Malcom's, Steel	Dec 1777-March 1778; April-May 1778 on command at Carlisle; sick Brunswick.
Raynolds/Randels, Joseph Private	April 15, 1777, Three Years	Second, Pell	Dec 1777 sick present; Jan-Feb 1778; March 1778 on command; April-May 1778; June 1778 payroll only.
Raynor, Ichabod Private	Nov 21, 1776, Duration of War	Fourth, Davis	Dec 1777-Jan 1778; Feb 1778 on command; March 1778 on party; April 1778 on guard; May 1778 sick in hospital; June 8, 1778 died.
Realy/Raely, James Private	Jan 16, 1777, Three Years	Second, Hallett	Dec 1777-Jan 1778; Feb 1778 payroll only; March 1778 sick in camp; April 1778; May 1778 payroll only; June 1778 sick in Pennsylvania.
Reamer/Roemer, Peter Private	Duration of War	Malcom's, Kearsley	Dec 1777 wounded hospital; Jan 1778 sick at Lancaster; Feb 1778 hospital at Lancaster; March 1778 Lancaster Hospital sick; April 1778 sick at Lancaster.
Reamer/Roemer, Philip Fifer	Duration of War	Malcom's, Kearsley	Dec 1777-April 1778.
Reed/Reid, Daniel/Danl Private	Duration of War	Malcom's, Black	Dec 1777 attending sick; Jan 1778 sick in quarters; Feb 1778; March 1778 sick present; April-May 1778 sick in camp.
Reed, Thomas Private	Dec 12, 1776, Duration of War	First, Copp	April 1778; May 17, 1778 deserted.
Rees, Martinus Private	Jan 7, 1777, Duration of War	First, Wendell	April-June 1778.
Reeves/Reves, Israel Private	Nov 21, 1776, Duration of War	Fourth, Titus	Dec-March 1778 sick absent; April 1778; May-June 1778 on furlough.
Regnier, Pierre Lieutenant Colonel	Nov 21, 1776	Fourth	Dec 1777 on command for the clothing of the regiment at Albany; Jan-May 1778; June 1778 in arrest
Reir/Rair, John Private	Oct 28, 1777, Duration of War	First, Finck	April-June 1778.
Relay, Lewis Private	Nov 15, 1776, Duration of War	First, Hicks	April-June 1778.
Rennols, Eli Private	May 5, 1778, Nine Months	Fourth, Smith	First appears on the muster roll for July 1778,

Revelea/Ravelia, Eselia/Eselea L. Private	Three Years	First, Van Ness, McCracken	April 1778; May 23, 1778 "exchanged for Sergeant Richards" and transferred to McCracken's Company; May-June 1778. See Richards, Simon.
Reyning, Jacob Private	Dec 14, 1776, Duration of War	First, Wendell	April 26, 1778 deserted.
Reynolds, Ebenezer/ Ebonezer Corporal	Jan 1, 1777, Duration of War	Fourth, Titus	Dec 1777-March 1778 sick absent; April 1778 sick at Albany; May 26, 1778 deserted.
Reynolds/Runnels, James Private	May 12, 1778, Nine Months	Second, Graham	May 1778; June 1778 on furlough.
Reynolds, James Private	Jan 1, 1777, Three Years	Fourth, Titus	Dec 1777-Feb 1778; March 1778 on main guard; April-June 1778.
Reynolds/Runnals, Timothy Private	Nov 21, 1776, Duration of War	Fourth, Sacket	Dec 1777-Jan 1778 on duty; Feb 1778; March 1778 sick in hutts; April 1778 sick present; May-June 1778.
Rich, Henry Corporal	Jan 1, 1777, Three Years	Second, Pell	Dec 1777; Jan 1778 on duty; Feb-May 1778; June 1778 on furlough at Bedford.
Rich, John Private	June 15, 1777, Three Years	Malcom's, Tom	Dec 1777; Jan-Feb 1778 on command; March-June 1778.
Richards/ Ritchards, Simon Private/Sergeant	Duration of War	First, McCracken / Van Ness	April 1778-May 1778; May 23, 1778 promoted to Sergeant and "exchanged for Lewis Revelia Capt V. Ness Compy"; June 1778 on command with Colonel Morgan. See Revelea, Eselia.
Richardson, William/Wm Private	Duration of War	Malcom's, Niven	Dec 1777; Jan 5, 1778 deserted.
Richmond, Benjamin Private	May 4, 1778, Nine Months	Second, Wright	June 1778.
Rider/Ryder, John Private	March 1, 1777, Three Years	Second, Pell	Dec 1777-May 1778; June-Aug 1778 on command at Valley Forge.
Riely/Rilley, John Private/Corporal	April 24, 1777, Duration of War	Malcom's, Lucas	Dec 1777; Jan-Feb 1778 on command; Feb 1778 promoted to Corporal; March-May 1778.
Riggs, Daniel Private	April 12, 1777, Duration of War	Fourth, Davis	Dec 1777-March 1778 sick absent; April-June 1778 sick at Danbury.

Riker, Abraham Captain	Nov 1, 1776	Second, Riker	Dec 1777; Jan-Feb 1778 on furlough; March 1778 sick in camp; April 1778; May 7, 1778 died.
Riley, James Private	Nov 18, 1776, Duration of War	First, Hicks	April-June 1778 on command General Schuyler's Guard.
Rinner, Jonathan Private	Nov 21, 1776	Fourth, Sacket	Only record is his name and date of enlistment on a muster roll dated September 14, 1778, at White Plains, New York.
Rion/Rayn, John Private/Corporal	Duration of War	Malcom's, Niven	Dec 1777-Feb 1778; Feb 1778 promoted to Corporal; April-May 1778.
Rippy, Elijah, Private	Duration of War	Malcom's, Niven	Dec 1777-Jan 1778; Feb 1778 sick in quarters; April 1778; May 1778 on fatigue.
Ritchie/Ricthie, Alexander/Alex Private	Jan 1, 1777, Duration of War	Fourth, Walker	Dec 1777-March 1778; April 1778 on command at Radnor; May 1778 on main guard; June 1778.
Ritchie, Charles Private	Nov 28, 1776, Duration of War	First, Graham	April-June 1778.
Ritchie, Isick/ Isaac Private	May 5, 1778	Fourth, Titus	First appears on muster roll for August 1778 as sick in Pennsylvania.
Ritter, Antoney/ Anthony Private	April 22, 1777, Duration of War	Malcom's, Lucas	Dec 1777; Jan 1778 sick in quarters; Feb 4, 1778 deserted.
Roach, William/Wm Private	May 5, 1778, Nine Months	Second, Riker	May-June 1778.
Roads, Jacob Private	May 5, 1778, Nine Months	Fourth, Sacket	June 1778 sick in Jersies.
Robbison/ Robinson, James Private	Jan 1, 1777, Duration of War	Fourth, Walker	Dec 1777-June 1778.
Robert, John 1st. Lt./Captain Lieutenant	March 17, 1777	Malcom's, Tom	Dec 1777-Jan 1778; Feb 1778 on command; March-April 1778 on furlough; May-June 1778; June 16, 1778 promoted to Captain Lieutenant.
Roberts, Caleb Private	Feb 17, 1777, Duration of War	Second, Pell	Dec 1777; Jan 1778 on main guard; Feb 1778 sick smallpox; March 1778; April 1778 payroll only; May 1778 on guard; June 1778 Pennsylvania sick.
Roberts, John Private	June 30, 1778, Nine Months	Fourth, Walker	June 1778 sick Crab Orchard.

Roberts, Jonathan/Jonn Private	April 30, 1777, Duration of War	Second, Riker	Dec 1777-June 1778.
Robertson/ Robison, Daniel/Danl Private	Duration of War	Malcom's, Niven	Dec 1777 sick in hospital; Jan 1778 sick in quarters; Feb 1778 sick in hospital; April 1778 sick hospital Reading; May 1778 sick Reading.
Robertson, James Corporal	Duration of War	Malcom's, Niven	Dec 1777-Feb 1778; April-May 1778.
Robertson, John Private	May 5, 1778	Second, Ten Eyck	June 1778 payroll only.
Robertson/ Robinson, Joseph Drum Major		Malcom's	Dec 1777-May 1778.
Robins/Robin, Evan/Even Private	May 5, 1778	Fourth, Marvin	May 1778 in inoculation; June 1778.
Robinson, James Private	May 5, 1778, Nine Months	Fourth, Davis	May 1778; June 16, 1778 died.
Robinson, William Private	May 5, 1778, Nine Months	Second, Pell	May 1778 in small pox; June 1778 sick at Brunswick.
Rocker, Joseph Musician/Private	June 13, 1777	First, Copp	March 25, 1778 reduced to Private; April 1778; May 1778 sick regimental hospital; June 1778 sick in hospital Cuckolds Town.
Rodgers/Rogers James Private	Three Years	Malcom's, Black	Dec 1777-Jan 1778; Feb 1778 on duty; March 1778 sick present; April-May 1778 sick in camp.
Rodgers/Rogers, Samuel Private	Three Years	Malcom's, Black	Dec 1777-Feb 1778; March 1778 on furlough; April-May 1778.
Roe, John Private	May 5, 1778, Nine Months	Fourth, Davis	May-June 1778.
Rogers/Rodgers, William/Wm Sergeant/Private	Dec 1, 1777, Three Years	Malcom's, Tom	Dec 1777-Feb 1778; March-April 1778 sick present; May-June 1778; June 1778 reduced to Private.
Romer, Peter Private	May 5, 1778, Nine Months	Fourth, Strong	May 1778; June 1778 sick in Jerseys.
Ronnels/Runnels, John Private	Jan 1, 1777, Three Years	Second, Pell	Dec 1777-March 1778; April 1778 on main guard; May 1778; June 1778 payroll only.
Roome/Rome, Benjamin Corporal/Private	Jan 1, 1777, Duration of War	Fourth, Walker	Dec 1777; Jan-March 1778 sick absent; April 27, 1778 reduced to Private; April-June 1778.
Roosa, Abraham Private	May 1, 1778, Nine Months	Second, Lounsbery	May-June 1778.

Roosa, Ary/Aron Corporal	May 1, 1777, Duration of War	Second, Lounsbery	Dec 1777-Jan 1778 sick in hospital at Fishkill; Feb 1778 sick in hospital; Feb 26, 1778 died.
Roosa, Jacob Private	May 1, 1778, Nine Months	Second, Lounsbery	May 1778; June 1778 on guard.
Rose/Roose, Andrew Private	Jan 1, 1777, Duration of War	Fourth, Walker	Dec 1777-May 1778; June 1778 tending the sick at Valley Forge.
Rose/Rosa, Isaac A. Ensign/2nd. Lt.	Nov 21, 1776	Fourth, Smith Davis	Dec 1777 sick absent; Jan 9, 1778 joined; Jan 22, 1778 resigned.
Rose, James Private	Dec 13, 1776, Three Years	Second, Hallett	Dec 1777-Jan 1778; Feb 1778 payroll only; March-April 1778; May 1778 payroll only; June 1778.
Rose, John Private	Nov 26, 1776, Duration of War	First, Copp	April-June 1778.
Rosman, Adam Private	May 9, 1777, Three Years	Fourth, Pearsee	Dec 1777 exchanged for John Williams. See Williams, John.
Rosman, Philip Private	Nov 28, 1776, Duration of War	First, Graham	April-June 1778.
Ross, William Private	Dec 15, 1776, Three Years	Fourth, Smith	Dec 1777; Jan-March 1778 sick in hospital; April 1778 sick Yellow Springs; May-June 1778.
Rotchery, James Private	Jan 23, 1777, Duration of War	First, Van Ness	April-June 1778.
Rotts/Roots, Martain/Martin Private	May 10, 1777, Duration of War	Malcom's, Lucas	Dec 1777-Feb 1778 sick in hospital; March 1778 on command; April-May 1778.
Royal, Peter Private	May 5, 1778, Nine Months	Second, Riker	May-June 1778.
Rudolph, Christopher Private	Duration of War	First, Wendell	April-June 1778.
Ruland/Rewland, Jehiel/Jehial Private	Nov 21, 1776, Duration of War	Fourth, Sacket	Dec 1777; Jan 1778 on party; Feb 1778; March 1778 on party; April-May 1778; June 1778 sick in Pennsylvania.
Rund/Rand, Simon/Symon Private	May 5, 1778, Nine Months	Second, Riker	May-June 1778.
Runnells/Runnols, Elijah Private	May 5, 1778, Nine Months	Fourth, Strong	May-June 1778.
Runnels, Joseph Private	May 5, 1778, Nine Months	Fourth, Strong	June-July 1778 sick in Pennsylvania.
Runnian, Benjamin/Benjm Private	Feb 1, 1777, Duration of War	First, Ten Broeck	April-June 1778.

Rushe, Anthony D. Private	Jan 1, 1777, Duration of War	First, Fourth	Only record is his name and date of enlistment on a muster roll dated September 14, 1778, at White Plains, New York.
Russell, James Private	Jan 24, 1777, Three Years	First, Van Ness	April 1778 sick Schnectady State of New York; May 1778 sick in Schnectady New York State; June 1778 sick in Schnectady Hospital.
Russell/Rissel, Jonathan Private	Nov 21, 1776, Duration of War	Fourth, Davis	Dec 1777-March 1778; April 1778 on fornight command; May-June 1778.
Ryan, Thomas Private	March 11, 1777, Duration of War	First, Graham	Muster rolls for April-June 1778 show him lame at Fishkill. The payroll for April 1778 shows he deserted on April 25, but he receives pay for the months of May and June 1778.
Ryckman, Wilhelmus Ensign	Nov 21, 1776	First, Hicks	April-June 1778.
Rynax/Rynex, William Sergeant	Nov 28, 1776, Duration of War	First, Copp	April-June 1778.
Sacket, Samuel Captain	Nov 21, 1776	Fourth, Sacket	Dec 1777-June 1778.
Sackett/Sacket, Peter Adjutant	Nov 21, 1776	Fourth	Dec 1777 sick at Goshen, New York; Jan-June 1778.
Sacknutt, John Private	May 5, 1778	Fourth, Smith	First appears on a muster roll dated September 14, 1778, at White Plains, New York.
Salisbury, Barent Staats/Staates 1st. Lt.	Nov 21, 1776	First, Copp	April-June 1778.
Salisbury, John Private	March 23, 1777, Duration of War	First, Copp	April 1778; May 1778 sick regimental hospital; June 1778 sick in hospital Cuckoldstown.
Salisbury, Joseph Private	March 18, 1777, Three Years	First, Graham	April-June 1778.
Saltsman, Peter Private	Jan 26, 1777, Duration of War	First, Finck	April-June 1778.
Sammons/Samons, Cornelius Private	May 5, 1778, Nine Months	Second, Riker	May 1778 sick in camp; June 1778 sick Valley Forge.
Samson, George Private	May 5, 1778, Nine Months	Second, Riker	May-June 1778.
Sandford/Sanford, Daniel Private	Nov 21, 1776, Duration of War	Fourth, Davis	Dec 1777-Feb 1778; March 1778 on command; April-June 1778.

Sandford, John Private	Jan 1, 1777, Duration of War	Fourth, Walker	June 1778 sick in Pennsylvania.
Sangh, Peter Private	Oct 28, 1777, Duration of War	First, Finck	April-May 1778; June 1778 on guard.
Santford/ Sandford, John Captain	March 11, 1777	Malcom's, Santford	Dec 1777 sick at Lancaster; Jan 1778 sick absent; Feb 1778 sick; March-April 1778; April 1778 lame at the hutts; June 1778. Oath at Valley Forge on May 11, 1778, last name appears as Sandford.
Sarjeson/Sargeson, William Drummer	Jan 8, 1777, Duration of War	Second, Pell	Dec 1777; Jan 1778 on command; Feb-June 1778.
Sattalley/Satally, Richard Private	Nov 21, 1776, Duration of War	Fourth, Titus	Dec 1777-March 1778 sick absent; April 1778 sick at Albany; May 26, 1778 deserted.
Saunders, Robert Private	March 16, 1777, Duration of War	First, Graham	April-June 1778.
Saxton, Gilbert, Sergeant	March 1, 1777, Duration of War	Fourth, Strong	Dec 1777-Feb 1778 on furlough; March 20, 1778 deserted.
Scates/Seates, James Private	March 11, 1777, Duration of War	Fourth, Strong	Dec 1777 sick in hospital; Jan-March 1778; April 1778 sick in quarters; May 1778 sick in hospital; June 1778 sick Pennsylvania.
Schellenburgh/ Shelenbergh, George Private	April 9, 1778, Three Years	First, Finck	May-June 1778.
Schriver/Scriver, Jacob N. Sergeant/Private	April 19, 1777, Duration of War	Fourth, Pearsee	Dec 10, 1777 reduced to Private; Dec 1777; Jan-Feb 1778 on party; March 1778 on general guard; March 19, 1778 transferred to the Commander-in Chief's Guard, and served until his death on Dec 1, 1780.
Schutt, Frederick/Fredk Private	May 5, 1778, Nine Months	Second, Ten Eyck	May 1778; June 1778 sick at Valley Forge.
Scott/Skoot, Elexander/ Alexander Private	May 5, 1778, Nine Months	Fourth, Strong	May-June 1778.
Scott, James Fifer	May 2, 1778	Second, Lounsbery	May-June 1778.
Scott, James Private	May 5, 1778, Nine Months	Fourth, Davis	May-June 1778.
Scott, John Private	Three Years	Malcom's, Black	Dec 1777-March 1778; April-May 1778.

Name	Enlistment	Regiment	Service
Scott, William Private	May 5, 1778	Second, Pell	
Scott/Scot, William/Wm Private	Duration of War	Malcom's, Kearsley	Dec 1777; Jan 1778 sick present; Feb-March 1778; April 1778 on command at the lines.
Scrivenor/ Schrivenor, Zador Private	March 11, 1777, Duration of War	First, Graham	April-May 1778 on command General Schuyler's guard; June 1778 on command General Schuyler's guard Saratoga.
Scudder, William 2nd. Lt.	Nov 21, 1776	First, Ten Broeck	April-June 1778.
Seager/Seager, Thomas Private		First, Van Ness	May-June 1778 sick in Albany Hospital.
Seamore/Siemore, Henry Private	Oct 24, 1776, Duration of War	First, Finck	April-June 1778.
Sedore/Sedere, John Private	March 20, 1777, Duration of War	Second, Wright	Dec 1777-May 1778; June-July 1778 sick Valley Forge.
Seeds, George/Geo. Private	Jan 1, 1777, Duration of War	Fourth, Walker	Dec 1777-June 1778.
Seeger, John Private	Duration of War	First, Wendell	April-June 1778.
Selfridge/ Sulfridge, William Quartermaster Sergeant		First	April 1778; April 1778 on duty; June 1778.
Sellers, Michael Private	Dec 7, 1776, Duration of War	Second, Hallett	Dec 1777-Jan 1778; Feb 1778 payroll only; March-April 1778; May 1778 payroll only; June 1778.
Serjeants/Serjeant, William Private	May 9, 1777, Duration of War	Malcom's, Santford	Dec 1777; Jan 1778 sick in hospital; Feb 1778 in hospital Reading; March 1778 sick in hospital; April 1778 Princeton; May 6, 1778 joined Invalid Corps.
Servise/Service, Philip Private	April 4, 1777, Duration of War	First, Copp	April-May 1778; June 1778 on command with Colonel Morgan.
Seton, William Private	May 5, 1778, Nine Months	Second, Graham	May 1778 sick small pox; June 1778 sick Cranbury.
Severe, Robert Private		Malcom's, Niven	April 1778 exchanged for John Dempsy.

Seward, John Private	April 13, 1777, Three Years	Malcom's, Tom	Dec 1777 sick absent; Jan-Feb 1778 sick in quarters; March 1778 on command; April 1778 sick present; May 1778 sick Regimental hospital; June 1778 sick Yellow Springs.
Shannon, Thomas Private	Oct 28, 1776, Duration of War	First, Hicks	April-June 1778.
Sharp, Lewis Private	March 11, 1777, Duration of War	First, McCracken	April-May 1778; June 1778 on command with Colonel Morgan.
Sharp, Thomas Private	Oct 24, 1776, Duration of War	First, McCracken	April-May 1778; June 1778 sick at Cuckolds Town.
Shavalier/Chevalier, John Private	March 11, 1777, Three Years	Fourth, Titus	Dec 1777-Jan 1778 on furlough; Feb 1778 on guard; March-April 1778; June 1778 sick in the Jersies.
Shaw, Ichabod Private	May 5, 1778, Nine Months	Second, Pelton	May-June 1778.
Shaw, William/Wm Sergeant	Duration of War	Malcom's, Kearsley	Dec 1777-March 1778; April 1778 on command at Carlisle.
Shearman/Shearmon, Jesse Private	Oct 26, 1776, Duration of War	First, Van Ness	April 1778 prisoner in camp; May 1778 taken by Colonel Cortlandt by prior date of Inlistment.
Sheely/Shely, John Private	Oct 7, 1777, Duration of War	First, Finck	April-May 1778; June 28, 1778 wounded & sent to Princeton Hospital.
Shelden/Sheldon, Joseph Private	May 30, 1777, Duration of War	Malcom's, Santford	Dec 1777-Jan 1778 sick at hospital; Feb 1778 in hospital Reading; March 1778 sick in hospital; April 1778 Reading Hospital; May 1778; June 1778 Yellow Springs.
Sherman/Shereman, Jesse Private	Dec 1, 1776, Three Years	Second, Graham	Dec 1777 payroll only; Jan-March 1778 on command artillery; April-June 1778.
Sherwood, Abraham Private	June 1, 1777, Three Years	Second, Lounsbery	Dec 1777-May 1778; June 1778 absent with leave.
Sherwood, Adiel/Adiele 1st. Lt.	Nov 21, 1776	First, Wendell, Ten Broeck	April 1778; May 1778 transferred to and took command of what had been Ten Broeck's Company; May 1778; June 1778 on command Valley Forge.
Sherwood, James Sergeant	Aug 21, 1777, Duration of War	Second, Pelton	Dec 1777 on furlough; Jan-March 1778; April 1778 payroll only; May 1778 on guard; June 1778.

Name	Enlistment	Regiment	Service
Sherwood/ Sherewood, Micijah/Micajah Private	Nov 21, 1776, Duration of War	Fourth, Sacket	Dec 1777-March 1778; March-June 1778 on His Excellency's Guard. He served in the Commander-in-Chiefs Guard until November 3, 1783.
Sherwood, Nathen/Nathan Private	Feb 26, 1777, Duration of War	Second, Pelton	Dec 1777; Jan 1778 on command; Feb-March 1778; April 1778 payroll only; May 1778 sick in the hospital; June 1778 Pennsylvania sick.
Shields/Shelds, John Private		Malcom's, Niven	Dec 20, 1777 deserted.
Shirdon/Shereton, Thomas Private	Duration of War	Malcom's, Niven	Dec 1777. Jan 1778 muster roll shows he deserted on January 20, 1778, but the payroll pays him for the entire month with the notation "put down in the muster roll as a deserter but since joined his compy." Feb 1778; April-May 1778.
Shirts, Hendrick Private	May 17, 1777, Duration of War	First, Wendell	April-June 1778.
Shockey/Shocky, Christian Private	Duration of War	Malcom's, Kearsley	Dec 1777-Jan 1778; Feb-April 1778 on furlough.
Shoemaker, Peter Private	April 28, 1777, Duration of War	Malcom's, Lucas	Dec 1777-Feb 1778 sick in hospital; March 1778 on command; April-May 1778.
Shove, Frederick Private	May 5, 1778, Nine Months	Second, Pelton	June 1778.
Showcraft/ Shoecraft, John Corporal/ Sergeant	Jan 1, 1777, Three Years	Second, Pell	Dec 1777-Jan 1778; Jan 4, 1778 promoted to Sergeant; Feb-June 1778.
Shutler, John Private	April 21, 1777, Three Years	Second, Hallett	Dec 1777-Jan 1778; Feb 1778 payroll only; March-April 1778; May 1778 payroll only; June 1778.
Shutts/Sheets, John Sergeant	Jan 3, 1777, Three Years	First, Hicks	April-June 1778.
Sibbio/Sibio, Thomas Sergeant/Private/ Sergeant	May 1, 1777, Duration of War	Fourth, Walker	Dec 1777-March 1778; April 1778 on party in Radnor; April 1778; June 15, 1778 reduced to Private; June 1778; July 15, 1778 promoted to Sergeant.

Sickells/Sickels, Garrett/Garet Sergeant	April 24, 1777	Malcom's, Lucas	Dec 1777; Jan 1778 on furlough; Feb-March 1778 on command; April-May 1778.
Silsbury/Silsby, David Private	Jan 25, 1777	Second, Graham	Dec 1777 payroll only; Jan-March 1778 sick at New Windsor; April 1778 sick near Goshen; May 1778 sick at Goshen; June 1778 Goshen.
Simmons, Caleb Private	May 5, 1778, Nine Months	Fourth, Smith	May 1778.
Simmons/ Simmonds, John Private	Nov 21, 1776, Duration of War	Fourth, Davis	Dec 1777; Jan 1778 on command at Gulf Mills; Feb-May 1778; June 1778 sick at Hopewell Jersey.
Simmons/ Simmonds, Joshua Private	Jan 1, 1777, Duration of War	Fourth, Walker	Dec 1777-May 1778; June 1778 on furlough North Castle.
Sin John/St. John, Tedious/Thadeus Private	May 5, 1778, Nine Months	Second, Pelton	June 1778.
Sinnott/Sinnot, Patrick Sergeant	Nov 21, 1776, Duration of War	Fourth, Davis	Dec 1777-May 1778; June sick Pennsylania.
Sisco/Sipeo, Dick Private	May 5, 1778, Nine Months	Fourth, Strong	May 1778; June 1778 sick Pennsylvania.
Sitzer, Barant Private	May 5, 1778, Nine Months	Fourth, Walker	June 1778 sick Pennsylvania
Skinner, Isaac Private	May 5, 1778, Nine Months	Second, Pelton	June 1778.
Slone/Sloan, Hugh Private	July 1, 1777, Duration of War	First, McCracken	April-June 1778.
Sloughter/ Slaughter, Jonas Private	Jan 20, 1777, Duration of War	First, Ten Broeck	April-June 1778.
Sloughter/ Slaughter, Nicholas Sergeant	Aug 6, 1777, Duration of War	First, Ten Broeck	April 1778; May 1778 sick present; June 1778 sick Valley Forge.
Slump, Martin Private	Oct 26, 1777, Duration of War	First, Ten Broeck	April-May 1778; June 1778 sick Princeton.
Slutt, Peter Private	Dec 7, 1776, Three Years	Second, Hallett	Dec 1777 waggoner; Jan 1778; Feb 1778 payroll only; March-April 1778; May 1778 on guard; June 1778.
Sly, Samuel Sergeant	Three Years	Malcom's, Black	Dec 1777 sick in hospital; Jan 1778 sick in quarters; Feb-May 1778.

Smalley/Smally, Timothy Private	Jan 1, 1777, Duration of War	Fourth, Walker	Dec 1777-Jan 1778 sick Albany; Feb-April 1778 sick in hospital Albany; April 1778 sick at Albany; June 1778.
Smily, Thomas Private	May 5, 1778, Nine Months	Second, Pelton	June 1778.
Smith, Benjamin Private	Dec 8, 1776, Duration of War	Fourth, Marvin	Dec 1777-March 1778 sick at Fishkill; April 1778; May 1778 sick in camp; June 1778.
Smith, Caleb Private	Dec 2, 1776, Duration of War	Second, Riker	Dec 1777 Tending Lieutenant Munday in Albany; Jan-Feb 1778 on furlough; March 1778; April 1778 sick in camp; May-June 1778.
Smith, Caleb Private	May 5, 1778, Nine Months	Fourth, Smith	First appears on muster roll for July 1778.
Smith, David Private	Jan 8, 1777, Duration of War	First, McCracken	April 1778; May 1778 sick regimental hospital; June 1778 sick at Cuckolds Town.
Smith, David Private	Nov 21, 1776, Duration of War	Fourth, Davis	Dec 1777-March 1778; April 1778 sick in camp; May-June 1778.
Smith, Elijah Private	May 5, 1778, Nine Months	Second, Riker	Dec 1777-April 1778; May 1778 sick in camp; June 1778.
Smith, Ezekiel Private	May 5, 1778, Nine Months	Second, Pelton	May-June 1778.
Smith, Gersholm/ Gersham Private	Nov 21, 1776, Duration of War	Fourth, Titus	Dec 1777-Feb 1778; March 1778 on command; April 1778 on command at Radnor; May 1778; June-Aug 1778 sick in Pennsylvania.
Smith, Gideon Private	May 5, 1778, Nine Months	Fourth, Smith	First appears on muster roll for July 1778.
Smith, Isaac Surgeon's Mate	Nov 21, 1776	Second	Dec 1777-June 1778.
Smith, Israel Captain	Nov 21, 1776	Fourth, Smith	Dec 1777; Jan-Feb 1778 on furlough; March-June 1778.
Smith, James Corporal/ Sergeant/ Private	June 1, 1777, Duration of War	Fourth, Sacket	Dec 1777 promoted to Sergeant; Dec 1777 recruiting; Jan-March 1778; March 20, 1778 reduced to Private; April-May 1778; June 1778 on command with General Poor.
Smith, John Private	Dec 3, 1776, Duration of War	First, McCracken	April-May 1778; June 1778 sick at Cuckolds Town.
Smith, John Sergeant	Jan 1, 1777, Duration of War	Second, Graham	Nov 1777-March 1778 sick at Fishkill; April-June 1778.

Smith, John Ensign	February 1777	Malcom's, Irvine	Dec 1777-Feb 1778; March 1, 1778 resigned.
Smith, John Private	May 5, 1778, Nine Months	Fourth, Smith	First appears on muster roll for July 1778.
Smith, Josiah Sergeant	May 5, 1778, Nine Months	Fourth, Titus	June 1, 1778 joined; June 1778.
Smith, Moses Private	Dec 23, 1776	Fourth, Smith	Dec 1777 sick absent Fishkill; Jan-April 1778 sick Fishkill; May-left sick Fishkill; June 1778.
Smith, Nathan Private	March 22, 1778 Duration of War	Fourth, Marvin	April 1778 under inoculation Fishkill; May 1778 sick Fishkill; June 1778.
Smith, Obediah Private	Nov 21, 1776, Duration of War	Fourth, Titus	Dec 1777-March 1778 sick absent; April 5, 1778 deserted.
Smith, Peter Private/Corporal	May 5, 1778, Nine Months	Second, Graham	May-June 1778; June 1778 payroll promoted to Corporal.
Smith, Richard Private	Dec 16, 1777, Three Years	Second, Hallett	Dec 1777-Jan 1778; Feb 1778 payroll only; March-April 1778; May 1778 sick in camp; June 1778.
Smith, Robert Sergeant	Dec 12, 1776, Duration of War	First, Finck	April-June 1778.
Smith, Thomah Private	Duration of War	Malcom's, Irvine	Dec 22, 1777 deserted.
Smith, William Private	July 4, 1777, Duration of War	First, McCracken	April-June 1778.
Smith, William Private	Jan 1, 1777, Three Years	Second, Ten Eyck	Dec 1777-Feb 1778 sick at Albany; March-June 1778.
Smith, William Private	Duration of War	Malcom's, Irvine	Dec 1777-Jan 1778 sick absent; Feb 1778 sick in hospital; March 1778 hospital; April 1778 Princeton Hospital; May 1778 sick Princeton; June 1778 Princeton Hospital.
Snow, Ephraim 2nd. Lt.	Nov 21, 1776	First, Copp	April-June 1778.
Snowden/ Snouden, John Private	Dec 7, 1776, Duration of War	Fourth, Marvin	Dec 1777-June 1778.
Snyder, Jacob Private	Jan 21, 1777, Duration of War	First, Wendell	April-May 1778; June 1778 sick at Hopewell Church in State of New Jersey.
Snyder, John Private	May 14, 1778, Nine Months	Second, Ten Eyck	May-June 1778.
Sohake, Jonathan Private	May 5, 1778, Nine Months	Second, Hallett	May 1778 on guard; June 1778.
Solyer, Zacheus Private	Oct 24, 1776, Duration of War	First, Hicks	April-June 1778.

Sotherland/ Sotharland, Samuel Private	May 5, 1778, Nine Months	Fourth, Strong	May 1778. As no one of this name appears on any other rolls, this man and the individual below may be the same.
Southerlin, James Sergeant	May 5, 1778, Nine Months	Fourth, Strong	June 1778. This individual and the man above may be the same.
Speers/Spiers, Jonathan Private	Nov 27, 1776, Duration of War	First, Hicks	April-May 1778; June 1778 left sick on the road from Pennsylvania.
Spicer, Jacob Private	Feb 3, 1777, Duration of War	Fourth, Titus	Dec 1777 doctor's waiter; Jan 1778 on command; Feb 1778; March 1778 on command; April-May 1778; June 1778 sick in Pennsylvania.
Spier, Joseph Private	May 5, 1778, Nine Months	Second, Pell	June 1778 sick at Coryells Ferry.
Spring, Nathaniel Private	Nine Months	Fourth, Titus	June 1, 1778 joined; June 1778 sick in Pennsylvania.
Springsteel/ Springtal, Christopher Private		Malcom's, Santford	Sept 1, 1777 deserted. Feb 22, 1778 taken confined Goshen Jail; March 1778 confined at Goshen; April 1778 broke Goshen jail.
Squirill/ Squirrell, Jacob Private	Dec 26, 1776, Duration of War	Fourth, Smith	Dec 1777; Jan-March 1778 sick in hospital; April 1778 sick Yellow Springs; May 1778 sick in camp; June 1778.
Stagg/Staggs, John Private	Dec 14, 1776, Duration of War	First, Van Ness	April-June 1778.
Stagg, John Paymaster	March 4, 1777	Malcom's	Dec 1777; Jan 12, 1778, appointed Brigade Major of Conway's Brigade. Oath at Valley Forge on May 29, 1778.
Stagg/Stag, John Private	Nov 27, 1776, Duration of War	Fourth, Pearsee	Dec 1777; Jan 1778 on party; Feb 1778; March 1778 on duty; April 1778 on party Radnor; May 1778 sick present; June 24, 1778 died.
Stall/Staal, Gerlock Private	Nov 2, 1777, Duration of War	First, Finck	April-June 1778.
Stanford, John Private	Jan 1, 1777, Duration of War	Fourth, Walker	Dec 1777-May 1778; June 1778 sick Pennsylvania.
Stanley, Daniel Private	Feb 1, 1778, Three Years	First, Van Ness	April 1, 1778 deserted.
Stansberry, William Private	Oct 23, 1777, Duration of War	First, Hicks	April-June 1778.

Name/Rank	Enlisted	Regiment/Company	Notes
Stanton, Benjamin/Benjm Private	May 5, 1778, Nine Months	Second, Wright	May 1778 smallpox; May 1778 muster roll shows "time of entering" as May 21, 1778; June 1778.
Staples/Steeples, Nathan Private	May 5, 1778, Nine Months	Fourth, Walker	May 1778; June 1778 sick Somerset.
Starr, George Private	Oct 20, 1776, Duration of War	First, Hicks	April-June 1778.
Statsman, John/Jean Private/Fifer	Duration of War	First, Ten Broeck	April-May 1778; June 1, 1778 promoted to Fifer; June 1778 sick at Princeton.
Steel, John/Jno Private	Jan 1, 1777, Duration of War	Second, Ten Eyck	Dec 1777-June 1778 sick at Haverstraw.
Steel, John Captain	January 1777	Malcom's, Steel	Dec 1777-Feb 1778; March 8, 1778 resigned.
Steenberg, Peter Private	May 7, 1778, Nine Months	Second, Pell	May-June 1778.
Stephens/ Stephans, Jesse/Justice Private	May 5, 1778, Nine Months	Fourth, Marvin	May 22, 1778 joined; May-June 1778.
Stephens/Stevens, Nathaniel/Nathl Private	Jan 19, 1777, Duration of War	Second, Wright	Dec 1777; Jan 17, 1778 deserted.
Stevens/Stephen, Peter/Petter Private	Duration of War	Malcom's, Niven	Dec 1777 sick nigh camp; Jan-Feb 1778 sick in quarters; April 1778 sick Yellow Springs; May 1778.
Stewart/Stuart, James Private	Duration of War	Malcom's, Irvine	Dec 1777-Jan 1778; Feb-April 1778 on furlough; May-June 1778 on command at Lancaster.
Stewart, John Private	May 5, 1778, Nine Months	Fourth, Titus	May 1778; June 1778 sick in Pennsylvania.
Stevens/Stephens, Abraham Private	Nov 20, 1776, Duration of War	First, Hicks	April-May 1778; June 7, 1778 deserted; June 20, 1778 returned from desertion; June 1778 on guard.
Stevenson/ Stephenson, John Sergeant	Jan 1, 1777, Duration of War	Second, Pelton	Dec 1777; Jan-March 1778 on command; June 1778 payroll only.
Stiles, Moses Private	Feb 28, 1777, Duration of War	First, Ten Broeck	April-May 1778; June 1778 sick Valley Forge.
Stillwell/Stilwil, Thomas Private	Feb 8, 1777, Three Years	Second, Wright	Dec 1777-March 1778; April 1778 sick in camp; May 1778 sick present; June 1778 sick Valley Forge.

Stillwill/Stilwil, James Sergeant	Jan 1, 1777	Second, Lounsbery	Dec 1777 sick in hospital at Albany; Jan 1778 sick in hospital; Feb 1778; March 1778 sick in hospital; April 1778 sick in State of New York; May 1778;June 1778 sick in State of New York.
Stitt, John Corporal	Dec 11, 1776, Duration of War	Fourth, Smith	Dec 1777 sick absent Albany; Jan 1778 sick in hospital; Feb 1778 sick in camp; March-April 1778; May 1778 on main guard; June 1778.
Stivers, Caleb Corporal/Private	Dec 3, 1776, Duration of War	Second, Pell	Dec 1777; Jan 2, 1778 deserted; March 1778 under sentence of Court Martial; March 21, 1778 enlisted; April 1778 on command at Swedesford; May 1778.
Stivers, Philip, Private	Jan 1, 1777, Duration of War	Second, Pell	Dec 1777-Feb 1778 sick absent; March-May 1778; June 1778 sick at Valley Forge.
St. Lawrence, George/Geo. Private	Jan 1, 1777, Duration of War	Fourth, Walker	Dec 1777-April 1778; May 1778 sick present; June 1778.
Stock, Charles Private	Oct 26, 1777, Duration of War	First, Ten Broeck	April-June 1778.
Stone, John Private	Duration of War	First, Finck	April-June 1778 on command General Schuyler's guard.
Stoutengen/ Stoutenger, George Private	Oct 27, 1776, Duration of War	First, Van Ness	April-June 1778.
Stranahen/ Straughen, James Private	Three Years	Malcom's, Black	Dec 1777-Jan 1778; Feb 1778 on command; March-May 8 1778.
Strang, Gilbert Ensign/2nd Lt.	Nov 21, 1776	Fourth, Sacket, Marvin	Dec 1777-Feb 1778 on furlough; Jan 9, 1778 promoted to Second Lieutenant and transferred to Marvin's Company; March 1778; April 23, 1778 resigned.
Stratton/Straton, Thomas Private	Duration of War	Malcom's, Santford	April 26, 1778 joined; April 1778; May 1778 in Regimental hospital; June 1778 hospital Princeton.
Strawbridge/ Trowbridge, Absolom Private	May 5, 1778, Nine Months	Second, Ten Eyck	May-June 1778.
Street, Samuel/Saml Private	June 1, 1777, Duration of War	Second, Wright	Dec 1777-April 1778; May 1778 sick present; June 1778 sick Valley Forge.

Name	Enlistment	Company	Remarks
Strong, John Private	May 5, 1778, Nine Months	Fourth, Strong	May-June 1778.
Strong, Nathan Captain	Nov 21, 1776	Fourth, Strong	Dec 1777-May 1778; June 1778 on furlough.
Suates, James Private	Dec 1, 1777	Fourth, Strong	Only record is his name and date of enlistment on a roll dated September 14, 1778, at White Plains, New York.
Succanox/ Succinox, Daniel Private	July 8, 1777, Three Years	Second, Graham	Dec 1777-Jan 1778; Feb 1778 sick in small pox; March 1778 sick in camp; April 1778; May 1778 main guard; June 1778.
Suckanut/ Suckanuck, John Private	May 5, 1778	Fourth, Smith	May 1778 sick in [Innoculation].
Sudlow, Samuel Private	March 16, 1777, Duration of War	First, Wendell	April-May 1778; June 1778 sick at Corryell's Town State of Pennsylvania.
Sullivan, Cornelius Private	Oct 17, 1777, Duration of War	First, Copp	April-May 1778; June 1778 sick in hospital Brunswick.
Sullivan/Suliven, James Private	Duration of War	Malcom's, Irvine	Dec 1777 on command with General Hand; Jan-April 1778 on command; May 1778; June 1778 guard Brunswick.
Sullivan, John Private		Malcom's, Irvine	Dec 1777 on command with General Hand; Jan-April 1778 on command;
Sullivan/Sulivan, Peter Private	April 8, 1777, Duration of War	Malcom's, Santford	Dec 1777 sick in hospital; Jan-June 1778.
Sutton, James Private	Nov 26, 1776, Duration of War	First, Copp	April-May 1778; June 14, 1778 deserted.
Sutton, Zachariah/Zackah Private	May 24, 1777, Three Years	Malcom's, Santford	Dec 1777-March 1778; April 1778 sick present; May 1778 in Regimental hospital; June 1778 Yellow Springs.
Sweed, William Private	May 5, 1778, Nine Months	Fourth, Strong	June 1778 sick in Jerseys.
Sweet, Caleb Surgeons Mate	May 1, 1777	First	April-June 1778.
Syles, Christopher Private	Dec 12, [ ] Duration of War	First, McCracken	April-May 1778; June 1778 sick at Brunswick.
Symon, Martin Private	April 14, 1776, Duration of War	Second, Hallett	Dec 1777-Jan 1778; Feb 1778 payroll only; March 1778 sick in camp; April 1778; May 1778 payroll only; June 1778 sick in Pennsylvania.

Syrine, James Private	Dec 15, 1776, Three Years	Second, Hallett	Dec 1777-Jan 1778 sick at Peekskill; Feb 1778 payroll only; April 1778 discharged.
Tably/Tabley, Jacob Private	Dec 5, 1776, Duration of War	First, Finck	April-June 1778.
Talbert, William Corporal	March 8, 1777, Three Years	First, McCracken	April-June 1778.
Talmadge, Joseph Corporal	Nov 21, 1776, Duration of War	Fourth, Davis	Dec 1777-May 1778; June-July 1778 sick Pennsylvania.
Talmadge/ Tallmadge, Samuel/Sam Sergeant	Nov 21, 1777, Duration of War	Fourth, Sacket	Dec 1777-Feb 1778; March 1778 sick in hutts; April-May 1778 sick present; June 1778 sick Pennsylvania.
Tapley/Taply, John Private	Duration of War	Malcom's, Irvine	Dec 1777-Jan 1778 sick absent; Feb 1778; March 1778 on command; April-June 1778.
Tapping/Topping, Daniel Sergeant	Nov 21, 1776, Duration of War	Fourth, Davis	Dec 1777-June 1778.
Tarrenty, Thomas Private	Jan 6, 1778	Fourth, Walker	Jan 29, 1778 deserted.
Taulman/ Tawlman, Peter Adjutant	July 1, 1777	Malcom's	Dec 1777-Feb 1778; March 1778 on furlough; April-May 1778. Oath at Valley Forge on May 11, 1778.
Taylor/Tayler, David Private	Duration of War	Malcom's, Black	Dec 1777-April 1778 on command; May 1778 on command at Walkill.
Taylor/Tayler, Thomas Private	Duration of War	Malcom's, Steel	Dec 1777; Jan 5, 1778 deserted.
Taylor, William Private	Feb 11, 1778, Three Years	First, Van Ness	April 15, 1778 deserted.
Tearse, Peter B. Adjutant	Nov 21, 1776	First	April-June 1778.
Teats/Teets, William Private	Three Years	Malcom's, Black	Dec 1777-Feb 1778 sick in quarters; March 1778; April 1778 sick present; May 1778 sick in camp.
Teets/Teats, Michael Private	Three Years	Malcom's, Black	Dec 1777-Feb 1778 sick in quarters; March 1778; April 1778 sick present; May 1778.
Teetsworth, Thomis/Thomas Private	Aug 20, 1777, Duration of War	Second, Pelton	Dec 20, 1777 deserted.

Templer/Templar, Thomas Private	May 10, 1777, Duration of War	Second, Wright	Dec 1777 tending sick; Jan 1778 on command pressing teams; Feb 1778 sick in quarters; March 1778; April 1778 sick in camp; May 6, 1778 dead.
Ten Broeck/ Tenbrook/ John C. 1st. Lt.	Nov 21, 1776	First, Ten Broeck, Wendell	For April 1778 he commanded what had been Captain McKeen's Company; in May 1778 he transferred to Wendell's Company; May 1778; June 1778 on command to East Town.
Ten Eyck, Abraham Pay Master	Nov 21, 1776	First	April 1778 on duty at Albany; May-June 1778.
Ten Eyck, Barent Captain	Nov 21, 1776	Second, Ten Eyck	Dec 1777 absent; Jan 22, 1778 discharged.
Ten Eyck/ Teneyck, John Private	March 22, 1777, Duration of War	Second, Pelton	Dec 1777 on guard; Jan-March 1778; April 1778 payroll only; May-June 1778.
Terboss/T. Bush, Simeon/Simon Sergeant	Jan 1, 1777, Three Years	Fourth, Sacket	Dec 1777-Jan 1778; Feb-March 1778 on furlough; April 1778; May 1778 sick present; June 1778 sick Pennsylvania.
Terry/Tarrey, Nathaniel Private	Jan 15, 1777, Three Years	First, McCracken	April-May 1778; June 1778 with Colonel Morgan.
Terry/Tery, Samuel Private	Feb 9, 1777, Duration of War	Fourth, Sacket	Dec 1777-April 1778; May 1778 sick present; June 1778 sick in Jersies.
Terwilleger/ Terwileger, Ary Vanatha/ Aron V. N. Private	May 1, 1778, Nine Months	Second, Lounsbery	May 1778 sick in camp; June 1778.
Terwilege, Jacobus/James Private	May 12, 1778, Nine Months	Second, Pell	May 1778 tending small pox; June 1778.
Terwilliger, John Private	May 12, 1778, Nine Months	Second, Pell	May 1778 tending S. Pox
Testard/Tetard, John Peter Chaplain	Nov 21, 1776	Fourth	Dec 1777 on furlough in State of New York; Jan-March 1778 sick absent; April-May 1778; June 1778 absent.
Thomas, Ezekiel Sergeant	Oct 18, 1777, Duration of War	First, Copp	April-June 1778.
Thomas, Henry Fifer	March 21, 1777, Duration of War	Second, Wright	Dec 1777-May 1778; June-Sept 1778 sick Valley Forge.

Thomas, James Private	May 5, 1778	Second, Ten Eyck	June 1778 payroll only.
Thomas, John Sergeant	Duration of War	Malcom's, Niven	Dec 5, 1777 deserted.
Thompson/ Thomson, Benjamin Private	Nov 21, 1776, Duration of War	Fourth, Sacket	Dec 1777-June 1778.
Thompson/ Thomson, Daniel Private	April 1, 1777, Three Years	Second, Graham	Dec 1777-Feb 1778; March 1778 on command with His Excellency. He transferred to the Commander-in-Chief's Guard on March 19, 1778, and served until April 1, 1780.
Thompson, Elias Private	May 5, 1778, Nine Months	Fourth, Smith	May-June 1778.
Thompson, James Private	Feb 17, 1777, Duration of War	First, Ten Broeck	April-June 1778.
Thompson, John Corporal	April 1, 1777, Three Years	Second, Graham	Dec 1777-June 1778.
Thompson, John Sergeant	Dec 7, 1776, Duration of War	Fourth, Marvin	Dec 1777-March 1778; April 1778 sick in quarters; May 1778 sick in camp; June 1778.
Thompson, Joshua Private	May 5, 1778, Nine Months	Second, Ten Eyck	May 1778 smallpox; June 1778 sick at Peekskill.
Thompson, Stanley, Private	May 5, 1778, Nine Months	Second	First appears on muster roll for Oct 1778.
Thompson, William Corporal	Sept 20, 1777, Duration of War	First, McCracken	April-June 1778.
Thompson, William Sergeant/Private	Jan 1, 1777, Duration of War	Second, Pell	Dec 25, 1778 deserted; June 1778 wounded at Princeton.
Tinble, Henry, Private	May 5, 1778, Nine Months	Fourth, Sacket	June 1778.
Tipperwine/ Tepperwine, Christian Private	Oct 24, 1777, Duration of War	First, Finck	April-June 1778.
Titus, John Private	March 5, 1778, Duration of War	First, Graham	April 25, 1778 deserted.
Titus, Jonathan Captain	Nov 21, 1776	Fourth, Titus	Dec 1777-Feb 1778; March 1778 on furlough; April 1778 sick in the Country at Pickland Pennsylvania; May 1778; June 1778 sick in Pennsylvania.

Titus, Jonathan Private	Nov 21, 1776, Duration of War	Fourth, Titus	Dec 1777-March 1778 on furlough; April-May 1778; June 1778 sick in Pennsylvania.
Tobin, Edward Corporal	Oct 18, 1777, Duration of War	First, Copp	April-May 1778; June 1778 sick in General Hospital Brunswick.
Tom/Tomm, Nathaniel Captain	March 17, 1777	Malcom's, Tom	Dec 1777; Jan-Feb 1778; March 1778; April 1778; May 1778 on command at regimental hospital; June 1778. Oath at Valley Forge on May 11, 1778.
Tompkins, Nathaniel Private	March 18, 1777, Duration of War	Fourth, Strong	Dec 1777-April 1778; May 1778 sick in hospital; June 1778 sick Pennsylvania.
Tool, John Private	Jan 1, 1777, Duration of War	Fourth, Walker	Dec 1777 sick in quarters; Jan-May 1778; June 1778 on command Wilmington.
Travis/Travas, Jacob Private	March 20, 1777, Duration of War	Second, Wright	Dec 1777-March 1778; April 1778 sick in camp; May 6, 1778 died.
Travis, Uriah Corporal	March 23, 1777, Three Years3	Second, Wright	Dec 1777-April 1778; May 1778 sick present; June 1778 sick at Valley Forge.
Trimmin/ Trimming, Jonathan/Jonathen Private/Corporal	Sept 3, 1777, Duration of War	Second, Pelton	Dec 1777; Jan 1778 on command Feb-June 1778; June 2, 1778 promoted to Corporal.
Trimmins/ Timmons, Abner Private	May 5, 1778	Second, Ten Eyck	June 1778 payroll only.
Trout, Adam Sergeant	Jan 1, 1777, Duration of War	Second, Ten Eyck	Dec 1777-Feb 1778 on furlough; March 1778; April 1778 on duty; May 1778; June 1778 payroll only.
Trout, Michael Fifer	Jan 1, 1777, Duration of War	Second, Ten Eyck	Dec 1777; Jan 2, 1778 deserted; March 18, 1778 returned; March 1778 under sentence of a Court Martial; April-May 1778; June 1778 payroll only.
Trowbridge see Strawbridge			
Tubbs, Stephen Private	May 5, 1778, Nine Months	Fourth, Davis	June 21, 1778 deserted.
Tubee/Tuby, John Private	Nov 21, 1776, Duration of War	Fourth, Titus	Dec 1777-March 1778; April-May 1778 sick in quarters; June 1778 sick in Pennsylvania.
Tully/Tulley, Samuel Private	March 26, 1777, Duration of War	First, McCracken	April-June 1778.

Tuman/Tumond, David Private/Drummer	Nov 21, 1776, Duration of War	Fourth, Titus	Dec 1777-Jan 1778 on furlough; Feb 1778; March 1778 promoted to Drummer; March 1778 sick present; April-June 1778.
Tuman/Tumond, Peter Private	Nov 21, 1776 Duration of War	Fourth, Titus	Dec 1777; Jan 1778 sick in quarters; Feb 1778 sick in camp; March 1778 sick present; April 1778; May 20, 1778 died.
Tuman/Tumond, Peter, Jr. Private	Nov 21, 1776, Duration of War	Fourth, Titus	Dec 1777-June 1778.
Turnbull, William/Willm Private	Nov 30, 1776, Duration of War	First, Graham	April-June 1778.
Turner, William Private	May 5, 1778	Second	First appears on rolls for Oct 1778.
Tuthill/Tuttle, Aariah/Agarick Sergeant Major	Nov 21, 1776, Duration of War	Fourth, Sacket	Dec 1777-Feb 1778; March-April 1778 on furlough; May-June 1778.
Tuthill/Tuttle, James Private	Jan 29, 1777, Duration of War	Fourth, Pearsee	Dec 1777-Feb 1778; March 1778 on duty; April 1778 sick in camp; May 29, 1778 died.
Tuttill, Solomon Private	May 5, 1778, Nine Months	Second, Pell	June 1778 sick at Valley Forge.
Tuttle/Tuthill, Joel Private	Jan 20, 1777, Duration of War	Second, Riker	Dec 1777; Jan 1778 on fatigue; Feb 1778 on command; March 1778 sick absent; April 1778 sick in camp; May 1778; June 1778 on furlough.
Van Beniscoten/ Benscoten, Elias Private	May 5, 1778, Nine Months	Fourth, Titus	May-June 1778.
Van Benschoten/ Van Bunschoten, Peter 2nd. Lt./1st. Lt.	Nov 21, 1776	Fourth, Pearsee/ Strong	Dec 1777; Jan 9, 1778 promoted to First Lieutenant and transferred to Strong's Company; Jan-June 1778.
Van Benthousen, Martin Private	March 13, 1777, Duration of War	First, Copp	April-June 1778.
Van Bueren/Van Buren, George Private	Jan 14, 1777, Three Years	First, Wendell	April-June 1778.
Van Cleak/Van Kleeck, Henry Private	Jan 1, 1777, Duration of War	Second, Ten Eyck	Dec 1777; Jan 1778 sick in quarters; Feb 1778; March-April 1778 on duty; May 1778 tending Lt. Livingston; June 1778 payroll only.

Van Cortlandt see Cortlandt

Vandamerk/ V. Damark, Zachariah Private	Jan 1, 1777, Duration of War	Second, Lounsbery	Dec 1777; Jan-March 1778 on furlough; April 1778 on week's command; May-June 1778.
Van Deboe, Jacob Private	Jan 3, 1777, Three Years	First, Hicks	April-June 1778.
Van De Bogart/ Van Debogart, Minant, Private	May 5, 1778, Nine Months	Second, Riker	May-June 1778.
Van Debogart, Nicholas Private	Dec 5, i776, Duration of War	First, Copp	April-June 1778.
Vandemark/ V. Damerk, John Private	May 1, 1778, Nine Months	Second, Lounsbery	May 1778; June 1778 sick at Fishkill.
Van Denburgh, Daniel Private	Dec 21, 1776, Duration of War	First, Van Ness	April 1778 on furlough by Colonel Van Schaick March 28, 1778 for 3 months; May-June 1778 on command General Schuyler's guard.
Van Dyck, Cornelius/Corns. Lt. Colonel	Nov 21, 1776	First	April 1778; May 1778 on command at East Town, June 1778.
Van Dyke/Van Dyck, Peter Sergeant	Oct 24, 1776, Duration of War	First, McCracken	April-June 1778.
Van Etten/ Van Atten, Peter Corporal	April 10, 1777, Three Years	Fourth, Pearsee	Dec 1777-March 1778; April 1778 sick in quarters; May 1778 sick in hospital; June 1778 sick Valley Forge.
Van Every/V. Every, Martain/Martin Private	Duration of War	Malcom's, Niven	Dec 1777-Jan 1778; Feb 1778 on furlough; April 1778 absent without leave; May 1778 sick in camp.
Van Gaasbeck, Thomas Ensign	April 6, 1777	Malcom's, Tom	Dec 16, 1777 resigned.
Van Hoevenbergh/ V Hoevenbargh, Rudolph/ Rhudolphus Ensign/2nd. Lt.	Nov 21, 1776	Fourth, Pearsee, Walker	Dec 1777 under arrest; Jan 9, 1778 promoted to Second Lieutenant and transferred to Walker's Company; Jan-June 1778.
Van Houser/ V. Hooser, Rynier/Rinear Corporal	May 24, 1777, Three Years	Fourth, Sacket	Dec 1777-June 1778.

Van Ness, Cornelius Private	March 10, 1777, Duration of War	Second, Pelton	Oct 23, 1777 deserted; June 5, 1778 enlisted; June 1778 sick in Pennsylvania.
Van Ness, David Captain	Nov 21, 1776	First, Van Ness	April 1778; Absent without leave since April 7, 1778.
Van Netten/ Vanetten, Jacobus Private	Jan 1, 1777, Three Years	Second, Lounsbery	Dec 1777-Feb 1778; March 1778 on command; April-June 1778.
Van Netten, James Private	Duration of War	Fourth, Walker	March 25, 1778 joined; March-April 1778; May 1778 sick in camp; June 1778.
Van Netten/Van Nelton, Joseph Private	Oct 27, 1776, Duration of War	First, Van Ness	April-June 1778.
Van Norden/ V Oorden, Albert/Alert Private	Duration of War	First, Finck	April-June 1778 on command General Schuyler's guard.
Van Renselaer, Nicholas 1st. Lt.	Nov 21, 1776	First, Graham	April 1778 General Schuyler's guard at Saratoga; May-June 1778 on command General Schuyler's guard at Saratoga.
Van Salsbury/ Van Salisbury, Cornelius Private	Jan 7, 1777, Three Years	First, Van Ness	April 1, 1778 deserted.
Vansaunt, John Private	May 5, 1778, Nine Months	Second, Wright	June 1778.
Van Schaick, Goose Colonel	Nov 21, 1776	First	April-June 1778.
Vashee/Vache, John Francis Surgeon	Jan 1, 1777	Fourth	Jan 1778; Feb 1778; March 1778 under an arrest; April-May 1778; June 1778 in arrest.
Van Slyck/ Van Slych, Martin Private	Duration of War	First, Finck	April-June 1778.
Van Snell, John Private	Duration of War	First, Van Ness	April-May 1778; June 1778 sick at Cuckolds Town.
Vantasel, Cornelius Private	March 24, 1777, Duration of War	Second, Wright	Dec 1777-March 1778; April 1778 on weeks command; May 1778 on detachment; June 1778.
Van Tassel/ Van Tosal, John Private	May 5, 1778, Nine Months	Fourth, Marvin	May-June 1778.

Van Valkenburgh/ Van Valkenburght, Bartholomo/ Bartholomew, 2nd. Lt.	Nov 21, 1776	First, Finck	April-June 1778.
Van Vorst, Christeaen/ Christian Private	Oct 26, 1776, Duration of War	First, Van Ness	April-June 1778.
Van Wagoner/ Van Wagener/Van Wagenen, Tunis Ensign	Nov 21, 1776	Second, Wright	Nov 29, 1777 appointed Forage Master; Dec 1777-March 1778.
Van Wert/Van Wort, Isaac 1st Lt.	Nov 21, 1776	Second, Wright	Dec 1777-Jan 1778 on furlough; Feb 1778 absent without leave; March-May 1778; June 1778 payroll only.
Van Wort/ Van Woert, Henry Quartermaster	Nov 21, 1776	First	April 1778; May 1778 on duty; June 1778.
Varnal/Varnil, John Private	Jan 1, 1777, Three Years	Second, Wright	Dec 1777 sick absent; Jan-Feb 1778; March 1778 on command; April-June 1778.
Varrian/Verrian, John Private	Jan 1, 1777, Duration of War	Second, Graham	Dec 1777; Jan 1778 on command; Feb-May 1778; June 1778 on furlough.
Veal/Veall, Jeremiah Private	Oct 25, 1776, Duration of War	First, McCracken	April-May 1778; June 1778 sick Corryell's Ferry.
Veile/Velie, Andrew G. Private	Jan 23, 1777, Duration of War	First, Hicks	April-May 1778; June 1778 wounded and in Princeton Hospital.
Vendewaker/ Venderwaker, James Private	April 4, 1777, Duration of War	First, Ten Broeck	April-June 1778.
Venice, John Private	Dec 7, 1776, Three Years	Second, Hallett	Dec 1777-Jan 1778 sick at Albany; Feb 1778 payroll only; March 1778 on duty; April 1778; May 1778 payroll only; June 1778.
Venier, Peter Private	May 5, 1778, Nine Months	Fourth, Marvin	June 1778 muster roll shows he joined on May 5, 1778; June 1778.
Vn Debogart/ V DeBogard, John Private	May 2, 1777, Three Years	Fourth, Pearsee	Dec 1777; Jan-March 1778 sick in hospital; April-May 1778; June 1778 on General Lee's guard.

Vrendenburgh/ Vredenburg, Isick/Isaac Private	Nov 28, 1776, Three Years	First, McCracken	April-June 1778.
Vrendenburgh/ Vredenburg, Peter Private Vredenburgh see Fredenburgh	Nov 28, 1776, Three Years	First, McCracken	April-June 1778.
Vunk/Vonck, Henry Private	Jan 15, 1777, Three Years	Fourth, Davis	Dec 1777-May 1778; June 1778 on furlough.
Vunk/Vonck, Peter Quartermaster	Nov 21, 1776	Fourth	Dec 1777-March 1778; March 24, 1778 discharged by order of a court martial.
V. Volkenborg/ V. Valkinburgh, Francis Private	May 5, 1778, Nine Months	Fourth, Pearsee	May-June 1778.
Wailen/Wheelon, Walter Private	Nov 7, 1776, Duration of War	First, Copp	April-June 1778.
Walker, Benjamin/Benj. Captain	Nov 21, 1776	Fourth, Walker	Dec 1777-Feb 1778; March 1778 acting Brigade Major; April-June 1778 Aide de Camp to the Baron Steuben. Oath at Valley Forge on May 22, 1778.
Walker, Edward Private	May 5, 1778	Fourth, Marvin	June 1778 muster roll shows he joined on May 5, 1778; June 1778.
Walker, Ermer Private	May 5, 1778	Fourth, Strong	First listed on roll dated September 10, 1778, at White Plains, NewYork.
Walker, George/Geo. Private	May 8, 1777, Duration of War	Malcom's, Lucas	Dec 1777-March 1778; April 1, 1778 deserted.
Walker, Israel Private	June 1, 1777, Duration of War	Second, Lounsbery	Dec 1777 on furlough; Jan 12, 1778 deserted; April-May 1778 in recruiting service; June 1778 recruiting.
Walker, John Private	Sept 9, 1777, Duration of War	Malcom's, Santford	Dec 1777-April 1778 waggoner; May 1778 waggoner camp; June 1778 Brunswick Hospital.
Walker, John Private	May 5, 1778, Nine Months	Second, Pell	June 1778.
Walker, Matthias Private	May 23, 1777, Duration of War	Fourth, Pearsee	Dec 1777-Feb 1778; March 1778 on duty; April-May 1778; June 1778 on [Gen.] guard.

Wall, Patrick Private	Jan 8, 1777, Duration of War	First, McCracken	April-June 1778 sick at Albany.
Wallace, William/Wm Corporal	Nov 15, 1776, Duration of War	First, Hicks	April-June 1778.
Wallicer/Walliser, Christian Private	March 11, 1777, Duration of War	First, Finck	April-June 1778 sick at Albany.
Walter, Jacob Private	Jan 20, 1777, Duration of War	First, Finck	April-June 1778.
Walter, Martin Private	Jan 20, 1777, Duration of War	First, Finck	April-May 1778; June 1778 waggoner to Brigade.
Walton, John Private	Oct 25, 1776, Duration of War	First, Finck	April-June 1778.
Ward, John Private	Feb 12, 1777, Duration of War	First, Finck	April-June 1778 on command General Schuyler's guard.
Ward, Robert/Robt. Drummer/ Drum Major	Aug 14, 1777, Duration of War	Fourth, Sacket	Dec 1777-Feb 1778; March 1778 sick in hutts; April 1778. His company muster roll shows he was promoted to Drum Major on May 1, 1778, but the regimental Field and Staff roll shows the promotion effective on April 27, 1778. May-June 1778.
Ward, Thomas Quartermaster Sergeant/ Sergeant	Three Years	Malcom's, Santford	Dec 1777; Jan 1778 reduced to Sergeant in Santfords Company; Jan-March 1778 on command; April 26, 1778 deserted.
Warden, Darius/Darias Private	March 4, 1777, Duration of War	Fourth, Strong	Dec 1777-June 1778.
Warder/Warden, Thomas Private	Oct 28, 1776, Duration of War	First, Van Ness	April-June 1778.
Warren, Edward Private	Nov 20, 1776, Duration of War	First, Hicks	April 4, 1778 deserted.
Warren, John Private	May 5, 1778, Nine Months	Second, Pelton	May 1778; June 1778 on guard.
Waterman, Samuel Private	May 5, 1778, Nine Months	Second, Ten Eyck	June 1778 sick at Valley Forge; August 1778 died Valley Forge.
Watkins, Benjamin/Benjm Private	Oct 24, 1776, Duration of War	First, McCracken	April-June 1778.
Watson, Major Private	March 11, 1777, Three Years	First, McCracken	March 5, 1778 returned from desertion; April-June 1778.
Watson, Robert/Robt Private	Duration of War	Malcom's, Niven	Dec 20, 1777 deserted.

Wattles, William/Wm Private/Sergeant	May 5, 1778, Nine Months	Fourth, Davis	May-June 1778; in June 1778 he was promoted to Sergeant.
Wattson/Watson, Thomas Sergeant	Duration of War	Malcom's, Kearsley	Dec 1777-Feb 1778; March 1778 sick present; April 1778 sick at New Ark.
Weaver, John Corporal	Nov 25, 1776	Fourth, Strong	Dec 1777; Jan 1778 sick in quarters; Feb 1778 sick in camp; March 1778; April 1778 on main guard; May-June 1778.
Webb, John Private	Jan 1, 1777, Duration of War	Second, Pell	Dec 1777-June 1778.
Webb, Nathaniel Sergeant	April 8, 1777, Three Years	Second, Lounsbery	Dec 1777-Jan 1778; Feb 1778 sick in camp; March-June 1778.
Wederwax, William Private	Jan 15, 1777, Three Years	First, Wendell	April-June 1778.
Wedge, Benjamin Private	May 5, 1778, Nine Months	Second, Pell	June 1778 sick at Valley Forge.
Weed, Abijah Musician	Oct 26, 1776, Duration of War	First, Hicks	April-June 1778.
Weed, Ezra Sergeant	Oct 24, 1776, Duration of War	First, Hicks	April-June 1778.
Weeks, John Private	May 5, 1778, Nine Months	Fourth, Sacket	May-June 1778.
Weesmiller, Hendrick Private	May 5, 1778, Nine Months	Second, Riker	May-June 1778.
Weissenfels/ Weisenfelts, Charles F. 2nd. Lt.	Nov 21, 1776	Second, Wright	Dec 1777-May 1778; June 1778 on furlough.
Weisenfels/ Weissenfelts, Frederick Lieutenant-Colonel	March 5, 1776	Second	Dec 1777-June 1778.
Welch, Isaac/ Isaak Corporal	Aug 4, 1777, Three Years	Fourth, Pearsee	Dec 1777-Jan 1778 sick at Whitemarsh; Feb 1778; March-May 1778 sick at Whitemarsh; June 1, 1778 deserted.
Welch, John Private	Nov 26, 1776, Duration of War	First, Copp	April-May 1778; June 1778 sick in Brunswick.
Welch, John Private	Nine Months	Fourth, Davis	June 1778.
Welch/Walsh, Joseph Private	Jan 1, 1777, Duration of War	Fourth, Walker	Dec 1777 sick in quarters; Jan 1778; Feb 1778 on duty; March-June 1778.

Welch, Thomas Private	Dec 23, 1776, Duration of War	First, Wendell	April-June 1778.
Welder/Wilder, Nehemiah Private	Duration of War	Malcom's, Kearsley	Dec 1777; Jan 1778 on guard; Feb 1778 guard; March 1778; April 1778 on command at Carlisle.
Weller, Amos Private	May 5, 1778, Nine Months	Second, Graham	May-June 1778.
Wells, John/Jno Private		Malcom's, Lucas	Dec 1777; Jan 1778 sick in quarters; March 1778 on command; April 15, 1778 deserted.
Wemp, Barent Private	Dec 28, 1776, Duration of War	First, Copp	April-May 1778; June 1778 absent without leave and supposed to be sick.
Wendell, Jacob H. Ensign	Nov 21, 1776	First, Van Ness	April 1778 sick in quarters; May-June 1778.
Wendell, John Private	Nov 16, 1776, Duration of War	First, Hicks	April-May 1778; June 1778 left sick on the road from Pennsylvania.
Wendell, John H. Captain	Nov 21, 1776	First, Wendell	April-June 1778.
Wentworth, John Private	June 1, 1777, Three Years	Second, Ten Eyck	Dec 1777-March 1778; April 1778 on command; May 1778 on furlough; June 1778 payroll only.
West, James Private	Oct 1, 1777, Three Years	Malcom's, Tom	Dec 1777-Jan 1778 not joined.
West, Williston Private	March 11, 1777, Duration of War	First, Graham	April-June 1778 on command General Schuyler's guard.
Westerfield/ Westervelt, David Private	May 5, 1777, Nine Months	Second, Riker	May-June 1778.
Westfall, Levi Private	May 2, 1777, Three Years	Fourth, Pearsee	Dec 1777-Feb 1778 sick at Rhinebeck; March-June 1778.
Whalen, Richard Private	Dec 28, 1776, Three Years	First, Wendell	April-June 1778.
Whaley, Timothy Private	May 5, 1778, Nine Months	Fourth, Davis	May-June 1778.
Wheeler, Henry Private	Jan 26, 1777, Duration of War	First, Ten Broeck	April-June 1778.
Wheeler, John Private	Jan 1, 1777, Duration of War	Fourth, Walker	June-July 1778 sick in Pennsylvania.
Wheeler, John Private	Jan 1, 1777, Duration of War	Fourth, Walker	Dec 1777-May 1778; June 1778 sick Pennsylvania.
Wheeler/Weeler, Richard Private	Dec 13, 1776, Duration of War	Second, Graham	Dec 1777 payroll only; Jan-June 1778.
Wheeler, Samuel Private	April 19, 1777, Duration of War	First, Ten Broeck	April-June 1778.

Wheeler, William Private	May 13, 1777, Three Years	Second, Lounsbery	Dec 1777-March 1778 on furlough; April-May 1778 sick State of New York; June 1778.
Wheeler, William Private	May 5, 1778, Nine Months	Second, Riker	June 1778 sick at Peekskill.
Whiley/Whyley, Edward Private	Jan 1, 1777, Duration of War	Second, Wright	Dec 1777-Feb 1778; March 1778 on command; March 19, 1778 to Commander-in-Chief's Guard.
Whisheck, George Private	Feb 20, 1777, Duration of War	First, Ten Broeck	April 1778; May 1778 sick present; June 1778 sick Valley Forge.
White, Andrew Ensign	Nov 21, 1776	Second, Pell	Dec 1777 sick absent; Jan-May 1778; June-Aug 1778 on command at Valley Forge.
White, Ephraim Private	Nov 21, 1776, Duration of War	Fourth, Davis	Dec 1777-April 1778; May 1778 sick in hospital; June 1778 sick Pennsylvania.
White, George Corporal	May 5, 1778, Nine Months	Fourth, Pearsee	May-June 1778.
White, James Corporal	Jan 1, 1777, Duration of War	First, Wendell	April-June 1778.
White, John Private	May 5, 1778, Nine Months	Second, Ten Eyck	June 1778 sick Peekskill.
White, Joseph Private	Dec 14, 1776, Duration of War	First, Van Ness	April-May 1778; June 1778 "invaluded" July 6, 1778. This is probably invalided, meaning he was unfit for service.
White, Philip Private	May 1, 1778, Nine Months	Second, Lounsbery	May-June 1778.
White, William Private	Jan 11, 1777, Duration of War	Second, Hallett	Dec 1777-Jan 1778; Feb 1778 payroll only; March 1778 on duty; April 1778; May 1778 payroll only; June-Aug 1778 sick at Valley Forge.
Whitehead, William Private	Jan 1, 1777, Duration of War	Fourth, Titus	Dec 1777; Jan 1778 sick in quarters; Feb 1778; March 1778 sick present; April-June 1778.
Whitman/ Whiteman, John Private	May 5, 1778, Nine Months	Fourth, Pearsee	May 1778; June 1778 dead.
Whitney, Jacob Private	Feb 1, 1777, Duration of War	Fourth, Walker	Dec 1777; Jan 1778 on party; Feb 1778; March 1778 sick in camp; April-June 1778.
Wickham, Stephen Private	Jan 1, 1777, Duration of War	Fourth, Pearsee	Dec 1777-March 1778 sick absent; April 1778; May 1778 sick in quarters; June 1778 sick in Pennsylvania.
Wicks, James Private	May 5, 1778, Nine Months	Fourth, Davis	May-June 1778.

Name/Rank	Enlistment	Regiment/Company	Service Record
Wier/Wair, James Sergeant	Duration of War	Malcom's, Niven	Dec 1777-Feb 1778; April-May 1778.
Wiesenfelts/ Wysenfelts, George Fifer	June 22, 1777, Duration of War	Second, Riker	Dec 1777-June 1778.
Wightman/ Wieghlien, Matthias Private	Duration of War	First, Finck	April 24, 1778 deserted; May 24, 1778 returned from desertion; May-June 1778.
Wilcott/Willcot, George Private	Duration of War	Malcom's, Kearsley	Dec 1777 sick in hospital; Jan 1778 sick Eastown; Feb-March 1778 at Bethlehem; April 1778 sick Eastown.
Wilcox/Wilcocks, John Sergeant	Feb 26, 1777, Duration of War	Second, Pelton	Dec 1777-Feb 1778; March 1778 on furlough; April 1778 on guard; May-June 1778.
Wiley, John Private	Duration of War	Malcom's, Kearsley	Dec 1777-Jan 1778 on command.
Wiley, Simeon Private	May 5, 1777, Nine Months	Second, Pell	June 1778 sick at Valley Forge.
Wilkerson, Thomas/Tho. Private	May 5, 1778, Nine Months	Fourth, Strong	May 1778; June 1778 sick Valley Forge.
Willcocks/ Willcox, Aaron Private	May 5, 1778, Nine Months	Second, Riker	May 1778; June 1778 sick Coryells Ferry.
Willet, John Private	Dec 18, 1776, Duration of War	First, Copp	April-June 1778.
Williams, Aron/Aaron Private		Fourth, Strong	Dec 1777; Jan 1778 sick in hospital; Feb 1778 sick absent; April-May 1778 left sick at Fishkill; June 1778 sick at Fishkill.
Williams, Charles Private	Nov 14, 1776, Duration of War	First, Hicks	April-June 1778.
Williams, Charles Corporal/Private	Jan 1, 1777, Duration of War	Fourth, Marvin	Dec 1777-Feb 1778 sick at Fishkill; March-April 1778; May 1, 1778 reduced to Private; May-June 1778.
Williams, Francis Private	Jan 25, 1778, Duration of War	Second, Hallett	April 1778; May 1778 payroll only; June 1778 sick in Pennsylvania.
Williams, James Private	May 5, 1778, Nine Months	Second, Wright	June 1778 sick Valley Forge.
Williams, John Private	July 29, 1777, Duration of War	First, McCracken	April-May 1778; June 1778 sick at Cuckolds Town.

Williams, John Private	May 9, 1777, Three Years	Fourth, Pearsee	Dec 1777; Jan 1778 sick in quarters; Feb 1778 sick in camp; March 18, 1778 died. See Rosman, Adam.
Williams, Race Sergeant	March 15, 1777, Three Years	Malcom's, Tom	Dec 1777-May 1778; June 1778 on command Brunswick.
Williams, Thomas Private	May 5, 1778	Second, Pell	June 1778.
Williamson, James Private	Nov 21, 1776, Duration of War	Fourth, Sacket	Dec 1777; Jan-Feb 1778 on party; March 1778 sick in huts; April-May 1778; June 1778 sick in Jersies.
Williamson, John Private	March 11, 1777, Duration of War	First, Finck	April-June 1778.
Willson, Walter Private	March 4, 1777, Duration of War	Fourth, Smith	Dec 1777-Feb 1778; March 1778 under guard; April-May 1778.
Wilson, Archibald Private	Aug 12, 1777, Three Years	Second, Lounsbery	Dec 1777 sick in camp; Jan-Feb 1778; March 20, 1778 deserted.
Wilson, James Private	March 19, 1777, Duration of War	First, McCracken	April-June 1778.
Wilson, John Private	May 7, 1778, Nine Months	Second, Pell	May-June 1778.
Wilson, Michael Private	Jan 14, 1777, Duration of War	First, Wendell	April-June 1778.
Wilson, Michel/ Michael Private	May 5, 1778, Nine Months	Fourth, Pearsee	May 1778; June 1778 sick in Jersey.
Wilson/Willson, Robert/Robt Private	Duration of War	Malcom's, Irvine	Dec 1777-Feb 1778; March-April 1778 command; May-June 1778.
Wilson/Willson, Samuel Private	Jan 5, 1777, Duration of War	Fourth, Sacket	Dec 1777; Jan 1778 sick in camp; Feb 1778 sick present; March 1778; April 1778 on duty; May-June 1778.
Wilson, Thomas/Thos Private	Three Years	Malcom's, Black	Dec 1777-Jan 1778; Feb-March 1778 on command; April-May 1778.
Winchell, John Private	May 7, 1778, Nine Months	Second, Pell	May 1778 sick in small pox; June 1778.
Winn/Wynn, John Private	Duration of War	Malcom's, Black	Dec 1777-Feb 1778; March-April 1778 sick present; May 1778.
Winn, Peter Private	March 10, 1777, Duration of War	First, Graham	April-June 1778.
Wintworth/ Wentworth, James Private	May 31, 1777, Three Years	Fourth, Titus	Dec 1777 sick absent; Jan 1778; Feb 1778 sick in camp; March 1778; April 1778 sick in quarters; May-June 1778 on furlough.
Wise, Daniel Private	May 5, 1778, Nine Months	Fourth, Pearsee	June 1778.

Witham, Joseph Private	Feb 19, 1777, Duration of War	Second, Hallett	Dec 1777; Jan 1778 sick in camp; Feb 1778 payroll only; March 1778 on duty; May 1778 sick in camp; June 20, 1778 died.
Witherick, George Private	March 19, 1777, Duration of War	First, Graham	April-June 1778.
Wolfe/Wolf, Michael Private	March 12, 1777, Three Years	First, Finck	April-June 1778.
Wood, Daniel Surgeon	August 1777	Malcom's	Dec 1777-May 1778. Oath at Valley Forge on May 11, 1778.
Wood, Peter Private	Feb 1, 1778, Three Years	First, Van Ness	April 15, 1778 deserted.
Wood, Robert Ensign	Nov 21, 1776	Second, Graham	Dec 1777 payroll only; Jan 1778; Feb 1778 on furlough; March 27, 1778 discharged.
Wood, William/Wm Surgeon's Mate	Aug 15, 1777	Fourth	Dec 1777-May 1778; June 1778 sick absent.
Woodcock/ Wodcock, Peter Private	Feb 20, 1777, Duration of War	First, Ten Broeck	April-May 1778; June 1778 on command with Colonel Morgan.
Woodmore/ Woodamore, Cornelius Drummer	Dec 1, 1776, Duration of War	Second, Graham	Dec 1777 payroll only; Jan 1778 on command; Feb 1778 sick in smallpox; March-June 1778.
Woodruff/ Woodruffe, Ephraim/Ephr. Sergeant	Jan 1, 1777, Duration of War	Fourth, Walker	Dec 1777-Feb 1777; March 1778 sick present; April 1778 sick in camp; May 1778; June 1778 sick Cranberry.
Wormly/Wormley, Jacob Private	March 14, 1777, Three Years	First, Ten Broeck	April 1778; May 1778 sick present; June 1778 sick Valley Forge.
Wormoet/ Warmoet, Christeaen/ Christian Private	Duration of War	First, Van Ness	April-June 1778.
Worrey, John Private	May 7, 1778, Nine Months	Second, Pell	May-June 1778.
Wright, Barick/Barach Drummer	Jan 14, 1777, Duration of War	Second, Wright	Dec 1777; Jan 1778 on fatigue; Feb-March 1778; April 1778 sick in camp; May 1778 sick absent; June 1778.
Wright, Benjamin Private	Oct 30, 1776, Duration of War	First, Copp	April-June 1778.
Wright, Jacob Captain	Nov 21, 1776	Second, Wright	Dec 1777 on furlough; Jan-June 1778.

Wurde, Daniel Private	May 5, 1777	Fourth, Pearsee	Only record is on a roll dated September 10, 1778, at White Plains, NewYork.
Wusills/Wesells, Nicholas Private	Duration of War	First, Van Ness	April-June 1778.
Wyatt, John Private	Dec 10, 1776, Duration of War	First, Wendell	April-June 1778.
Wyllis/Willis, James Private	Nov 20, 1776, Duration of War	First, Hicks	April-June 1778.
Wyre/Wyer, Jeremiah Private	Jan 1, 1777 Duration of War	Fourth, Sacket	Dec 1777-June 1778.
Yets/Yetts, John Private		Malcom's, Tom	Feb 1778 taken the 1st of February and now confined New Windsor; March 1778 confined; April 25, 1778 deserted.
Yorus, John Private	May 5, 1778	Second, Wright	June 1778 sick at Valley Forge.
Young, Christopher Private	Dec 7, 1776, Duration of War	First, Copp	April-June 1778.
Young, Guy 1st. Lt.	Nov 21, 1776	First, McCracken	April-June 1778.
Young, John Private	Jan 1, 1777, Three Years	Second, Hallett	Dec 1777-Jan 1778; Feb 1778 payroll only; March 1778 on duty; April 1778; May 1778 payroll only; June 1778.
Youngs, David Private	Three Years	Malcom's, Black	Dec 1777-Jan 1778 sick in quarters; Feb-April 1778; May 1778 on command at ye lines.
Zeronius/Zeranius, Christopher Private	March 21, 1778, Duration of War	First, Ten Broeck	April-June 1778.

158

BIBLIOGRAPHY

The following publications were not used in compiling the above lists. However they can provide additional information for researchers on the Valley Forge Encampment, and the Delaware and New York men in the American Revolution. Many of these are available on HathiTrust and other on-line sites.

Aimone, Alan, and Barbara. "'Brave Bostonians': New Yorkers' Roles In The Winter Invasion Of Canada." *Military Collector and Historian* 36 (1984): 134-150.

_____. "Organizing and Equipping Montgomery's Yorkers in 1775." *Military Collector and Historian* 28 (1976): 53-63.

Anderson, Enoch, *Personal Recollections of Captain Enoch Anderson, An Officer of the Delaware Regiments in the Revolutionary War*, ed. Harry Hobart Bellas, Wilmington: Historical Society of Delaware, 1896.

Anderson, "Journal of Lieutenant Thomas Anderson of the Delaware Regiment, 1780-1782." *Historical Magazine*. 2nd. ser., (1867): 207-11.

Bastian, Joe, "The Delaware Regiment in the Battle of Long Island," *Archeology* 30 (Fall 1978): 21-25.

Bellas, Henry H. *A History of the Delaware State Society of the Cincinnati From Its Organization to the Present Time. To Which is Appended a Brief Account of the Delaware Regiments in the War of the Revolution.* Wilmington: Historical Society of Delaware, 1895.

Caleb P. Bennett and Wm. Hemphill Jones "The Delaware Regiment in the Revolution," *The Pennsylvania Magazine of History and Biography* 9 (1886): 451-462.

Benninghoff, Herman O. III. *Valley Forge: A Genesis for Command and Control.* Gettysburg, Pa: Thomas Publications, 2001.

Bleeker, Leonard. *The Order Book of Capt. Leonard Bleeker, Major of Brigade in the Early Part of the Expedition Under Gen. James Clinton, Against the Indian Settlements of Western New York, in the Campaign of 1779.* New York: Joseph Sabin, 1865.

Bockstruck, Lloyd DeWitt. *Revolutionary War Bounty Land Grants Awarded by State Governments*. Baltimore: Genealogical Publishing Co., 1996.

Bodle, Wayne K. The *Valley Forge Winter: Civilians and Soldiers in War.* University Park, Pa: Penn State University Press, 2002.

_____. "Generals and 'Gentlemen': Pennsylvania Politics and the Decision for Valley Forge" *Pennsylvania History: A Journal of Mid-Atlantic Studies*, 62 (1995): 59-89.

_____. "The Vortex of Small Fortunes: The Continental Army at Valley Forge, 1777-1778." Ph. D. Dissertation, University of Pennsylvania, 1987.

Bodle, Wayne K. and Jacqueline Thibaut. "Valley Forge Historical Research Report." 3 vols., unpublished, (1980).

Bulletin of the Fort Ticonderoga Museum. numerous relevant articles.

Burr, Aaron. *Memoirs of Aaron Burr, With Miscellaneous Selections From His Correspondence.* ed. Matthew L. Davis. 2 vols. New York: Harper & Brothers, 1836-1837. For Malcom's Regiment.

Bush, Martin H. *Revolutionary Enigma: A Re-Appraisal of General Philip Schuyler of New York*. Port Washington, N. Y.: Ira J. Friedman, 1969.

Chadwick, Bruce. *George Washington's War: The Forging of a Revolutionary Leader and the American Presidency*. Naperville, Ill.: Sourcebooks, Inc., 2004.

Champagne, Roger J. *Alexander McDougall and the American Revolution in New York*: Schenectady: New York State American Revolution Bicentennial Commission, 1975.

Clark, Murtie June. *The Pension Lists of 1792-1795, With Other Revolutionary War Pension Records*. 1991; reprint, Baltimore: Genealogical Publishing Co., 1996.

Clinton, George. *Public Papers of George Clinton*, 10 vols. New York and Albany: State of New York: Wynkoop Hallenbeck Crawford Company, 1899.

Cubbison, Douglas R. "Col. Rudolphus Ritzema in Albany, 1776." *Military Collector and Historian* 61 (2009): 313-315.

Dawson, Henry B. *Westchester-County, New York, During the American Revolution*. Morrisania: Privately printed, 1886.

Delafield, Maturin L., ed. "Colonel Henry Beekman Livingston," *Magazine of American History* 21 (1889): 256-58.

Delaware Archives. 5 vols. Wilmington: Public Archives Commission of Delaware, 1911-1919.

Dickens, Charles W., ed. "Orderly Book of Caleb Prew Bennett at the Battle of Yorktown, 1781," *Delaware History*, 4 (1950): 105-148.

"Delaware Memorial at Valley Forge," *The Pennsylvania Magazine of History and Biography*, 39, (1915): 69-79.

Egly, T. W. Jr. *Goose Van Schaick of Albany, 1736-1789: The Continental Army's Senior Colonel*. (The Author, 1992)

_____. *History of the First New York Regiment, 1775-1783*. Hampton, N.H.: Peter E. Randall, 1981.

Fernow, Berthold, ed. *New York in the Revolution*. Albany: Weed, Parsons & Company, 1887

Fish, Nicholas. "Selections from the Correspondence of Major Nicholas Fish, of the Army of the Revolution," *Historical Magazine*, 2nd ser., 5 (1869): 203-205.

Fleming, Thomas. *Washington's Secret War: The Hidden History of Valley Forge*. N. Y.: HarperCollins, 2005.

Gano, John. "A Chaplain in the Revolution: Memoirs of the Rev. John Gano," *Historical Magazine*, 4 (1861): 330-35.

Gardner, Asa Bird. "The New York Continental Line of the American Revolution," *Magazine of American History* 7, (1881): 401-419.

Gerlach, Don R. *Proud Patriot: Philip Schuyler and the War of Independence, 1775–1783.* Syracuse: Syracuse University Press, 1987.

Godfrey, Carlos E. *The Commander-in-Chief's Guard: Revolutionary War* Washington, D.C.: Stevenson-Smith Co., 1904; reprint, Baltimore: Genealogical Publishing Co., 1972.

Greenwood, John, *The Revolutionary Services of John Greenwood of Boston and New York, 1775-1783*, New York, 1922.

Hall, William. "Colonel Rudolphus Ritzema." *Magazine of American History* 2 (1878): 162-67.

Hancock, Harold Bell. *Liberty and Independence: The Delaware State during the American Revolution.* Wilmington: Delaware American Revolution Bicentennial Commission, 1976.

_____. *The Loyalists of Revolutionary Delaware.* Newark: University of Delaware Press, 1977.

Hefter, J. and Calvin W. Hurd., "Colonel David Hall's Regiment, Delaware Line, 1777-1783," *Military Collector and Historian* 18 (1966): 48-50.

Heitman, Francis. *Historical Register of Officers of the Continental Army during the War of the Revolution, April 1777 to December 1783.* Washington, D.C: Rare Book Shop Publishing Co.; reprint, Baltimore: Genealogical Publishing Co., 1969.

Hill, Steven. *The Delaware Cincinnati, 1783-1988.* Bryn Mawr, Pa.: Dorrance & Company, 1988.

Hufeland, Otto. *Westchester County During the American Revolution 1775-1783.* White Plains: Westchester County Historical Society, 1926.

Index of Revolutionary War Pensions. Washington, D.C.: National Genealogical Society, 1966.

Jackson, John W. *Valley Forge: Pinnacle of Courage.* Gettysburg, Pa: Thomas Publications, 1992.

Journals of the Provincial Congress Committee of Safety and Council of Safety 1775-1777. Vols. 1 & 2, Albany: Thurlow Weed, 1842.

"Journal of Col. Rudolphus Ritzema," *Magazine of American History* 1, (1877), 98-107.

Judd, Jacob. "The Unknown Philip Van Cortlandt: Loyalist," *New York History*, 64, (1983), 395-407.

_____. *The Van Cortlandt Family Papers. Vol. I: The Revolutionary War Memoir and Selected Correspondence of Philip Van Cortlandt.* Tarrytown, N. Y.: Sleepy Hollow Restorations, 1976.

Ketchum, Richard M. *Saratoga:Turning Point of America's Revolutionary War.* N. Y.: H. Holt, 1997.

Kirkwood, Robert, *The Journal and Orderly Book of Cap. Robert Kirkwood of the Delaware Regiment of the Continental Line.* ed. Joseph Brown Turner. Wilmington: Historical Society of Delaware, 1910.

Koetteritz, John B. *Andrew Finck.* Little Falls, N. Y.: The Author, 1906.

Krueger, John William. "Troop Life at the Champlain Valley Forts During the American Revolution," Ph. D. dissertation, State University of New York at Albany, 1981.

Kwasny, Mark V. "Partisan War in the Middle States: The Militia and the American War Effort Around the British Stronghold of New York City, 1775-1783," Ph. D. dissertation, Ohio State, 1989.

Lauber, Almon W., ed., *Orderly Books of the Fourth New York Regiment, 1778–1780, the Second New York Regiment, 1780–1783, by Samuel Tallmadge and Others, with Diaries of Samuel Tallmadge, 1780–1782, and John Barr, 1779–1782.* Albany: The University of the State of New York Press, 1932.

Lefferts, Charles M. *Uniforms of the American, British, French, and German Armies in the War of the American Revolution 1775-1783.* N. Y.: New York Historical Society, 1926.

Loane, Nancy K. *Following the Drum: Woman at the Valley Forge Encampment.* New York: Barnes & Noble. 2009.

Leggett, Abraham, *The Narrative of Major Abraham Leggett of the Army of the Revolution,* ed. Charles I. Bushnell, New York: Privately printed, 1865.

163

Livingston, Henry. "Journal of Major Henry Livingston, of the Third New York Continental Line, August to December 1775," ed. Gaillard Hunt *Pennsylvania Magazine of History and Biography*, 22 (1898): 9-33.

Lobdell, L. S. ed., "The Four New York Regiments," *Magazine of American History* 26 (1891), 147-50.

Londahl-Smidt, Donald M. "Notes Concerning the Uniform of the Delaware Battalion in 1776," *Military Collector and Historian* 19 (1967): 9-11.

Luzader, John. *Decision on the Hudson: The Battles of Saratoga.* Washington, D.C.: National Park Service, 1975.

_____. S*aratoga: A Military History of the Decisive Campaign of the American Revolution.* N. Y.: Savas Beatie, 2010.

McBarron, H. Charles, Jr. "Colonel David Hall's Regiment, Delaware Line, 1777-1783," *Military Collector and Historian* 18 (1966): 48-49.

McBarron, H. Charles, Jr. and Simpson, James P. "Colonel John Haslet's Delaware Regiment, 1776," *Military Collector and Historian* 17 (1965): 49-51

McDougall, William L. *American Revolutionary: A Biography of General Alexander McDougall.* Westport, Conn.: Greenwood Press, 1977.

McGuire, Thomas J. *The Philadelphia Campaign Volume I: Brandywine and the Fall of Philadelphia.* Mechanicsburg, Pa.:Stackpole, 2006.

_____. *The Philadelphia Campaign: Volume Two: Germantown and the Roads to Valley Forge.* Mechanicsburg, Pa.: Stackpole, 2007.

McMichael, James, "Diary of Lieutenant James McMichael of the Pennsylvania Line, 1776-1778," *Pennsylvania Magazine of History and Biography*, 16, (1892): 129-159.

Manders, Eric I. "Notes On Troop Units In The New York Garrison, 1775-1776." *Military Collector and Historian* (25): 18-21.

_____. "Notes On Troop Units In The Northern Army: 1776, Continental Units And State Levies." *Military Collector and Historian* (1975): 8-12.

Metcalfe, Bryce. *Original Members and Other Officers Eligible to the Society of the Cincinnati, 1783-1938.* The Society of the Cincinnati.

Moyne, Ernest J. "Who Was Colonel John Haslet of Delaware?" *Delaware History*" 13 (1969): 283-300

Munsell, Joel. *Annals of Albany.* Albany, N.Y.: 1871.

New York in the Revolution as Colony and State. Supplement, Vol. 2. Office of the State Comptroller. Albany: J, B. Lyon Company, 1904.

Muster and Pay Rolls of the War of the Revolution, 1775-1783, Part 1, Collections of the New-York Historical Society for the Year 1914 (New York: The Society, 1916).

Muster and Pay Rolls of the War of the Revolution, 1775-1783, Part 2, Collections of the New-York Historical Society for the Year 1915 (New York: The Society, 1916).

Neagles, James C. and Lila L. Neagles. *Locating Your Revolutionary War Ancestor: A Guide to the Military Records.* Logan, Ut.: The Everton Publishers, 1983.

Newcomb, Benjamin H. "Washington's Generals and the Decision to Quarter at Valley Forge. *The Pennsylvania Magazine of History and Biography*, 117 (1993): 309-329.

New York, Division of Archives and History. *The Sullivan-Clinton Campaign in 1779, Chronology and Selected Documents.* Albany: University of the State of New-York, 1929.

Orderly Book of the Northern Army at Ticonderoga and Mt. Independence From October 17, 1776 to January 8, 1777, Albany: J. Munsell, 1859.

Pagano, Francis B. "An Historical Account of the Military and Political Career of George Clinton, 1739-1812." Ph. D. dissertation, St. John's University, 1956.

Peden, Henry C., Jr. *Revolutionary Patriots of Delaware, 1775-1783.* Bowie, Md.: Heritage Books, 1996.

Peterson, Clarence S. *Known Military Dead during the Revolutionary War.* Baltimore, 1959; reprint, Baltimore: Genealogical Publishing Co., 1967.

Pierce's Register. *Register of the Certificates Issued by John Pierce, Esquire, Paymaster General and Commissioner of Army Accounts for the United States, to Officers and Soldiers of the Continental Army Under Act of July 4, 1783.* 1915; reprint, Baltimore: Genealogical Publishing Co., 1987.

Poucher, J. Wilson. "Colonel Lewis Du Bois." *Proceedings of the Ulster County Historical Society of 1935-1936:* 15-33.

Putnam, Israel, *General Orders Issued by Major-General Israel Putnam when in Command of the Highlands...1777,* ed. by Worthington C. Ford, Brooklyn, N.Y., 1893.

Reid, W. Max. "A Diary of the Siege of Fort Schuyler." *Magazine of History* 3 (1906): 90-104.

Ritzema, Rudolphus, "Journal of Col. Rudolphus Ritzema of the First New York Regiment August 8, 1775 to March 30, 1776." *Magazine of American History,* 1, (1877): 98-107.

Roberts, James A. comp. *New York in the Revolution as Colony and State.* Albany: Press of Brandow Print, 1898.

Robinson, Thomas P. *"Some Notes on Major-General Richard Montgomery, "* New York History, 37 (1956): 388-398.

Rodney, Caesar. *Letters to and from Caesar Rodney, 1756-1784.* ed. George Herbert Ryden. Philadelphia: University of Pennsylvania Press for the Historical Society of Delaware, 1933.

Rodney, Thomas. *Diary of Captain Thomas Rodney, 1776-1777.* ed. Caesar A. Rodney. Wilmington Historical Society of Delaware 8 (1888)

Scharf, John Thomas. *History of Delaware 1609-1888.* 2 vols. Philadelphia: L. J. Richards & Co., 1888.

Scott, John Albert. *Fort Stanwix and Oriskany* Rome, N.Y.: Rome Sentinel Co., 1927.

T*he Journal of William Scudder,* ed. F. J. Sypher. Ann Arbor: Scholars' Facsimiles & Reprints (2005).

Seymour, William. *A Journal of the Southern Campaign, 1780-1783.* Wilmington: Historical Society of Delaware. 1896.

Shannon, Anna "General Alexander McDougall: Citizen Soldier, 1732-86." Ph.D. dissertation, Fordham University, 1957

Sims, Lynn Lee "The Military Career of John Lamb", Ph. d. dissertation, New York University, 1975.

Smith, William, *Historical Memoirs from 16 March 1763 to 25 July 1778 of William Smith,* ed. William H. W. Sabine, N. Y.: New York Times Original Narratives, 1958.

Spaulding, Ernest W. *His Excellency George Clinton (1739-1812), Critic of the Constitution.* New York: Macmillan Co., 1938.

Swiggett, Howard. *War Out of Niagara.* 1933; reprint, Port Washington, N.Y.: Ira J. Friedman, Inc., 1963.

Thomas, Howard. *Marinus Willett, Soldier Patriot, 1740-1830.* Prospect, N. Y.: Prospect Books. 1974.

Trussell, John B. B., Jr., *Birthplace of an Army: A Study of the Valley Forge Encampment.* Harrisburg: Pennsylvania Museum and Historical Commission, 1976.

U. S. Congress, Walter Lowrie and Walter S. Franklin, eds. *American State Papers; Documents, Legislative and Executive, on the Congress of the United States, from the First Session of the First to the Second Session of the Seventeenth Congress, inclusive; Commencing March 4, 1789, and Ending March 8, 1823. Class IX Claims.* Washington, D.C.: 1834. Contains much information on thousands of Revolutionary War service claims filed in Congress. See McMullin, Phillip W. *Grassroots of America,* for a thorough index.

U. S. House of Representatives. *Resolutions, Laws, and Ordinances, Relating to the Pay, Half Pay, Commutation of Half Pay, Bounty*

Lands...Officers and Soldiers of the Revolution...and to Funding Revolutionary Debt. 1838; reprint, Baltimore: Genealogical Publishing Co., 1998.

U. S. War Department. *Letter from the Secretary of War, Communicating a Transcript of the Pension List of the United States - June 1, 1813.* Washington, D.C., 1813; reprinted as *Revolutionary Pensioners; a Transcript of the Pension List of 1813.* Baltimore: Genealogical Publishing Co., 1959.

U.S. War Department. *Letter from the Secretary of War, Transmitting a Report of the Names, Rank and Line of Every Person Placed on the Pension List, in Pursuance of the Act of 18th March 1818.* Washington, D.C., 1820; reprint, Baltimore: Genealogical Publishing Co., 1955.

Waldo, Albigence, "Valley Forge 1777-78: The Diary of Surgeon Albigence Waldo of the Continental Line," *Pennsylvania Magazine of History and Biography*, 21, (1897): 299-325

Ward, Christopher L. *The Delaware Continentals.* Wilmington: The Historical Society of Delaware, 1941.

Weaver, Philip D. "Update on 4th New York Uniforms in 1775," *Military Collector and Historian* 55 (2003): 247-48.

_____. "Yet Another Update on 4th New York Uniforms in 1775: When a Jacket is a Vest," *Military Collector and Historian.* 60 (2008): 255-258.

Whitely, William G. *The Revolutionary Soldiers of Delaware* (Papers of the Historical Society of Delaware), No. 14, Wilmington 1895.

Wild, Ebenezer, "The Journal of Ebenezer Wild (1776-1781)...." *Massachusetts Historical Society Proceedings*, 2nd ser., vol. 6, (1890): 78-160.

Willet, William M. *A Narrative of the Military Actions of Colonel Marinus Willet, Taken Chiefly From His Own Manuscript.* New York: G. & C. & H. Carvill, 1831.

Zlatich, Marko. "The American Soldier—A Delaware Version of 1777," *Military Collector and Historian* 19 (1967): 58-59.